Running a Hole in the Wind:

Hidden
Horses
Found

Conrad Crease

By Conrad Crease

The Desert Baron: Friedrich, A Warrior For All Seasons

Finding the Hidden Horse: Profiles of Long Shots

BLUE MAX PRESS LLC
1607 Berkshire Avenue
Myrtle Beach, SC 29577

Copyright 2013 Conrad Kenneth Crease
All rights reserved.

ISBN: 1491249528
ISBN-13: 9781491249529

To Lillian's children:
Craig, Elaine, Brian, and Vanessa; thoroughbreds all…

ACKNOWLEDGEMENTS

Once again thanks to my former racing partner Marvin Small for his encouragement, suggestions and invaluable insights, and to the knowledgeable Rich Meyer whose synapses travel just slightly slower than the speed of light, making him the best handicapper of thoroughred horse races that I have known in my over 40 years of service in the punter wars.

Additional recognition is due the Bloodstock Research Information Services (Brisnet). Their early, middle, and late pace numbers were invaluable in constructing the formula that is the foundation of the *Finding the Hidden Horse* software program that has produced so many long shot winners for its users over the past two years.

The examples reprinted are the property of Brisnet.

FORWARD

So many things in life turn on an accident or an epiphany. And, unless you belong to the school that believes in predestination, we are all subject to the "chaos theory," that branch of science concerned with the behaviour of complex systems in which tiny changes can have major effects. That theory is the study of nonlinear dynamics in which seemingly random events are actually predictable from simple deterministic equations.

Over my some 40 years of battle in the punter wars, I have watched too many times a horse win at box-car odds, causing me to ask: Was that race a boat, a fix? Too many times I didn't find the answer, until one day at Oaklawn I watched a long shot horse that – from a review of the racing form – appeared to have little chance of hitting the board, much less of winning the race. Had I been using the FHH application, I wouldn't have let that race pass without getting down some win and twice as much to place money on that horse.

This work is the explanation of that rationale.

INTRODUCTION

The human brain is no match for the computer when it comes to the speed with which it calculates and iterates: the computer is no match for the human brain when it comes to intuitive reasoning. And until the computer can intuitively reason, it is only a tool; nothing more, nothing less. Its redeeming feature is the lightning speed with which it can compute. Unlike the human brain it never forgets, nor does it experience fatigue. Much depends on the mind of the writer of the code. Which will it be: garbage in, garbage out; or genius in, genius out?

Notwithstanding the remarkable success of *Finding the Hidden Horse: Profiles of Long Shots*, I have made an honest effort not to replow ground first turned over with that work. The FHH software application for handicappping thoroughbred horse races has been on the market for over 27 months: the examples herein are the incontrovertible results made possible by this remarkable tool designed for the serious handicapper.

The facts speak for themselves: *res ipsa loguitor!*

CKC
August, 2013

CONTENTS

Acknowledgements	vii
Forward	ix
Introduction	xi
1. The Punter's Dream	1
2. Sixteen iterations	21
3. Early Scores	33
4. The Nature of Risk	43
5. On Touts and Tipsters	53
6. Hidden Horses Found	63
7. The Morning Line: What Good Is It?	85
8. A New Horse in the Barn	101
9. Their First Dance	129
10. Trainers and the Games They Play	147
11. In the Land of Long Shot Hunters, Patience is King	161
12. Where Would We Be Without Numbers?	197
Addendum	207
Bibliography	209

Chapter 1

THE PUNTER'S DREAM

"Is all that we see or seem but a dream within a dream?"
EDGAR ALLEN POE

Psychologists tell us that many dreams are simply wish-fulfillment expressions of our sub-conscious. They also contend that most gamblers have compulsive-obsessive personalities; that they really want to lose. I have yet to see sufficient clinical data supporting that conclusion, but will readily grant that over four decades I have seen a scattered few punters who didn't know when to quit until the punter's dream turned into a nightmare, and they lost everything: money, other valuable possessions, homes, wives, mates, friends, and – saddest of all – their self-respect. As Kenny Rogers famously sang: "Ya gotta know when to hold 'em and know when to fold 'em."

This treatise is not about losers; it's about winners and what it takes to win in this challenging, frustrating, yet magnificent game of thoroughbred horse race handicapping that has been my avocation for more years than I now care to admit. For ten years, from the mid 80s to the mid 90s, I was fortunate enough to be the managing partner of the Prairie Pride Farms Racing Stable, and an owner and breeder of some of those magnificent descendants of the immortal Eclipse. Racing on the Midwest circuit: the now destroyed Ak-Sar-Ben in Omaha; the Woodlands in Kansas City; Remington Park in Oklahoma City, and Oaklawn Park in Hot Springs, Arkansas; our stable of over a dozen horses enabled us to stand in the winner's circle often enough to pay the feed, board, and training bills. We kept a runner at the track as long as the horse was winning at least half its keep; for – to be honest – we played for the love of the game.

After the disbursement of our stable in 1995 – it was either that or the disbursement of my lovely wife – I came away with an insider's knowledge of some of the more mundane if no less important details of what it takes to win a horse race.

The first if not the most important question the novice handicapper must ask is: Is the game honest?

Aye, there's the rub. (I sense Shakespeare turning over in his grave.) Remembering my first experience with dishonesty at a game of chance takes me back to my early years, as a nine year old to be exact. You know how kids love a carnival; one set up its tents and rides not far from our home on the outskirts of the city, the calliope and merry-go-round music floating enticingly to our front porch. My father, with few dollars to spare, gave me one to splurge as I saw fit on the carnival rides that only cost a dime; in those hard times a dollar was a dollar. At the entrance to the carnival stood one of those child alluring machines (you can still see them today at entrances to drug and grocery stores), games of chance; you put your dime in the coin slot, then attempt to manipulate the miniature crane and the large four cornered claw in order to snag one of the flashy toys and stuffed animals piled up so enticingly below.

Putting my dime in the slot, I carefully manipulated the forked claw above the toy soldier I was eyeing. Close, ever closer, slowly I moved the jaws of the claw above the target prize. I remember thinking: it's mine! And for a dime! All I had to do was close the menacing jaws, and so I did. The jaws slammed shut – empty. No matter, I remember thinking, I had come close and still had nine tries left to win the soldier, lying on his back, looking up at the open jaws of the claw; did I imagine it, or was there a cynical smile on his face?

I'm ashamed to have to tell you that I stood at that thieving machine, and blew my whole dollar – a dollar I knew my father had worked hard to earn – in nine more futile tries. Several times I came close; once grasping the soldier in the claw, pulling him half way up before he fell from its tenuous hold. Never getting into the carnival, I skulked home: if I had possessed a tail it would have been dragging between my legs.

"Well, brother, did you have fun at the carnival?" My father asked upon my arrival at our front porch.

Fighting back a tear, I couldn't answer for a minute or two.

"What's the matter, son?"

I blurted out what had happened, and that I thought the machine was rigged.

Slowly, he sat down with me at the edge of the porch. In his patient, slow, but steady way of talking he offered some advice I've never forgotten.

"Brother, as the years come on you will learn that when it comes to money and gambling, for that's what you were doing, things are not always as they appear at first glance."

I had, he mildly admonished, "paid too much for my whistle," relating Benjamin Franklin's famous warning to wide-eyed innocents: "Take care that you don't pay too much for your whistle."

Pulling another dollar out of his billfold, Dad sent me back to the carnival. On entering the gate I gave a knowing sneer to the robber machine and to its turbaned head atop, then spent my dollar on cotton candy and rides on the merry-go-round and Ferris wheel.

I was 35 when I saw and bet on my first thoroughbred horse race at the old New Orleans wood frame Fairgrounds – since burned to the ground. Lady Luck easily seduced me into what turned out to be a life long affair when she allowed me to cash a ticket on my first try. I was smitten, and as we all know, love is blind. At that time it never occurred to me that a thoroughbred horse race at a state sanctioned track might be fixed. At that time I believed the game was honest, that all parties to the contest wanted to win, probably because I *wanted* to believe that. I was disabused of that naïve notion when, a few years later, I ran across an experienced handicapper to whom I put the question: "Do you think the game is on the up and up?"

Phoenix Phil smiled that sardonic grin for which he was noted: "I think most horse races are square. Occasionally, they aren't."

Phil then told me of the time he got a call from one of his reputation challenged friends, telling him to get out to the track for the last race of the day as the 4 horse was coming in. The friendly tout didn't say: "The race is fixed." Phil went on to say that the same friend had made a couple of similar calls before that had paid off handsomely. The 4 horse, of course, "came in," winning at generous odds.

Human nature being what it is, Phil's recounting of the tip he received was not necessarily proof that those races were less than honest; I had to admit, however, that the tips were at best remarkable coincidences. Over the years many punters have tried to give me a tip at the track, giving it as if they had inside information; no doubt straight from either the trainer or the horse's mouth. Typically, they would assert: "The 3 is gonna win this race!" What I think they really meant was: "I think the 3 is the winner: I hope the 3 wins!" It didn't take long for me to conclude that tips from other punters were worth exactly what you paid for them — nothing.

Phil went on to say he believed the great majority of thoroughbred horse races are honest tries by most owners, trainers, and jockeys; especially at the big time tracks.

"If I didn't believe that I wouldn't be playing the game."

I knew that the legendary Phoenix Phil was a shrewd gambler and an experienced handicapper, so his answer was good enough for me. Besides, I wanted to believe in the integrity of the game;

as surely most – if not all – punters do. Years later, however, I was party to an incident at a small Nebraska track that brought some lingering doubts to the fore, where they remained until I entered the game some 25 years ago as an owner and breeder, becoming an insider.

In my early handicapping days I was a form player, a chalk chaser. My attitude toward the Daily Racing Form past performance records was: what you see is what you get. And I read every thoroughbred horse race handicapping book I could find; only a few were worth the time.

So it was that Lillian Louise and I often made weekend trips to this small Nebraska town with a population of about 20,000, and about a five hour trip due north from Wichita, to play the horses as it was our wont to do in the springtime of our youth. Our goal was to get away for the weekend, to have some fun, paying for our trips with our winnings, which we were often able to do.

On a weekend in September many years ago, a rather unpleasant incident occurred involving your humble handicapper and several jockeys at a bush track in a small Nebraska town. Two results are sure to follow upon the loss of a punter's temper at the race track: 1 – the punter does something stupid, and 2 – the punter does something stupid. This can prove to be exceedingly dangerous to the punter's person and billfold. I have to admit that in my callow youth I had a bad temper; it remains with me today, the difference is that I've learned to control it.

On the first day at the track Lil and I cashed some nice tickets; we were fresh, relaxed, and eager. The next day we thought we had located a sure thing (ha-ha) in the second race. We had not yet learned the horseplayer's rule written in stone; when it comes to horse racing there is no such thing as a sure thing. After reviewing the horse's past performances in the Daily Racing Form (it's interesting that the DRF calls the records of a horse's past races *performances* rather than simply records), we didn't see how our pick could get beat; assuming the race was honest, unless the horse stumbled, or was hit out of the gate, or the jockey fell off – which happens more often than the casual observer might think. Unfortunately, everyone else who read the form saw what we had seen and came to the same conclusion; that the horse was probably a "mortal lock," as my friend the dog racing tip sheet writer was overly fond of asserting about his picks.

We reasoned that we might get $3.60 to $3.80 to place, as none of the other runners were less than 4/1 with five minutes to post. We agreed to bet half our winnings of the previous day (not an insubstantial amount) on the highly touted favorite to place.

I neglected to mention that the meet's top jockey was in the saddle and the horse was trained by the meet's leading trainer. The track announcer, sometime handicapper and morning line setter, went on for some ten minutes touting his "can't lose" pick to win the race. The crowd took the bait and so did we. We bet quite a bit of money on the mortal lock, more than we should have, less than we could have, but win or lose our standard of living wouldn't have changed.

As I trained my binoculars on everyone's hopeful, the runners stood ready in the gate. The flag went up: the bell rang; the gates flew open; the field leapt forward – except for the favorite. Our horse, the crowd's horse, the morning line setter's tout, didn't appear to be in any hurry to leap forward. Leisurely, it seemed to me, our horse strolled out of the gate, giving the field about a seven length lead. My stomach turned over; it was a six furlong race over a five furlong track! The jockey, having a firm hold on the reins, pulled the horse's head down, bowing it's neck, the high strung animal fighting to be free from the rider's restraint. The horse was a natural front runner following its breeding and training; in seven previous races it had never been worse than third at the quarter mile marker.

Was I witnessing a "stiff," a "boat " race?

As the race unfolded the "crowd's hope" began to make up some ground, but as the field approached the final turn our favored steed was still some five lengths back. A hundred yards into the stretch, the jockey finally put his whip to the no doubt by then confused animal, then beat the hell out of our mortal lock all the way to the finish and, either for show to the crowd or out of anger, whacked it a few more times after the race was over. Our hope, the crowd's hope, the announcer's mortal lock, finished a fast closing fourth, some five lengths behind the 18/1 winner.

Smoke coming out of my ears, I was certain I had just seen a fixed race! Red in the face I'm sure, I stood up, starting down the grandstand steps.

Lil grabbed my arm: "Where are you going?"

"To see a man about a horse!" I threw back, charging toward the rail where I knew the jocks would be passing on their way to the jock's room. Several passed by before my target arrived.

"Nice stiff, Smith!" The accusation was loud enough for Smith and two other jocks to hear.

They stopped: three heads swung in my direction. Coolly, I stared back. I'm not sure how I would have reacted had they jumped the rail and headed toward me, but I stood my ground.

Saying nothing, they moved on.

On arriving back at our seats, my lovely punting partner asked: "What did you think you were accomplishing?"

"Nothing. And I sure won't try to accomplish it again."

After much commiserating and rationalizing of our loss of half the previous day's winnings, over a whiskey sour for me and a glass of white wine for her, we discussed over dinner the day's unpleasantness.

"You really think the jock deliberately pulled the favorite? He's the leading rider and the trainer leads the trainer standings. Aren't we just being sore losers?" The always level headed Lil queried, as was her common sense wont to do.

"Looked like he pulled the horse. Of course, we can't prove it nor can the crowd."

By this time, my temper cooling to a simmer, I suggested that perhaps I was wrong, perhaps the trainer was using the race to attempt to teach the horse to rate, to save something for the stretch rather than charging out of the gate at full throttle, but reaching the finish line nearly out of gas.

"Besides," she offered, "even if *that* race was fixed, it doesn't necessarily prove that most races are. You'll never be able to convince me that all or even most horse races are fixed. Thieves fall out; someone would eventually squeal. Remember, we're playing at a bush track. What do you suppose the winner's share was for that race?"

"About three thousand."

"I rest my case," she sweetly smiled, hitting the nail squarely on its head, as usual.

A recent example of an apparent "monkey business" race occurred on 12/5/2012 in the ninth and final race at Remington Park, a mile and 70 yard $7,500 claimer with a purse of $12,800 for Oklahoma bred three year olds and up which had never won two races. This race was not quite at the bottom of the class barrel, neither was it much above it. The field of 11 had run a combined total of 184 races without achieving their second win; an average of nearly 18 losing tries per runner. That's the type of race that often produces double digit winners; a fertile field for Hidden Horse Hunters to find long shot candidates.

The FHH application tabbed the top three contenders as the 4, 3, 1. The 4, Triticale, had the best work of the field: five furlongs in 60 seconds; believe me, that's a hot work for Remington Park. The horse was also getting five pounds for the apprentice jockey allowance; seven pounds from four horses and five pounds from the rest of the field. It appeared to me that Triticale was the sole front speed. His morning line odds were 30/1. Which was I to believe; the morning line setter or my System? I made my usual long shot bet to win and twice as much to place on the System's number one contender, the 4.

THE PUNTER'S DREAM

I was ruminating about what to do with my 4 in the exotics when I noticed something odd in the pps regarding the 5 horse, Jenna's Reply; he had run 20 races without posting his second lifetime win; he had won a grand total of $17,677 (an average of $884 per race); in his last five races he had left the gate at odds of 31/1, 34.3/1, 39.9/1, 40.6/1, and 23.6/1, respectively! In addition, his works were lousy and the trainer would have the bettors believe that Jenna's Reply didn't work out in the two months prior to this race. In spite of the above, the intrepid morning line setter posted the horse's odds at an unbelievable 6/1! The horse was 15/1 on the board with about five minutes to post. Considering all of Jenna's Reply's apparent negatives, I thought his morning line should have been about 100/1 and wasn't about to make a straight bet on it; but the more I thought about it the more I came to the conclusion that something odd was up. I finally concluded: "That's the rat that's going to beat me!"

I ended up boxing the 4 with the 1, 3, 5 in exactas then used the 4, 5 over the 1, 3, 4, 5 over all in trifectas and tabbed a fifty cent super box of the 1, 3, 4, 5. The 4 left the gate at odds of 26/1, the 5 at 14/1, the 3 was the odds-on favorite, and the 1 was 22/1. I noticed that the odds on most of the field were gyrating in wide swings; this often happens at the second tier tracks that have modest betting pools.

I was astounded when the gates opened: Triticale, the 4, broke dead last; how could I have been so wrong? Meantime, Jenna's Reply was forwardly placed per the chartwriter: "Jenna's Reply was never far back along inside, responded to handling to take command along rail mid stretch, kept to task and drew off late." Meanwhile: "Triticale well back at the half, circled leaving far turn, responded to handling while mid track, finished well to get up for second."

The race finished 5, 4, 3, 1 - lighting up the odds board with box car figures: a $460.80 two dollar exacta; an $1,152.80 two dollar trifecta, and a dime super for $446.00. It was a nice hit for me and I took the money, but the wine of winning this race left a sour taste. Clearly, betting the 5 horse was not from handicapping the race; I had just smelled a rat and made a lucky gamble.

Though of course no one could prove it, this race – insofar as the winner is concerned – had all of the earmarks of a "monkey business" race. While casting no aspersions on any individual, the facts speak for themselves: *res ipsa loquitor*. Perhaps Jenna's Reply had imbibed a goodly swig of "Argentina Joy Juice" about which runs the ubiquitous rumor around many tracks that no state racing board chemists have yet been able to detect the performace enhancing elixir. I would rather think that, than suggest that any of the other jockeys had any part in the ridiculous outcome of that race. In the alternative, you would think that Jenna's Reply's connections would have some explaining to do.

To add insult to injury, the announcer rubbed the crowd's nose in it, exclaiming in his mid-stretch call: "Jenna's Reply takes the lead! He just has more gears than anyone else, that's all there is to it! Jenna's Reply has made a mockery of it down the stretch!"

It appears fair to assume that the mockery of that race was not made by the horse.

If you Google "horse race fixing" quite a number of illuminating entries are available.

THE PUNTER'S DREAM

NINTH RACE
Remington
December 5th, 2012

1 MILE 70 YARDS. (1.384) CLAIMING. Purse $12,300 (includes $2,300 OBP - Oklahoma Bred Pgm) FOR ACCREDITED OKLAHOMA-BRED THREE YEAR OLDS AND UPWARD WHICH HAVE NEVER WON TWO RACES. Three Year Olds, 120 lbs.; Older, 122 lbs. Claiming Price $7,500. (Clear 61)

Value of Race: $12,300 Winner $6,844; second $2,588; third $1,504; fourth $570; fifth $284; sixth $85; seventh $85; eighth $85; ninth $85; tenth $85; eleventh $85. Mutuel Pool $25,033 Pick 3 Pool $6,160 Pick 4 Pool $18,830 Daily Double Pool $8,847 Exacta Pool $19,552 Superfecta Pool $14,461 Trifecta Pool $15,106

Last Raced	#	Horse	M/Eqt	A/S	Wt	PP	St	¼	½	¾	Str	Fin	Jockey	Cl'g Pr	Odds $1
17Nov12 9RP⁶	5	Jenna's Reply	L b	5G	122	5	3	5¹	6½	5¹	1¹	1⁴	Cardoso D	7500	14.50
14Nov12 9RP¹²	4	Triticale	L	3G	115	4	11	11	10½	7½	2ʰᵈ	2¾	Risenhoover S	7500	26.50
10Nov12 9RP³	3	N C C Troubador	L b	3G	120	3	2	6²	7¹	4½	3½	3¹	Berry M C	7500	0.70
06Nov12 9RP⁶	1	Spodie Odie		5G	122	1	9	8⁴	8¹	9ʰᵈ	5ʰᵈ	4¹¾	McNeil E	7500	22.60
14Nov12 9RP¹⁰	6	Sinners Angel		3G	120	6	4	7¹	5¾	3¹	4ʰᵈ	5³	Medina J A	7500	13.00
10Nov12 9RP⁴	10	Rumorsboutme		3G	120	10	7	4½	2¹	2²	6¹	6¹½	Compton P	7500	4.90
10Nov12 9RP⁹	8	Prince Rillian	L b	3G	120	8	1	2½	3¹	6½	8¹⁰	7¹½	Birzer A	7500	19.40
22Sep12 9RP⁶	11	Big Demon	L b	3G	120	11	5	1³	1³	1²	7¹	8¹⁰½	Wethey, Jr. F	7500	7.10
06Nov12 9RP⁹	7	Drill Stem	L	5G	122	7	8	10²½	11	8½	9¹½	9²¼	Landeros B C	7500	31.60
10Nov12 9RP¹³	9	Chrome Deputy	L b	4G	122	9	6	3²	4ʰᵈ	10	10	10	Quinonez B	7500	83.70
27Oct12 9RP¹⁰	2	Tied On		3G	120	2	10	9⁵	9⁴	11	11	11	Cunningham T	7500	18.10

OFF AT 10:14 Start Good. Won driving. Track Fast.
TIME :23⅘, :48², 1:14², 1:41, 1:45⁴ (:23.60, :48.47, 1:14.40, 1:41.12, 1:45.95)

$2 Mutuel Prices:
5 - JENNA'S REPLY 31.00 13.00 4.80
4 - TRITICALE 21.60 14.80
3 - N C C TROUBADOR 2.10

$2 EXACTA 5-4 PAID $460.80 $2 SUPERFECTA 5-4-3-1 PAID $8,939.20
$2 TRIFECTA 5-4-3 PAID $1,152.80

Chestnut Gelding, (Ap), by Wood Reply - Amy's Three by Cachuma. Trainer Griggs Veronica. Bred by Charles Golden(OK).

JENNA'S REPLY was never far back along inside, responded to handling to take command along rail mid stretch, kept to task and drew off late. TRITICALE was back at the half, circled leaving far turn, responded to handling while mid track, finished well to get up for second spot. N C C TROUBADOR was allowed to settle early, came five wide into lane, moved up to loom danger mid stretch, flattened out in late going. SPODIE ODIE saved ground while unhurried for half, came four wide into stretch, finished with a mild mid track rally. SINNERS ANGEL forwardly positioned along inside into stretch, moved into contention mid stretch, gave way. RUMORSBOUTME chased pace for half, faded in lane. PRINCE RILLIAN stalked leaders for half, faded. BIG DEMON hustled to front, set pace for three quarters, dropped back. DRILL STEM never threatened. CHROME DEPUTY forwardly positioned outside rivals for half, faded steadily thereafter. TIED ON was never far back, broke down top stretch, tanned off.

Owners- 5, Golden Charles M.; 4, Angle Jerry ; 3, Black Hawk Stable ; 1, Johnson Trudy ; 6, Charlton V. Joan; 10, Patterson Randy ; 8, Neff Roger D.; 11, Ivan Holmes Partnership One ; 7, Listen Robert L; 9, Garrison Scott K.; 2, Porter Bob

Trainers- 5, Griggs Veronica ; 4, Lozano Martin ; 3, Hartman Chris A.; 1, Adams Michael T.; 6, Charlton Brent W.; 10, Gleeson Tyrone ; 8, Neff Roger D.; 11, Caster Boyd ; 7, Listen Robert L.; 9, Garrison Scott K.; 2, Seaton Skad

Breeders- 5, Charles Golden (OK); 4, Kelly Thiesing (OK); 3, Mr. & Mrs. Lake Newcomb (OK); 1, John M. Lowder (OK); 6, Vena Joan Charlton (OK); 10, Handy D. Patterson (OK); 8, Roger D Neff (OK); 11, Harvey Bryant (OK); 7, Robert L. Listen (OK); 9, Scott K. Garrison & Davant Latham (OK); 2, Doyle D. Williams (OK)

Scratched- Watch Me Explode(29Nov12 9RP¹²), Mr. Lawton(26Nov12 9RP⁹), Big Sky Okie(24Oct12 9RP¹)

$2 Daily Double (1-5) Paid $116.60; Daily Double Pool $6,847.
$2 Pick Three (6-1-5) Paid $439.80; Pick Three Pool $6,160.
$2 Pick Four (12-6-1-5) Paid $14,119.20; Pick Four Pool $18,830.

Best Work

FHH Contenders from internet screen: 4, 3, 1

COPYRIGHT 2012 BLOODSTOCK RESEARCH INFORMATION SERVICES

Three Jockeys Held in Race Fixing Probe

Jockey Kieren Fallon is among 16 people arrested today in a police probe into corruption within horse racing and fixing the outcome of races.

More than 130 police officers raided 19 addresses across Suffolk, North Yorkshire, South Yorkshire and Hertferdshire, and arested a number of people for alleged conspiracy to defraud. It is understood the allegations involve more than 80 races over the past two years.

Trainer Karl Burke and jockeys Darrel Williams and Fergal Lynch were also understood to have been arrested.

(UK Daily Mail.)

Don't the names Kieren Fallon and Fergal Lynch (who apparently escaped the authorities' clutches for he had a mount in the 2012 Breeder's Cup races) have a certain distinctive Dickens-like ring to them? And there's horse race fixing in Hertferdshire, of all places?

Horse Racing-Fixing Probe Welcomed in Victoria State

Racing Victoria (RV) have welcomed the announcement of an inquiry into race fixing in horse…racing which have made headlines across Australia. Racing Commissioner Sal Perna said that an investigation would be launched covering thoroughbred, harness, and greyhound racing, August 20 and be concluded by Sept. 14.

"We welcome today's announcement," RV chief executive Rob Hines said in a statement on Thursday."

Addressing reporters, Perna expressed belief that the industry is largely free from corruption.

(Reuters, Thursday, August 16, 2012.)

They *welcome* an investigation? Why, what track wouldn't welcome an investigation into race-fixing at their track? And, of course, the wise thing to do in any criminal investigation is to announce to the press the exact dates the investigation will begin and end.

Race Fixing Claims Investigated at 3 Michigan Tracks

Search warrants were executed earlier this week.

Authorities say they believe as many as 30 owners, drivers, trainers, and gamblers conspired to fix the outcome of certain harness horse races run at three Michigan tracks. The Michigan State Police and the Michigan Gaming Control Board executed search warrants today at three southeast Michigan homes as part of an ongoing investigation into fraudulent wagering at the tracks. Police say the case involves races at Hazel Park Raceway, Northville Downs and Sports Creek Raceway in Swartz Creeks. The tracks themselves aren't under investigation and have been cooperating with investigators.

(From OTB, Bill Jempty, Friday, March 5, 2010 – Detroit Free Press.)

What? The races are crooked at Sport Creek Raceway in Swartz Creeks?

7 Plead Guilty to Race Fixing in Pa. Two Owners, Five Riders at Penn National Face Fines, up to Five Year Terms.

Two owners and five thoroughbred jockeys have agreed to plead guilty to fixing races earlier this year at Penn National Race Track, federal prosecutors said yesterday. Under the plea agreements, filed yesterday in U.S District Court in Harrisburg, each of the owners and jockeys could get up to five years in prison and fined $250,000.

(Baltimore Sun, Jay Apperson, December 1, 2000.)

Shades of Casablanca! There's race fixing going on in the industry? There's horse races actually being fixed in the US of A? As Jonathan Winters might have put it: "What the hell kind of a deal is that? I've been ta two hog callins and a county fair and I aint never seen nothin like that!"

In U.K., Dubai Sheik's Horse Trainer Is Banned

The governing body for horse racing in Britain disqualified one of the country's elite trainers for eight years for administrating banned substances to more than a dozen horses, bringing a high-profile doping scandal to the world of English racing.

Trainer Mahmood Al Zaroomi has admitted to administering a banned substance to 15 horses under his care – which belong to the ruler of Dubai, Sheik Mohammed Bin Rashid Al Maktoum, and his prestigious Godolphin stables – said the watchdog, the British Horseracing Authority.

"The circumstances in this particular case are exceptional not only on account of the profile of the owner in question, but also the number and the caliber of the horses involved," BHA Chief Executive, Paul Bitter said. The BHA race-day testing returned only 14 positive tests during all of 2012.

(Truncated from Wall Street Journal, Joshua Robinson, April 26, 2013.)

THE PUNTER'S DREAM

Fat chance that bettors in the UK, Australia, Michigan, and Pennsylvania will quit playing the races at the tracks in their jurisdictions, for uninformed bettors are like moths drawn to the flame of beating the horse racing game; afflicted by, yet drawn to the magnet that is the punter's dream. They will persist in spite of recent and persistant revelations in England, Australia, Michigan and Pennsylvania, for they *want* to believe, even as you and I want to believe, placing our wagers in the belief that thoroughbred horse racing is, by and large, an honest game.

Many years ago I finally quit chasing the chalk, coming to the conclusion that if a race were to be fixed it would probably involve "killing" the favorite. The only time I use a favorite now is to include it in my exotic bets; though seldom do I use it on top in my exacta, trifecta, and superfecta plays. Over time favorites historically lose two of three races. While a winning percentage of .333 is a huge number in baseball, it's a loser at the track. Yet chalk chasers persist in their lemming-like pursuit of favorites, and the crowd too often responds by betting these over touted horses down to 4/5 or less. Over the years I have seen innumerable 3/5 horses finish up the track, triggering huge prices for show tickets. I'm incredulous that any experienced horse player will actually put good money on a horse that will pay just $3.20 for a $2.00 ticket, *if it wins!* Generally, I will pass a race in which the favorite has been bet down to 3/5 or less.

When I hit my $15,000 superfecta, the details of which were set out in *Finding the Hidden Horse: Profiles of Long Shots,* I remember thinking as I constructed my bets for the last race of the day, "What if the favorites die?" On this strictly gambling impulse, and as I was on track money for the day, I bet the four highest odds runners, using the front runner over three other long shots boxed underneath. If I had not come to be prejudiced against favorites due to my experience of tearing up so many tickets on them, I doubt I would have asked the question that brought me that big hit: What if the favorites die?

Some six years ago, after watching a string of long shots win without apparent supporting form, I began to keep track of the times this happened. Thereafter, when I saw horses win at 10/1 or more, I went back to the Daily Racing Form to see if I could locate any important variables that I and the crowd had missed that could have reasonably predicted a top effort of a long shot winner in that race.

Such a search is *algorithmic:* a search for repetitive patterns. After over two years of collecting the data, I and my fellow punter for some twenty years constructed a paper and pencil system that later became the software application: *Finding the Hidden Horse.* After reviewing and subsequently promoting the book, Dave Powers of the California Handicapper asked if the strategies set out in the book could be demonstrated wholly within the Brisnet past performances. It was a pleasure to work with his program writer, Len Czyzniejewski, to produce the software version of the paper and pencil system. The best seller application has now been on the market for over two years. It has proven to be one of the most accurate and consistent race result predictors on the market. Originally intended for long shot players, it has been highly accurate at all price levels.

This chapter began by asking the question: Is thoroughbred horse race wagering an honest game? Notwithstanding the apparent monkey business that has been going on in the United Kingdom, Australia, Michigan, Pennsylvania, and no doubt as well in many other jurisdictions, the following updates of the results to date for the FHH race winner selection software solidly supports the conclusion that – at least at the big league tracks – thoroughbred horse races are, by and large, honestly contested.

Let's leave the final word to Phoenix Phil, one of the more successful thoroughbred horse race handicappers that I know.

"Most races are square. Occasionally, they aren't."

Chapter 2

SIXTEEN ITERATIONS

"Everything should be as simple as possible, but not simpler."
ALBERT EINSTEIN

The FHH thoroughbred handicapping software program was not quite ready for prime time when the gates opened for the 2011 Run for the Roses. More's the pity, since our pencil and paper method on which the application was based gave Animal Kingdom something more than a passing shot at the win. After sixteen iterations of the program code, FHH was more than ready to take aim at the Preakness. Upon completion of the program's beta version, I well remember Len asking: "So Shackleford's your horse?" I think he thought the system's tabbing that horse as the winner was beginner's luck. Luck was not a factor in the computation of Shackleford's monster 112 mid-pace number in the Derby. The actual "tells" - variables that made up his system point total that tabbed the horse as the top contender – are set out in the following: Author's Guide to Successful use of the FHH software.

No twenty minutes per race handicapping is necessary when using the program; the system does it for you – in a millisecond. Once you have downloaded the chosen race card from the Brisnet comma delimited PP Single Data Files and loaded it into the program, the interface screen appears. You choose the race and note the scratches in the boxes in the upper left corner of the screen. The headings of the first three columns, left to right, indicate the saddle cloth number, post position, and the name of each horse. The remaining columns are headed by the following identifications:

1. M/L Morning Line.
2. TOT These are the total "tell" points awarded to each horse by the system's analysis.
3. WO-F The distance of the current best workout since the horse's last race.
4. WO-T The time of the workout.
5. W/Os Points awarded for workouts.
6. TRB Indicating the horse had a troubled last race.
7. CUT Identifies and awards points to horses that are cutting back in distance from last race.
8. START Identifies Brisnet best E-1 number and ties from horse's last three starts.
9. S PTS Points awarded for best starts of last three races.
10. MID Identifies Brisnet best E-2 number from last three starts.
11. M-PTS Points awarded for best middle pace and ties from last three starts.

12. LATE Identifies Brisnet best E-3 number from last three starts.
13. L-PTS Points awarded for best late pace and ties from last three starts.
14. WGT Gives the number of pounds off from last race.
15. W-PTS Points awarded for weight off from the horse's last race.

I strongly recommend that the Program user take the time to study the above listing and the following explanations of how the "tell" points are established.

How the "Tell" Points are Awarded

WORKS: Three points are awarded for the best current work of the field. (Current works are defined as workouts since a horse's last race, and will note if its trainer has left his or her horse in the barn since its last race.) For first time starters, three points are awarded for the best *published* work and ties. Two points for up to three other horses and ties for the next best works. No differential is made for the distance of the race.

TROUBLE: One point is awarded for each horse whose last race was "troubled." The program uses 16 definitions of "trouble." The reader may fairly ask: "Why give points to a negative variable?" Since the program was originally intended as a guide to identifying probable long shot candidates, and as many long shots have a troubled previous race, the trouble notation gives the handicapper a "heads up."

CUTBACK: If the current race is shorter in distance than the horse's last race, and the last race was at a mile or more, points are awarded as follows:

For a horse that was within two lengths of the front at the six furlong marker in the previous race, award three points.

If the horse was within three to four lengths of the front at the six furlong markers, award two points.

If the horse was within five lengths of the front at the six furlong marker, award one point.

If the current race and the race from which the horse is cutting back is less than eight furlongs, and a horse was within two lengths from the front at the head of the stretch, award three points.

If a horse was within three to four lengths from the front at the head of the stretch, award two points.

If a horse was within five lengths of the front at the head of the stretch, award one point.

A substantial majority of "cutback winner" horses are those natural front runners that couldn't stay up at the farther distance. (Notably Shackleford, who led the Derby to the eighth pole before packing it in, then wired the field in the sixteenth of a mile shorter distance of the Preakness. His monster mid-pace figure of 112 in the Derby foretold his Preakness win. Yet the betting public let him leave the gate at 13/1 and change.)

A substantial number of long shot winners are "cutback" horses. Novice handicappers and unsophisticated bettors frequently overlook this important tell.

START: In a current sprint (seven furlongs or less) award three points to the best start and ties from the Brisnet E-1 designation, then two points each to the next best three horses and ties.

In a route award two points to the best E-1 start and ties, then one point to each of the next best three starts and ties.

Best start is the best start of the horse's last three races.

While a good start is important, it is the *least* predictive of winners at any distance, and especially in route races. And, surprisingly, front speed does not win all that many sprints of five to five and one half furlongs.

MIDDLE PACE: In a sprint (seven furlongs or lesss) award three points to the best mid-pace and ties or Brisnet E-2 number, then award two points for the next best three and ties.

In a route award two points to the best mid-number and ties, then one point each to the three next best and ties.

Best mid-pace is the best number of a horse's last three races.

In the intermediate distances a substantial number of winners come from horses with superior mid-pace numbers. (Shackleford's most important tells in the 2011 Preakness were his mid-pace number from the Derby, and he was cutting back.)

LATE PACE: In a sprint award two points for best late pace and ties, then one point each to the next best three and ties.

In a route award three points for best late pace number and ties, two points each to the next best three and ties.

In the two years to date that the FHH program has been on the market our records conclusively support our contention that the single most predictive "tell" of winners of any race, at any distance, on any surface; but especially on the turf - is late pace.

WEIGHT: In routes only, award three points for a horse carrying seven pounds or more less than in its last race; two points for five or six pounds off, and one point for a horse carrying three to four pounds less than in its last race. This feature will give the user a "tell" on foreign horses that are first time runners in the United

States, because foreign horses usually carry heavier weights than in the states.

This tell is the least important of the variables, but you should never a ignore a horse that, in addition to having substantial weight off in the current race from its last race, also has creditable numbers in at least one of the other variables. This tell has produced some giant priced winners; not very often, but you ignore this variable at your peril of missing a long shot winner.

The program awards the "tell" points that produce the top four contenders and ties. These appear in the lower left of the screen headed: Contenders 1, 2, 3, 4 and ties. To the right of each contender and at the head of the column marked "tells" are the total points awarded for each contender. The maximum points earnable are 21. Special attention should be given to any horse that earns ten or more tell points, and to any horse that has at least a three point margin over the next best total point earner.

In the lower right of the screen, opposite the CONTENDER boxes, appear four categories and columns headed by BEST. The categories are: WORKS, START, MID, and LATE.

In the Best Work line will appear first the saddle cloth number; in the next box to the right appears the distance of the work, and to the right appears the time of the work.

In the Best Start line appears the saddle cloth number and the Best Start number to the right.

In the Best Mid line appears the saddle cloth number and the Best Mid number to the right.

In the Best Late line appears the saddle cloth number and the Best Late number to the right.

These boxes – the Best in Category boxes – are used by the system (their correlation with the contender horses having been determined by algorithmic research) as "confirming" factors that have a direct bearing on the contender's tell numbers. When the FHH user finds that one or more of the top contenders also appear in one or more of the Best in Category boxes, this is generally confirmation of a probable best bet. (We will go over this point again in later specific examples.)

EXAMPLES

In the 2011 Preakness the FHH program identified the 5, Shackleford, as the number one contender with a total of seven points, two points higher than the number two contender. This was "confirmed" by his best mid-pace Derby number of 112. The indicated betting strategy was to bet Shackleford to win and twice as much to place.

In the 2011 Belmont the program identified Ruler on Ice as the top contender, because of his monster late pace number of 110. The Belmont track handicappers and the morning line setter touted the public off by tabbing Ruler on Ice with a ridiculous morning line of 20/1. It was no surprise to FHH users that the Ruler, dancing home on top in the slop, paid a cool $51.60, 26.00, and 13.60. When the System's number four contender finished second, FHH had given its users a $928.00 exacta that was accomplished by running Ruler on Ice up and back with the screen horses.

As South Carolina is not a horse race betting state, my eldest asked if I would place a bet for him. Assuring him that his credit was good with me, I put $20 to win on the Ruler's nose for him. He was able to buy a badly needed new set of tires with his winnings.

On a sour note, one of the punters we solicited for the FHH software progam e-mailed Len: "Can you prove you picked Shackleford and Ruler on Ice *before* the races ran?" Of course we could, but we decided not to give such a "doubting Thomas" the time of day. It was his loss and it couldn't have happened to a more loss deserving guy.

On May 28, 2011, in between the Preakness and the Belmont, the system scored a huge win in the fifth race at Hollywood Park. The top four system contenders were the 5, 1, 3, 8. The 1, 5, and 8 were at morning lines of 6.8/1, 3/1, and 4/1, respectively. The 3, Slane Castle, was tied with the 1 and 8 for the number two contender in the system. With just a few minutes to post the 3 was 70/1! When Slane Castle crossed the finish line on top, paying $143.80, 44.80, and 15.20, we knew we had a winner with the FHH program.

On May 30, 2011, the system covered Arlington, Belmont, and Hollywood; picking 22 winners of 30 races. All of the winners came from one of the top four contenders as listed by the system in the lower left corner of the interface screen. 13 winners were "confirmed," each appearing in one or more of the Best in Category boxes in the lower right section of the screen. Half of the winners came from the system's top or tied for the top contender. Six winners came from the system's number two or tied for second contender. Five winners came from the system's number four contender or tied. A remarkable 17 of the 22 winners from the 30 races covered came from one of the system's top two contenders and ties. Eureka! It was clear that the Finding the Hidden Horse computer handicapping application was a winner.

SUGGESTED BETTING STRATEGIES

The general strategy is to bet one of the top two contenders, or both if the odds are a value. When one or both of the top two contenders are confirmed by one or more "Best in Category" boxes, run the top horse or two up and back with the remaining "screen" horses in exactas and trifectas. If you feel like swinging for the fences, box the screen horses underneath the key confirmed horse or horses from the top two contenders in supers. With the advent of dime supers, a five horse box costs $12; some of these bets often pay off in four figures.

Once the sorting is completed, the user needs to examine the track odds at about ten minutes to post, noting the odds on each of the system's first four contenders and ties. A problem arises when there are more than four top contenders due to one or more contenders being tied for fourth. In order to get the contenders down to four, the handicapper must go "inside the numbers" and attempt to separate the ties. The method that has worked best is to add the pace numbers - start, mid, late - to get a total pace number. In case of further ties (for instance, the total pace numbers on two or three of the tied contenders are not separated by more than three points), the handicapper then uses the best late pace number in a route, or the best mid pace number in a sprint. Often the numbers are too close to eliminate any of the ties; in that case you either spread bet or pass the race. An exception to this rule is that, regardless of a horse's total pace number, never eliminate a horse that is confirmed with at least one "Best in Category."

When the user finds mild to moderate overlays on any of the top four contenders, the next step is to check the Best in Category boxes in the lower right half of the screen. These are frequently value bets, especially when one or more of the contenders is at odds of 10/1 or more. For instance, if the number one contender has total points that are at least two points higher than the next contender and is also best in at least one of the Best in Categories, that horse is "confirmed" as a value bet and frequently is the key horse to use in structuring your exotic bets. In back testing the results since the release of the program, 58% of the winners have come from one of the system's top two contenders.

The program was conceived and dedicated to the proposition that long shot winners have in common certain "tells," or variables, that the general betting public, learned track handicappers, and fuzzy minded morning line setters overlook; or, for whatever reasons, ignore. In practice the system identifies many form or chalk horses while constantly searching for the tells that point to a solid long shot candidate.

The system was constructed on the mathematically scientific foundation of the above simple yet highly predictive variables that consistently point to a top effort by the top "tell" point horses as defined in the program and displayed on the interface screen. Two years of back checking several thousand race results, searching for repetitive algorithmic patterns, and applying the *laws of probability* and the theorem of *regression to the mean,* produced this consistent money maker of a program; an invaluable aid to professional and novice punters alike.

The Finding the Hidden Horse thoroughbred horse race handicapping software program requires that the user have nominal handicapping ability coupled with a strict adherance to the rule of common sense. The program's microscopic eye reads the past performance single comma delimited file from Brisnet in a millisecond, consistently revealing solid plays – long shots, middle shots, or short shots – to the hidden horse hunter.

Chapter 3

EARLY SCORES

"Nothing is more frequently overlooked than the obvious."
T. HOYNE

Early feedback from FHH users was not only encouraging, but in many cases the results were sensational. Always cognizant that the huge payoffs being reported by the users might be a case of beginner's luck, we recorded many of the responses.

E-mail from sophisticated user Ed Raven:

I got back late last night from my annual trip with the family to Lake George and Saratoga. We went to the track on Wed. 8/31 and had much success. The day started with the first and Hammock, a triple confirmed horse with a 3 point advantage over the second pick. Near post time he was 7-1 on the board so I made a substantial win bet with twice as much to place. This pick was also confirmed by some home grown numbers that I also use. I wheeled him in the double, since race 2 was a crapshoot. Hammock won and paid $17.00 to win. The DD came back $325 after a $41 horse won the 2nd. Great start to the day and a guaranteed profit. Gotta love it!!!

The other winners on the day were:

Race 6 – Top pick Count Catamount wins @ $6.40 and a cold exacta of $41.40.

Race 7 – Top Pick wins @ $9.40, cold exacta of $16.20 and cold trifecta of $55.00.

Race 8 – Top pick wins @ $8.40, exacta of $92.50, pick 3 - $128.

Race 9 – Top pick double confirmed, wins @ $7.50, pick 3 - $154.50.

It was a great day and the entire family had fun and best of all came away winners. I must say that I did not bet the short priced winners, but the family did and they were thrilled that they had so many winners.

On Saturday, I actually caught this race that you mentioned. I had the $35.20 winner and $802 exacta, but did not get the $6,000 tri as I put the 3 over the 1, 5, 6, over all. I did not put all in the second spot like you did. I never thought of doing that. Oh well, live and learn.

How did you decide to use all in the second slot instead of the third slot as usual in this race. I'm still dumbfounded by that.

Hi Ed,

The *all* bet can be useful when you are locked into your key horse that happens to be a long shot like the 3. As I said in the recap, I used the all in both first and second with the 3 because I knew the exacta would be big if the 3 got there first or second.

I learned a lot about constructing exotic bets from my dog racing friends when you couldn't play the horses in Wichita. You are right that most alls are done in third and fourth positions but I was so convinced that the 3 would get there that I thought it was worth a shot that another long shot could get there with the 3. (Half the field were long shots.) I thought it was a good gamble. It certainly wasn't handicapping – and I really liked the 1, 5, 6. In a 10 horse or more field I will frequently do an all for first and second when I really like my first pick. It has frequently been a good gamble.

When I get the time I want to discuss with you how best to break the ties when there are 2, 3, or 4 horses tied for fourth contender as I try to get the system's contenders down to four.

The inception of the concepton of the FHH handicapping software program:

Hi Dave,

A perfect example of applying the strategies set out in *Finding the Hidden Horse: Profiles of Long Shots* occurred in the sixth race at Santa Anita on Thursday, January 27, 2010, when a 60/1 long shot candidate was correctly identified by the system, finishing second and paying $34.20 to place, keying a $2 exacta of $216.90, a $2 trifecta of $923, and a superfecta of $3,939.60.

The system's first step is to determine the four best pre-race workout horses. The 3 was best at 4 furlongs in :46 2/5, the next best work was the 7 at 4 furlongs in :47, the 3rd best work was the 1 at 5 furlongs in :59 3/5, and the 4th best work was the 5 at 4 furlongs in :47 2/5. There were 2 tells on the 1, indicating the horse was ready for a top effort, notwithstanding his poor efforts in his only 2 races. Betting the 60/1 to win with twice as much to place; boxing the 4 lowest pre-race workout horses nailed the exacta, trifecta, and the superfecta at juicy prices.

And that is with the betting favorite winning!

Hi Conrad – If everything needed is in the pps, Len could likely program it and we could offer it to our software customers.

Hi Dave,

Yes, since the system is based on algorithms; that is, repetitive patterns or "tells" that are in the past performances of most long shot winners. When I finish working the race by pencil there are certain numbers that I work from. The remarkable thing is that if the system can't find a long shot candidate it will otherwise pick the logical contenders. The example I used of the 60/1 horse being identified as a probable long shot candidate by the system is an excellent case on point.

The "form" handicapper probably wouldn't have touched that horse with a ten foot pole, but he had two of the most important tells; that is, one of the four best pre-race workouts (those after his last race and before the current one) of the field and he was the sole cutback horse in the race. I know, his trainer had a pitiful record, but the figures said that horse had a shot to hit the board, just as the figures of the 2/1 winner of that race tabbed him for a big race. He had the best work of the field and had by far the best late pace figure.

The system uses seven basic variables with some refinements. These variable can all be pulled from the Brisnet past performances.

(2/5/2011)

While on the subject of the records of the trainers of long shot winners, most long shot winners do not have trainers in the top 10 trainer standings; one of the reasons the crowd lets them leave the gate at double digit odds. The FHH software system does not include, nor does it give any weight to the jockey or trainer records or jockey-trainer combination records; that is, no tell points are awarded for those variables, although those records are accessible in the program in the white columns above the main screen. The system is only interested in seven simple variables, or "tells;" current works, troubled previous race, cutbacks, start, middle-pace, late pace, and weight off from the previous race.

Early User Feedback:

Al K – I loaded Penn – 4 of 9 winners, including $48.00 winner in fourth. And Hollywood – 6 of 9 winners (all first or second picks), including $48 winner on top in eighth. Had the late pick 4.

Lou P – I purchased your system from RPM a few days ago and am very impressed.

Pat – Konrad, could you please put me on your update list for the Hidden Horse. Love the program. Love the book. Read it 3 times. Hit a $113. horse at MTH yesterday. Today $37.00 horse at MTH just boxing the top two horses produced a nice exacta around $300...a remarkable program.

Charles R –Thanks for your prompt response and information. I was lucky yesterday at Monmouth (race 8) with the FHH second choice #10, as the first choice (#1) was scratched. Boxing the FHH second choice with the post time favorite, I hit an exacta for $303.80. Yet and still, I definitely want to study and understand the results and feedback you send us to maximize and optimize the use of such a POWERFUL selection method.

Ed Raven – Can't thank you enough for your help…Race 3 – as you said, the 2 was double confirmed with low figs, but at 6/1 had to take a shot. He won and paid $15.30, 6.60. Had the exacta for $63.60 and the tri for $275.00 Profit $505. Race 8 – You know the results here! Having won yesterday and up today and having like this race a lot, I decided to push the envelope and make substantial wagers here. WOW!!! Both the 3 and 5 wento off at 13.7/1. Huge exacta of $320.80 and tri at $3,295!!! Race 9 – Decided to include the other screen horse, the 5 in my boxes…hit the tri that came back at $1,422.80.

An incredible day, to say the least. This is by far and away the best system I have ever purchased. It uncovers horses that the public overlooks very often, and often at incredible prices…

Larry M – Thanks for a great book, program, and all the help each day with your tutorial lessons. I have finally been able to find the long shots that I've missed in the past. Please continue to keep me updated.

Joe E – A bit late on the response of BC day. FHH had a really nice day on BC Saturday. The two horses I really loved were Little Mike and Trinniberg, and to have FHH listing them on the contender list was icing on the cake for me. I also hit the BC Classic Superfecta… My tout for the Classic was that Game On Dude would not run well and wouldn't even hit the board and that is why I threw him completely out of my super play. Trust me, I learned a long time ago that experts are wrong most of the time and when they are right they are the super chalk picks.

I am very anxious to try out FHH at Gulfstream...have always considered it to be a longshot play track. Actually thinking of going down there this year during the Eclipse Award event as there is also a Tournament at GP as well. Be nice to have FHH give me the winning picks for that contest.. Well thanks again for the updates and can't wait until you finish your current project. Have a very happy Thanksgiving Day! I know that I am very thankful for FHH and would like to thank you for sharing it with all of us.

P.S. I am pretty sure that FHH tabbed the winner at Holywood on Saturday, November 10, in the seventh race that paid $91.60 to win.

(Author's note: yes, the System nailed it.)

John M – Thank you for getting back to me as soon as you did. The information on your selections and betting strategies are priceless. WOW!!! What a Saturday at Keenland. In 60 years of playing horses I never had a day like that one...attached...your results of the fourth race...A great piece of work. You should be proud of it.

(Author's note: No doubt the next hat I buy will have to be a larger size to accommodate the swelling of the temporal encasement of my grey matter.)

Several of the above users have commented about "confirmed" horses, so a few words of explanation are in order. When an FHH user opens the interface screen, two sets of boxes appear on the lower half of the screen: one is to the left and headed "Contenders;" to the right appear four boxes headed "Best in Category." The Categories are: Works, Start, Mid, Late; these variables are "confirming" when they apply to one of the top contenders. Double confirming indicates that a horse is best in two categories, and is triple confirmed when best in three categories. (To my knowledge there have only been two instances in the past two years of a horse being best in all four categories.)

Early User Updates

On 7/1/2011, the system was tested in 31 races at Arlington, Belmont, and Churchill Downs; 83% of the winners came from one of the System's top four contenders and ties. Of these 26 winners, 16 were confirmed with at least one Best in Category variable; 20 of the 26 winners (64%) came from one of the system's top three contenders.

On 6/18/2011, the system was tested in 39 races at Arlington, Belmont, Churchill Downs, and Mountaineer (to see how the system would perform in the minor leagues). 32 winners (82%) came from one of the system's top four contenders and ties. 22 of these winners (69%) came from one of the system's top two contenders; 23 of the 32 winners (70%) were confirmed in at least one of the Best in Category variables; 7 were double confirmed.

Over the two day test, 58 winners (80%) came from one of the system's top four contenders and ties. 25 winners came the system's top contender; 41 winners (71%) came from one of the system's Best in Category variables; 12 of those were double confirmed.

HIDDEN HORSE SYSTEM TABS $94.80 WINNER IN 7TH AT MONMOUTH 9/10/2011; BELMONT TABS $56.80, $48.40 WINNERS IN 5TH AND 9TH ON 9/11/2011!!!

EARLY SCORES

Monmouth 9/10/2011 Race 7:

Winner #2 contender tied, confirmed with B/S, tied for third B/M
$94.80 34.20 12.80
Place #4 contender tied
Show Best Late
Fourth #2 contender tied
$2 exacta $599.60
$2 trifecta $2,788.00
$2 superfecta $6,356.20

Belmont 9/11/2011 Race 5:

Winner #4 contender, 2nd B/L, 3rd B/S **$56.50 15.00 7.00**
Place #3 contender, B/L
Show #1 contender
$2 exacta $240.50
$2 trifecta $719.00

Belmont 9/11/2011 Race 9:

Winner #3 contender tied, B/S **$48.40 16.60 13.80**
Placed #2 contender
Showed Best Late
$2 exacta $332.00
$2 trifecta $2,260.00

As a general rule, anytime a long shot (M/L of 10/1 or more) appears as one of the system's top four contenders, that horse should be bet, especially if it is confirmed with at least one Best in Category, for the system has found a tell or tells that the morning line setter and the betting public have overlooked. The standard system long shot play is to win and twice as much to place.

Because the challenges of thoroughbred horse race handicapping appear highly complicated, many novice handicappers assume at first glance that the variables are so many that it's probably best for them just to concentrate on the hot trainers and jockeys. Many beginners, knowing little of breeding or the history of this high strung hot blooded breed, just play the jockeys. The Finding the Hidden Horse software application reduces the nearly infinite number of variables involved in analyzing a horse race to seven simple "tells."

Neither jockey's nor trainer's records are included in the awarding of tell points by the system. It's all about the *horse,* and the answer to the most important question of all in the handicapping puzzle: what is the *present physical condition* of the horse? Is it ready to put in a top effort? The tells of the FHH system point the way for serious players, pointing them to the fields in which hidden horses hide, waiting to be found by the astute and persistent Hidden Horse Hunter.

Chapter 4

THE NATURE OF RISK

"...to lead you to an overwhelming question
Oh do not ask 'what is it?'
Let us go and make our visit."
T. S. ELIOT

The gambling urge is one of mankind's most primordial of instincts. Next to the abuse of controlled substances and alcohol, obsessive-compulsive gambling is a major cause of bankruptcies, broken marriages and homes; often leading to the disintegration of entire families. If it were practically possible, state gaming boards should require that all bettors who want to gamble at state sanctioned sites be given a short test — constructed by credentialed psychiatrists — to determine if the bettor is more likely than not a compulsive-obsessive personality. With its power to regulate the gaming industry within its jurisdiction, the state should require that every state sanctioned gaming source, horse track, and casino bar those individuals who are so designated from entry, including online websites. In other words, all gamblers who want to gamble at state sanctioned tracks or casinos would be required to qualify for a bettor's license issued by the state. That will happen, of course, the day after hell freezes over.

It doesn't take long for addicted compulsive gamblers to "whack out" as they are pulled into the spiraling downward vortex of betting too much, too often; feeding the need for feeling the "rush" of winning. It is only after they have gone through their cash, borrowing to the hilt on whatever collateral they have (usually their homes) and – in too many cases – stealing what they can get away with. Like alcoholics, they have to sink to the bottom of the barrel; then, and only then will they seek help for their addiction. In my early years of risk-taking I have been to the edge of the vortex more times than I care to admit, but was always able to pull back from the edge of disaster, for I knew when to quit.

Before I was introduced to horse race gambling, I dabbled in most of the other games of chance, never settling on one until many more years of trial and error. I was a poor crapshooter as I couldn't remember all of the rules. Though mathematics has been my bag (by profession a tax accountant), I wasn't any better at blackjack. I have never spent a dime on the numbers game, otherwise known as the state lottery. I was, however, a fair poker player, preferring the rather mundane Jacks or Better. As far as the one-armed bandits are concerned, the average player doesn't stand half a chance, primarily because the casino owners have basic human nature on their side; human nature not having changed since mankind first stood upright. Experts estimate that 70 percent of players are ahead of the game at some point in their casino visit, yet 90 percent leave as losers, having succumbed to one of the seven deadly sins – greed. As the noted philosopher Pogo famously asserted: "We have met the enemy, and he is us!"

When I visit the local casino I play video poker; one of the few gambling games in which I contend that the gambler has half a chance, for it's clearly a game of skill. Lotto, Keno, and Roulette players may as well throw their money in the gutter, as those games are strictly games of chance involving numbers over which the player has no control. Even when you play a game – Jacks or Better – in which the top hand, a royal flush, rarely pays more than $4,000 in a one dollar game for hitting a perfect hand (against which the odds are 43,000 to 1); you can readily see why a casino permit is – in a manner of speaking – a license to steal.

In the last 20 years competition for the gambling dollar has expanded exponentially. The floodgates opened after state after state discovered they could get into the numbers game with only token resistance from their voters; after all, the net proceeds were to be used for the general public good, were they not?

Just a few years ago, casinos and pari-mutuel horse and dog racing were illegal in the state of Kansas; today, the Kansas Star Casino is 20 minutes from my door, and from my desktop computer through simulcasting I can lawfully bet on every horse or dog track in the country, in addition to Australia, New Zealnd, and Dubai. A few days ago the Kansas Star Casino management announced to our local press that for the full year they would "win" over 189 million dollars. Obviously, they are proud of the nearly 16 million dollars a month ($500,000 a day) in winnings that they suck from this city of over 400,000, the aircraft building capital of the world.

Within 60 miles from my front door are four casinos; three just across the border in northern Oklahoma. At least the players benefit from the disclipines of competition forced upon the casinos because word gets around fairly fast when one casino gets a reputation for having tight slots. You can be sure that there is no chance of the casinos losing money: there is no risk for them, because the state guarantees them a more than generous margin of profit. All the casinos need to do to stay afloat is to consistently draw enough moths to their flame to pay their fixed overhead. That's the answer to the question often asked by slot players when just a single cherry hits: Why all the bells and whistles?

After more decades than I now care to admit, I have settled on two games of chance; video poker for entertainment; thoroughbred horse race handicapping for serious money. The Finding the Hidden Horse software program has been a gift from Lady Luck to most, if not all of its users, not the least of whom am I. The program has given me consistent profits and some spectacular hits, leaving me eternally grateful to Len Czyzniejewski for his brilliant coding of the original paper and pencil method.

Many users have asked how the system was constructed so that only seven simple variables could be so consistently predictive of the winners of thoroughbred horse races. Most systems on the market use a nearly infinite number of variables: jockey and trainer records, combination jockey-trainer records, breeding, trainer's records on various surfaces, track bias (inside, outside, or the middle) and many more variables too numerous to mention. So many of the handicapping and betting systems sold to the betting public are remarkably complicated; although I'm not referring to straight race selection subscription services (The California Handicapper, for instance) that for a month or for a track season charge a fee for telling the subscriber: "Bet this horse!"

The journey to simplicity that the FHH system began with was an exhaustive study of the laws of probability. Such laws could never exist without numbers, a subject that has fascinated me since the day I aced binary mathematics. Readily admitting that I am analytic to a fault (and just as readily attested to by my four children), I believe that all colleges; conservative, progressive, or if by some miracle – apolitical; owe to their students an advanced curriculum for in depth studies of the *laws of probability*, an apolitical course if ever there was one.

"Without numbers, there are no odds and no probabilities; without odds and probabilities, the only way to deal with risk is to appeal to the gods and the fates. *Without numbers, risk is wholly a matter of gut.*" (Emphasis added.) From *Against the Gods: The Remarkable Story of Risk.* (Peter L. Bernstein, John Wiley & Sons, Inc., New York, 1998.)

On the day I write this page I'm playing Belmont, one of my favorite tracks. One of the track's intrepid handicappers pointed out that in the last three days there were 18 straight failures by morning line and betting favorites; failing to recognize that this was an explicit criticism of the morning line setter and the track's handicappers, who too often lead the betting public down the primrose path. Have you noticed how often, after a race in which their highly touted favorite has failed, they just can't bring themselves to say: "Gee, we're sorry the favorite didn't get there. We were wrong." Yet the tracks put them out there as experts, and the public bites. Pay no attention to the announcers and the track handicappers; they will drive you up the wall. Turn the video sound down and figure the race out for yourself.

After 18 straight losses by favorites, would you – considering the law of probabilities – believe the favorite in the current race to be a good or a bad bet? A case can be made for either proposition, but the law of probabilities suggests that it might be a good idea to include the favorite, at least in your exotic bets, for the reason that the 18 race losing streak by favorites was several times over one standard deviation from the mean, or average. The odds of a favorite winning a particular race are one in three or .333, for favorites over time lose two of three races. And yes, the favorite won the instant race, bringing the mean of favorite wins over the last 19 races to .05263.

It's unusual for long shots (arbitrarily defined as winners at odds of 10/1 or more) to win two consecutive races; it's rare for them to win three in a row, and to the best of my memory, I don't believe I have witnessed long shots win four consecutive races during my handicapping experience of some 40 years. Today at Belmont two consecutive long shots won at prices of $79.80 and $30.00. What do you think the odds were for another long shot to win the next race? They would be difficult to precisely calculate, but surely the chances would be considerably less than 50/50 that a $20.00 or more winner would follow. In other words, there's a solid chance that the next race winner will be more formful than the previous two races. The next two races were more formful; the winners paying $11.80 and $10.60.

Conversely, when you see four or five favorites win in a row, the law of probabilities dictates that the card is due for a long shot win, for the *mean* will rule. Prejudiced as I am against favorites; partial as I am to long shots; I have to keep reminding myself that the law of probabilities has not - nor will it ever be – repealed.

THE NATURE OF RISK

The theorem of *regression to the mean* dictates that the probability of favorites winning percentages for the next 19 races at Belmont will be considerably more than the mean of .333 as the results revert, or regress, toward the historical average for winning favorites. Conforming to the law of probabliity, this is invaluable information for the Belmont punter over the next week or two, for the *law of probability* and the theorem of *regression to the mean* are joined at the hip when solving the problem of predicting with any regularity the outcome of any thoroughbred horse race.

As Nobel prize winner Daniel Kahneman, author of *Thinking Fast and Slow,* puts it: "The very idea of regression to the mean is alien, difficult to communicate and comprehend." (Farrar, Straus and Giroux, New York, 2011.) Nevertheless, the twin principles of causal probability and regression to the mean are crucial in building any handicapping system purporting to represent a consistent and valid predictor of the probable winner of any thoroughbred horse race.

The strongest pillar upon which the system's foundation was set asks the question: What is the *present physical condition* of the horse we are examining? Assuming we are not in possession of inside information (which is more often than not worthless), we must limit the examination to the horse's past performances in either the Daily Racing Form or the Brisnet records. The System uses Brisnet because of the detailed breakdown of the pace figures. Both publications are invaluable to the punter; the DRF gives us the Beyer number, Brisnet does not. The specific variable that answers the question as to the present condition of the horse being examined is *recency*.

Through trial and error over substantial back checking data, the following variables were discarded: most money won to date;

overall winning percentages of the horse, jockey, or trainer; quality of breeding; past class; class droppers or climbers; and a few more, none of which relate in a positive way to recency. The goal was to simplify the handicapping process, not to complicate it. Many systems I have seen use upward of 20 variables in their calculations. As one of my dog playing friends commented when horse racing came to Wichita through simulcasting at our local dog track: "In dog races the variables are few, with few exceptions each field consists of eight dogs, but in thoroughbred horse racing the variables are nearly infinite." In constructing the system we were determined to use only the variables necessary to produce consistent, reliable predictions of a probable top effort by any of the horses being examined in the current race.

We can probably generally agree that in the short run anything can happen. I've seen days at the track when my worst handicapping nightmare occurred; favorite after favorite after favorite won race after race after race. No matter, given enough races the average, or mean, will prevail. The larger the number of races the more likely the results will regress to the mean. On the other hand, I have had days when I have hit three consecutive long shot winners. Again, given the law of large numbers, it's probably not a good idea to back long shots in the next few races, for regression to the mean is sure to follow. If it were possible for Brisnet and or the DRF to keep track of and publish a daily running average of favorites winning at a specific track; that would be a huge handicapping aid to all punters, especially the hunters of hidden horses.

The regression to the mean hypothesis tells us that when results get too far away from the average of past results over time, there is a

THE NATURE OF RISK

gravitational pull back toward the mean in an over or under propostion; the more races covered, the more accurate the mean.

So *recency* was the overriding variable on which the FHH system was constructed; the most important of the variables, though no tell points were awarded for it. The question arose: *how* recent? Would the answer be too recent, or not recent enough? What was the "just right" number of back races the system needed to analyze in order to pinpoint the most important variables of the system? Should we just use a horse's last race to plug in our variables or all of the past performances printed in the form? The answer was determined by an algorithmic search; the critical analysis and trial and error examination of hundreds of past performance examples.

For the remarkable success of the system, the magic number was three; not one, nor five; not two, nor four – simply *three*; by remarkable coincidence – or not – a Fibonacci number! (Leonardo Pisano, AKA Fibonacci, was the "greatest European mathematician of the middle ages." His series of numbers – 0, 1, 1, 2, 3, 5, 8, 13, 21, 34 to infinity – demonstrates recurring patterns in nature that suggest the patterns of growth in man and nature are not spontaneous, but caused by and subject to immutable mathematical formulas, or preset patterns. Our organs, teeth, and bones are Fibonacci numbers; they also govern the branching in trees and the arrangements of leaves on a stem. Stock traders have devised Fibonacci trading systems that correlate to the theorem of *regression to the mean*.) They are magic numbers, and should be studied by any serious handicapper. It would be instructional to all punters to determine what percentage of races are won over time by horses carrying Fibonacci numbers.

Chapter 5

ON TOUTS AND TIPSTERS

"Sit down before fact like a little child, and be prepared to give up every preconceived notion, follow humbly wherever and to whatever abyss Nature leads, or you shall learn nothing."
T. H. HUXLEY

Spring usually comes late to Kansas: the winters can be a quarter year of grey skies and slushy streets, or the ground frozen for too long. The fortunate denizens of the Arkansas mountains are blessed with an early spring, usually arriving in mid February. So it was that Lil and I for many years looked forward to the opening of the Oaklawn Park meet in Hot Springs. That was long before I entered the game as an owner and breeder of thoroughbred horses. Even though February was in the middle of tax preparation season, we would often steal away for a three day weekend of playing the horses and rekindling our relationship with a mini-honeymoon. The fresh mountain air was invigorating in more ways than one, whetting our appetites for food and fun; renewing our relationship by each thinking of the other without the distractions of business and family. We always came home in an elated mood, whether or not we had won or lost at the track.

It was at Oaklawn that I bought my first tip sheet from the hustlers hawking their selections just outside the entrance to the grandstand. "Get your tip sheets here! Four winners yesterday! Only a dollar!" (That was a long time ago, when you could buy the Daily Racing Form for fifty cents.) After a couple of weekends in which I bought a tip sheet each day we played, I realized that the purveyors of handicapping wisdom for a dollar were just following the morning line setter for the track, touting mostly favorites. When later I refused one of the tipsters, he persisted by accompanying us to the entrance, until in desperation he hectored: "But it's only a buck!" Whereupon I deferred to the "cheapskate" of his tone by buying another tip sheet. Lil sweetly smiled as I gave it to her to give to another couple as we entered the grandstand in which the tip sheet sellers could not hawk their wares. Later, we encountered hucksters selling tips without the bother and expense of printing and paper. Their sales pitch was delivered by word-of-mouth; their customers sought them out rather than the other way around. It was a nearly perfect con.

One spring Saturday at Hot Springs I was witness to a masterful swindle perpetrated on several credulous bettors. We always liked to sit in one of the last two highest rows of the grandstand so that we could be closer to the betting windows, in addition to having a panoramic view of the mile long track. On the way back from the betting window I noticed a crowd of about a dozen punters gathered around an individual who kept pointing to his program, gesticulating to the crowd around him. My curiousity aroused, I moved closer, asking one of the bystanders at the edge of the circle what was going on.

"This guy has picked three straight winners, two were long shots!"

"Really?" I politely replied. "Good for him!"

"For fifty bucks he'll mark the rest of your program." I had been around the tracks long enough to recognize a shill when I saw one. "Thanks, anyway," I tossed back on the way to our seats.

"He likes the three horse in this race," he persisted.

Brushing him off, I replied: "Good for him."

Back at our seats, I discussed it with my beautiful punting partner. We examined the Daily Racing Form past performances of the tipster's 3 horse and found it wanting; we liked the 4. Nevertheless, human nature being what it is, and the 3 horse being 20/1 on the board, Lil suggested and I agreed to put 20 bucks on the 3 in addition to a solid bet on our pick, the 4.

You can guess what happened: the 3 wins in a walk and our 4 horse finishes second. Wow! Four hundred bucks for our 20 dollar bet, plus place money on our 4 and a five dollar exacta for $456.

"That guy must have inside information!" Lil suggested.

"Maybe. Maybe not. Let's give him a test."

After cashing the bets, I sauntered over to the enlarging crowd now circling the tipster. He was collecting a lot of fifties from the excited punters. In a conspiratorial tone he cautioned each sucker to: "Keep it down. We don't want this to get around, if too many of you are on the same horse it will knock our odds down."

I sprang for the fifty and he gave me the 2 horse in the next race. Taking the bait, we tabbed the tipster's horse for fifty bucks to win. I can't exactly say that we were overly surprised when the 2 finished dead last by 20 lengths. I turned to Lil: she turned to me; laughing at ourselves, we hugged and kissed. We had been both the victims and the beneficiaries of an ingenious con. Searching for the tipster in the area in which he had last been seen, it came as no surprise that he was nowhere to be found.

Telling Lil that I would be back in about ten minutes, I decided to do a little reconnoitring of the grandstand. The Oaklawn Park building is huge, with several floors and many betting areas. I reasoned that it would be easy enough to place several tipsters at strategic distances so that track management would have a difficult time sending a guard to investigate unusual crowds gathering around a tipster placed a substantial distance from other tipsters. On the first floor at the opposite end of the grandstand where we were seated, I found another tipster pointing to his program and gesticulating to a crowd circling him. Seems he had picked four races in a row; for fifty bucks he would mark your program.

Arriving back at our seats, laughing as I sat down, I said to Lil: "Of course, it's a con! It's a ring. If there are eight horses in a race, each of them gives out a different horse until they have covered the field. One of them is always going to have the winner. So seven were losers, the tipster with the winner attracts a crowd of punters eagerly pumping fifty bucks apiece into the hands of the "genius" tipster. After the race the seven losers move to different areas, repeating the process; the winner reeling in another set of suckers. We were lucky enough to be on the winner."

"And we only had to give back fifty bucks," Lil laughed. "Our lucky day."

It may be unfair to describe as "touts" the group of former trainers on the east coast who offer to provide bettors winners for a fee, usually $50 to $60 for a day's card. And, of course, they have "special" promotions for the Triple Crown and the Breeders' Cup races. To hear them tell it they never miss, their customers are always winners. No doubt many of you have been solicited by mail from most of them. They always have unbelievable winning records that they ask us to accept at face value, for who among us is going to take the considerable time it would take to verify their claims.

Many years ago – when I had not yet reached the level of handicapping sophistication to which I now aspire – I bit on the bait that a particularly well known former trainer mailed to me. When I called to subscribe for a week-end "special," I was put through to the "personal assistant" to the legendary, now retired trainer who made his living by selling tip sheets. After taking my order, the shill asked what kind of bettor I was. When he learned that I was something considerably more than a two dollar week-end bettor, he put me through to the great man himself.

In spite of the problem we had in communicating – I was methodical; he was impatient – he assured me he had one hell of a deal for me. Seems he had gathered together a group of about 15 "sophisticated bettors" and the upshot was that they were all going to pool their bankrolls and make a killing through a betting coup that was being set up by him and his widespread track contacts. He wanted me to believe that he knew practically all of the owners, trainers, and clockers at the big time eastern tracks and that he was sometimes privy to "inside information." For just fifteen hundred he would let me in. As soon as I replied that I would think about it and get back with him, the phone went dead. It was *caveat emptor* (let the buyer beware) in spades. So make sure that latin phrase is your motto the next time you are tempted to spring for a tip sheet.

Another east coast tipster announced that in last year's Sunshine Millions their organization hit 5 of 6 races! They actually bragged about picking winners paying $3.60, $5.20 and $6.20 at Gulfstream in the Millions races there and winners of $4.00 and $6.60 at Santa Anita for the same event. And, of course, they would have the subscriber understand that they are "in the know" with various track insiders: "At Santa Anita we're in constant touch with trainers, trip handicappers, clockers, sheet boys, handlers – and especially jockey agents. Mike Smith, Joe Talamo and Rafael Bejerano make their money off purses, not fees, so the "reps" work night and day to find out which horses are rounding into form and ready for a top effort. This is where one hand wipes the other: We give them our "inside info" - they give us theirs! This is as good as it gets – and our results prove it – SO GET ON BOARD!"

Sure, that's the way to win at this game! Pay attention to what jockey agents, trainers, trip handicappers, handlers and "sheet boys" have to say about a horse's chances. I wonder why the word *con* suddenly comes to mind. If they truly have all of this "inside information" at their disposal, why sell it to the public for piddling amounts? Why not put their own money where their mouth is and rake in the winnings that they are so sure will follow?

There are only half a dozen or so books on handicapping thoroughbred horse races that are, in my opinion, worth the time and money (hopefully, mine included). Most of them were written in an honest effort to impart the experience of the author to the novice punter. Unfortunately, most of them are complicated and difficult to follow with the exception of Andy Beyer's racing tomes: *Beyer on Speed* and *The Winning Horseplayer*. (The latter published in 1983 and the former in 1994 by Houghton Mifflin Company; New York, New York.)

The Winning Horseplayer was primarily about betting strategies rather than the finer points of handicapping and for that reason, alone, it deserved the recognition it received from the racing publication industry and its self-styled "expert handicappers." It's difficult to argue with most of the points Andy makes in his book, with the exception of his statement on page 186: "It is best not to base many handicapping decisions on published workout information." My ten years of owning, breeding, and racing thoroughbreds taught me that published workouts are one of the most valuable of variables in evaluating the present physical condition of a horse. Of course, the trainer doesn't *always* ask the horse for its *best* in every workout; the FHH program is only interested in the horse's best published workout since its last race – that's when the trainer asked for an all out effort. The horse may have run three lousy works since then, but we are only concerned with the best work when we know the trainer asked the horse to extend itself. In the case of two year olds, we are only interested in the first time starter's best published work since it was put into training, no matter the recency of the work. Of course, the punter would prefer that the best work be the most recent work, but I have caught a lot of two year old first time starter winners by simply using the horse's best work, no matter the timeliness of it. And especially if the work is the best of the race.

Beyer on Speed was published nearly 20 years ago and has withstood the test of time by validating Andy's revolutionary concept of a single "speed figure" for every horse in every race at every track in the country, published daily by *The Daily Racing Form*. In my opinion, it simplifies the handicapping equation in the extreme. Nevertheless, the FHH application does not use it as one of the variables of its formula. I have found the Beyer Numbers to be most useful in Grade One and Grade Two Stakes, but not so effective at the lower rungs of the racing ladder. Yet many punters use it exclusively in making their betting decisions. The final judgement on speed handicapping is probably best left to a friend of Andy's who told him for years: "It doesn't matter how fast they run; it's how they run fast that counts."

One of the more thorough and comprehensive treatments of the myriad problems that face the serious handicapper is Michael Pizzolla's *Handicapping Magic*. (I.T.S Press, Las Vegas, 2000.) In addition to being a successful punter, Michael is also an attorney. The law as well as the accounting profession requires its practitioners to have an eagle eye for detail; the successful handicapping of thoroughbred horse races requires that handicappers be no less meticulous in their search for the variables that will identify horses that are ready for a solid effort in the race being examined.

Pizzolla is also a world class sleight-of-hand magician who has performed before heads of state and royalty; surely, an exceedingly interesting and revealing avocation for a man of the law. He is the first to admit that there is no single magic secret to successful thoroughbred handicapping; it's all hard work, demanding acute concentration for considerable periods of time. He is of the opinion that the subject is so immensely complicated that no one person can possibly master all of the subtle nuances involved. Asserting that thoroughbred handicapping is much too complex to be reduced to simple rules, he has produced a 433 page tome in which he thoroughly covers the handicapping challenge by introducing to the punter the concepts of his trademarked Pace Balanced Speed, Form Cycle Window, Projected Power Fraction; and something called the Fulcrum Pace — all of which, though difficult to understand, are well worth the serious handicapper's study.

His observation that it is extremely difficult to make money at this game by making many bets not counter to the crowd are borne out in the foundation premise of the Finding the Hidden Horse software application. Many self-styled handicapping experts agree with Pizzola's contention that the handicapping process is too complicated to lend itself to a few mechanical rules. However, the record of the FHH System for the past two years demonstrates that it's possible to reduce the variables required to consistently predict the outcome of thoroughbred horse races by using just seven variables that separate the wheat from the chaff. Each of these variables is assigned a point value number that determines the top four contenders and ties: the system is not simple; neither is it complicated. Its foundation is simply the use of a modicum of common sense applied to the *law of probabilities* joined with the theorem of *regression to the mean*.

Chapter 6

HIDDEN HORSES FOUND!

"The battle is not always to the strong, nor the race to the swift, but that's the way to bet."
DAMON RUNYON

No matter how the contest looks on paper the race still has to be run, for *there's many a slip 'tween the cup and the lip* on the way to the finish line. The experienced handicapper has learned the hard way that there are several races on any card that are simply unplayable. Generally, I won't make a bet on a horse with odds of 7/5 or lower unless in that race the FHH program has located a promising long shot candidate to hook with that favorite in the exotics. Another generally passable race is one in which there are three or more horses with odds of 3/1 or lower. The two year old races should be passed when there are four or more first time starters. Experience has taught me that I'm fortunate if I can find half of the card's races playable. It took me a long time to learn that the world would probably not end if I did't play *every* race on the card. Today, my predilictions for the most playable races are routes, especially on the turf. My favorite classes of races are three year olds and up maidens of any class, and three and up non-winners of two races. The FHH software has been particularly adept in tabbing long shot winners from those two race classes.

Included in the cost of buying the FHH software application has been the update service I've provided at least weekly since May of 2011. Following are selected examples of some of the more remarkable long shot winners selected by the System.

FHH TABS $177.50 WINNER IN 5TH AT FINGER LAKES; $673 EXACTA; $5,488 TRI; DIME SUPER FOR $8,419: HAS SOLID BREEDERS' CUP PLAYS!!

On 11/3/2012 the FHH interface face screen for the 5th at Finger Lakes presented:

TELLS	M/L	POST
10=7	5/1	1/1
1= 6	20/1	56/1
3= 6	5/1	13/1
2= 4	3/1	2.5/1
4= 4	20/1	88/1
5= 4	15/1	46/1
7= 4	5/1	9/1

BEST IN CATEGORY

Work = 4 4   fur:48.4
Start = 10   95
Mid = 10   94
Late = 3, 6   82

In separating the four horses tied for #4 contender, the bettor should *always* include the confirmed horses; those with at least one Best in Category. The confirmed horses were the 3, 4 and the double confirmed 10 (the odds-on favorite at 1/1). As the system attempts to limit the contenders to just four horses, the tie breaker rule is to add the three pace numbers: start, middle, and late pace for a total pace number. The exception to this rule is that when one of the tied contenders is a *confirmed* horse, you don't throw it regardless of a better total pace figure by one of the other tied horses. In this case, the rule was to throw the 5 and 7, leaving the top five contenders as the 10, 1, 3, 2, 4. In analyzing the odds board the 1 and the 4 nearly jumped off the page to an experienced hidden horse hunter for the #2 contender tied and the #4 contender tied sported odds of 56/1 and 88/1. The system bet was to run the 10 up and back with the screen horses; the 1, 2, 3, 4, 6, in exactas, trifectas, and supers. Then to make straight bets to win and twice as much to place on the long shots 1 and 4.

The race comes 4, 10, 1, 3.

The winner pays **$177.50 38.20 12.00; $2 exacta $673; $2 trifecta $5,488; Dime Super $8,419.65!**
Note that the winner had Best Work; place horse had Best Start and Middle Pace, and the fourth place finisher had the Best Late Pace.

This race was a perfect example of the FHH program's ability to pull out of the form a long shot that, after a cursory look at its past performances, you wouldn't have touched with the proverbial ten foot pole. Yet, digging deeper, the form revealed that the winner had worked four furlongs in :48 2/5 on 10/26 – just eight days before the race; it was the best by far of Martina Bride's last twelve workouts and a particularly exceptional work for Finger Lakes. Additionally, the horse had been off for two months and was returning to the track with a *new* trainer; always an important variable to examine carefully. Always give a close look to a horse with these kinds of tells, especially when it is returning to the track freshened by the layoff and a new trainer and entered in a nearly bottom of the barrel race for $4,500 claimers consisting of three year olds and up, non-winners of two races.

HIDDEN HORSES FOUND!

FIFTH RACE
Finger Lakes
November 3rd, 2012

6 FURLONGS. (1.08¹) CLAIMING. Purse $8,000 FOR FILLIES AND MARES THREE YEARS OLD AND UPWARD WHICH HAVE NEVER WON TWO RACES. Three Year Olds, 121 lbs.; Older, 124 lbs. Non-winners of a race since October 3 Allowed 2 lbs. A race since September 3 Allowed 4 lbs. Claiming Price $4,500. (Showery 46)

Value of Race: $8,000 Winner $5,400; second $1,800; third $900; fourth $450; fifth $180; sixth $90; seventh $90; eighth $90. Mutuel Pool $21,521 Pick 3 Pool $2,843 Pick 4 Pool $11,548 Daily Double Pool $3,742 Exacta Pool $23,586 Superfecta Pool $11,230 Trifecta Pool $18,304

Last Raced	#	Horse	M/Eqt.	A/S	Wt	PP	St	¼	½	Str	Fin	Jockey	Cl'g Pr	Odds $1
28Aug12 4FL9	4	Martina Bride	L	4F	120	4	7	6¹	5³	2hd	1nk	Rohena J M	4500	87.75
05Oct12 7FL3	10	Terry Teresa	L	3F	119	9	1	1¹	1½	1²½	2⁴½	Flores J	4500	1.00
27Jly12 9Cby8	1	Next Top Model	L b	5M	114	1	5	3²	3¹	3¹	3¹½	Rodriguez G	4500	56.25
20Oct12 9FL1	3	Simply Stunning	L	3F	121	3	6	5hd	7³	6¹	4²½	Rodriguez J	4500	13.00
26Oct12 7FL3	7	My Three Daughters	L b	4F	120	7	2	9	9	7½	5¹	Perez M	4500	9.10
12Oct12 2FL3	6	At the Palace	L bf	3F	117	6	9	4¹	4½	5¹	6¹½	Ignacio R	4500	4.00
22Oct12 4FL3	2	Miss Directed	L b	3F	120	2	4	2hd	2¹	4¹	7³	Davila, Jr. M A	4500	2.50
11Oct12 4FL12	9	Columbia Falls	L bf	5M	120	8	3	7½	8hd	9	8⁵½	Sone J	4500	33.50
23Oct12 1FL6	5	Kwazy Kwisp	L b	3F	119	5	8	8½	6hd	8½	9	De Diego E	4500	46.00

OFF AT 1:53 Start Good For All But AT THE PALACE. Won driving. Track Muddy (sealed).
TIME :22², :46², :59⁴, 1:14¹   (:22.40, :46.54, :59.93, 1:14.23)

$2 Mutuel Prices:
4- MARTINA BRIDE 177.50 38.20 12.00
10- TERRY TERESA 2.60 2.10
1- NEXT TOP MODEL 10.80

$2 EXACTA 4-10 PAID $673.00 $1 SUPERFECTA 4-10-1-3 PAID $84,195.50
$2 TRIFECTA 4-10-1 PAID $5,488.00

Gray or Roan Filly, (My), by Say Florida Sandy - Country Blue by Runaway Groom. Trainer Gonzalez Ulises. Bred by Amy Boll & Jody Boll(NY).

MARTINA BRIDE was unhurried early, gained some two from the rail on the turn, eased out, took dead aim on the leader and under the whip as along in time. TERRY TERESA broke on top, set the pace off the rail, well clear a furlong out and then couldn't last. NEXT TOP MODEL was well placed along the rail, continued inside in the lane and finished with interest. SIMPLY STUNNING four wide up the backstretch, took the two path on the turn, angled out and made a mild bid. MY THREE DAUGHTERS lagged back while seven wide up the backstretch, entered the lane along the rail and then failed to fire. AT THE PALACE broke slow, saved ground early, angled out four wide into the turn, in striking distance into the lane and tired. MISS DIRECTED tracked along the three path, moved closer to the leader while four wide at the top of the lane and faded. COLUMBIA FALLS six wide up the backstretch, three path around the turn and tired. KWAZY KWISP broke sluggishly, saved ground and tired.

Owners- 4, Gonzalez Ulises ; 10, Lewis Mark J.; 1, Ross John P.; 3, DiStasio Richard A.; 7, Hernandez Enrique ; 6, Mitre Box Stable ; 2, River Card Stable ; 9, Windy Lea Farms ; 5, Murphy Timothy P.

Trainers- 4, Gonzalez Ulises ; 10, LeCesse Michael K.; 1, Ross John P.; 3, Markgraf David ; 7, Hernandez Enrique ; 6, Buckley Jonathan B.; 2, Acquiano James S.; 9, Buckley Jonathan B.; 5, Murphy Timothy P.

Breeders- 4, Amy Boll & Jody Boll (NY); 10, Patricia Generazio (FL); 1, John D. Murphy (KY); 3, Richard Distasio (NY); 7, Wellspring Stables (NY); 6, David Cassidy (NY); 2, Brent Fernung & Crystal Fernung (FL); 9, Windylea Farm/Philip J. O'Neill (NY); 5, Richard Zwirn & Kay Zwirn (NY)

Scratched- Isamu(16Oct12 9FL7)

$2 Daily Double (2-4) Paid $272.00; Daily Double Pool $3,742.
$2 Pick Three (7-2-4) Paid $2,131.00; Pick Three Pool $2,843.
$2 Pick Four (2/4-7-2-4) Paid $11,544.00; Pick Four Pool $11,548.

BEST WORK!
BEST START!

Winner 4 FHH #4 contender tied, confirmed by Best Work

COPYRIGHT 2012 BLOODSTOCK RESEARCH INFORMATION SERVICES

What to do with the layoff horse? That is the question. Should the punter wait for the horse's second try or back it in the first race back? That requires an examination of the work pattern since being put back into training. First, how long was the layoff? Second, what was the horse's performance in his last race? A good example occurred in the ninth race at Arlington on 6/30/2013 in a one mile 40k turf allowance contest. The 4 horse, Captain Marvin, had been off since his race of November 8, 2012; a full 238 days. That indicated a serious injury. He returned to training on April 13, 2013; since then he worked ten times. One of the works (on May 5, 2013) was a bullet of 4 furlongs in :47.2, best of 48 that worked that day at that distance at that track, indicating that Captain Marvin was physically ready to race. In the current race the horse had by far the Best Work and the Best Late Pace of the race, two variables supporting his fitness for his first try off a long layoff. As conventional wisdom among the "experts" is that you have to give the horse an out before backing him in a serious bet, the crowd let him leave the gate at the generous odds of 12.2/1. It should have come as no surprise to hidden horse hunters that Captain Marvin brought home the bacon as a $26.40 winner. The System and the pp's showed him to be the fresh and rested horse as he easily won the turf route contest.

NINTH RACE
Arlington
June 30th, 2013

1 MILE. (1.33²) (Off The Turf) ALLOWANCE. Purse $40,000 FOR THREE YEAR OLDS AND UPWARD ILLINOIS REGISTERED, CONCEIVED AND/OR FOALED WHICH HAVE NEVER WON $8,800 ONCE OTHER THAN MAIDEN, CLAIMING, OR STARTER OR HAVE NEVER WON TWO RACES. Three Year Olds, 120 lbs.; Older, 124 lbs. Non-winners of a race at a mile or over since May 30 Allowed 2 lbs. (Races where entered for $25,000 or less not considered). Lane 1. (If the management considers it inadvisable to run this race on the Turf Course, it will be run on the main track at One Mile). (Clear 80)

Value of Race: $40,000 Winner $24,000; second $8,000; third $4,000; fourth $2,000; fifth $1,200; sixth $267; seventh $267; eighth $266. Mutuel Pool $142,722 Pick 3 Pool $10,026 Pick 4 Pool $28,457 Pick 5 Pool $11,198 Pick 6 Pool $1,807 Pick 9 Jackpot Pool $4,773 Daily Double Pool $18,260 Exacta Pool $93,269 Jackpot High-5 Pool $7,944 Superfecta Pool $44,899 Trifecta Pool $70,498

Last Raced	#	Horse	M/Eqt.	A/S	Wt	PP	St	¼	½	¾	Str	Fin	Jockey	Odds $1
08Nov12 ^{8}Haw^{9}	4	Captain Marvin	L	4G	122	1	8	8	8	$6^{2\frac{1}{2}}$	$4\frac{1}{2}$	$1\frac{1}{2}$	Martinez S B	12.20
19Jun13 ^{8}AP^{2}	7	January Bee	L	5G	122	4	1	$1\frac{1}{2}$	$1^{1\frac{1}{2}}$	1^{1}	$1^{1\frac{1}{2}}$	$2\frac{3}{4}$	Hernandez R M	4.30
27Apr13 ^{5}Haw^{9}	6	Prince Cheval	L	4G	122	3	4	$4^{2\frac{1}{2}}$	4^{1}	5^{hd}	5^{1}	3^{nk}	Torres F C	17.50
01Jun13 ^{9}AP^{7}	8	Smokin Glock	L	3C	118	5	5	5^{4}	$5^{3\frac{1}{2}}$	$4\frac{1}{2}$	6^{3}	$4\frac{3}{4}$	Emigh C A	5.70
01Jun13 ^{3}AP^{1}	5	Cammack	L	3C	118	2	7	6^{hd}	6^{hd}	7^{3}	7^{6}	$5^{1\frac{1}{4}}$	Perez E E	2.40
08Jun13 ^{8}AP^{10}	13	Lahshad	L b	3G	118	8	2	$3^{1\frac{1}{2}}$	3^{1}	$3^{3\frac{1}{2}}$	3^{hd}	6^{1}	Perez E	12.60
01Jun13 ^{9}AP^{5}	9	Ultimo Trago	L b	3C	118	6	3	$2\frac{1}{2}$	2^{2}	2^{1}	2^{hd}	$7^{13\frac{1}{2}}$	Castro E	2.90
08Jun13 ^{8}AP^{6}	11	Tall Grass Cat	L b	3G	118	7	6	7^{3}	7^{1}	8	8	8	Desormeaux K J	7.10

BEST WORK!

OFF AT 5:17 Start Good. Won driving. Track Fast.
TIME :24¹, :48, 1:12⁴, 1:25², 1:38 (:24.30, :48.08, 1:12.83, 1:25.41, 1:38.18)

$2 Mutuel Prices:

4- CAPTAIN MARVIN	26.40	14.00	8.20
7- JANUARY BEE		5.80	4.40
6- PRINCE CHEVAL			7.80

$2 EXACTA 4-7 PAID $112.00 $1 JACKPOT HIGH-5 4-7-6-8-5 PAID $0.00 Carryover Pool $5,987
SUPERFECTA 4-7-6-8 PAID $226.32 TRIFECTA 4-7-6 PAID $250.50

Dark Bay or Brown Gelding, (Mar), by Kitten's Joy - Somethingtreasured by Charismatic. Trainer Gabriel, Jr. G. Leo. Bred by Nikolaus Bock(IL).

CAPTAIN MARVIN was reserved in last off the inside in the opening half, advanced readily four deep on the turn to gain contention nearing upper stretch, was fanned five wide racing through the stretch but continued with a steady effort to prevail in time under firm handling. JANUARY BEE moved to the fore from the break, dictated the pace on a narrow margin a bit off the inside racing into the turn, maintained the advantage while shifting well out racing into upper stretch but was collared late. PRINCE CHEVAL, held up tracking off the first flight while angling inside early, saved ground to upper stretch and continued willingly inside foes to late stages to close the gap. SMOKIN GLOCK was rated just out of striking distance outside a rival in the opening stages, steadily drew into contention between foes racing into upper stretch, then altered course four deep avoiding close quarters in midstretch but continued willingly in that path to the end. CAMMACK swerved out avoiding traffic in early stages, was collected to track between foes well off the second flight racing into the turn, gradually drew into contention racing into upper stretch, then shifted out six wide in the last furlong to make some belated progress. LAHSHAD tracked the pace three deep from within striking distance early, lost some ground to the leaders racing into the bend, made a steady effort to challenge in that path nearing upper stretch but emptied out leaving the furlong marker. ULTIMO TRAGO, in touch with the pacesetter between foes in the opening stages, prompted the leader racing to upper stretch and gave way. TALL GRASS CAT was guided to the inside early tracking the leaders from out of striking distance and never mounted a serious challenge.

Owners- 4, Diamond Racing Inc. and Janssen, Jay and Joan ; 7, Stirtz William ; 6, Casa De Caballos ; 8, Asiel Stable ; 5, Team Block ; 13, Law Dog Stables, Inc. ; 9, Hernandez Racing Club ; 11, Virginia H. Tarra Trust

Trainers- 4, Gabriel, Jr. Leo G.; 7, Becker Scott ; 6, Aguirre Roy ; 8, Silva Carlos H.; 5, Block Chris M.; 13, Hansen Andrew M.; 9, De la cerda Armando ; 11, Block Chris M.

Breeders- 4, Nikolaus Bock (IL); 7, R & R Stables (IL); 6, Casa de Caballos, Ltd (IL); 8, Asiel Stable (IL); 5, Team Block (IL); 13, Elizabeth Valando, Alexander J. Lee &Steven A. Mari (IL); 9, Salvador Hernandez (IL); 11, Virginia H. Tarra Trust (IL)

Scratched- Lighthouse Pride(01Jun13 ^{10}AP^{7}), Big Man in Black(08Jun13 ^{6}AP^{5}), He's Dann Good(05Jun13 ^{3}AP^{1}), Run Right At It(19Oct12 ^{6}Haw^{9}), Cardston(08Jun13 ^{8}AP^{2}), Excellent Chance(19Jun13 ^{8}AP^{8})

$2 Daily Double (3-4) Paid $117.20; Daily Double Pool $18,260.
$1 Pick Three (1/6/9-3-4) Paid $269.50; Pick Three Pool $10,026.
PICK 4 3-1/6/9-3-4 PAID $522.10
-3-1/6/9-3-4 PAID $1,566.05 $1 Pick Six (6-4-3-1/6/9-3-4) 4 Correct Paid $25.50; Pick Six Pool $1,807; Carryover Pool
PICK 9 JACKPOT 2-5-6-6-4-3-1/6/9-3-4,PAID $1,014.31 7 Cogrect Carryover Pool $22,382

Data provided or compiled by Equibase Company, which includes data from The Jockey Club, generally is accurate but occasionally errors and omissions occur as a result of incorrect data received by others, mistakes in processing and other causes. Equibase Company and Bloodstock Research Information Services, Inc. and Thoroughbred Sports Network disclaim responsibility for the consequences, if any, of such errors, but would appreciate being called to their attention. Copyright 2013

Winner 4 - 238 day layoff - Best Work, Best Late Pace

COPYRIGHT 2012 BLOODSTOCK RESEARCH INFORMATION SERVICES

RUNNING A HOLE IN THE WIND: HIDDEN HORSES FOUND

The Breeders' Cup races are always a challenge because of the many foreign horses entered that have not run in this country. I have been gathering a data base on foreign horses in order to decipher the chartwriter's usually cryptic descriptions and too often nearly unintelligible comments. 2012's cup races were no exception. The bottom line is that you probably have to pass the races in which more than one foreign horse is entered, unless you can get at least a general idea of the foreign steed's style of running: whether it is a front runner, a mid-pace stalker, or a late pace closer.

FHH TABS 9 WINNERS OF 15 CUP RACES! LONG SHOTS OF $32.60, 20.40, 36.60, 29.40; EXACTAS $50.60, 95.80, 136.40, 54.80; TRIFECTAS $121.80, 115.20, 220.80, 249.40; SUPERS $323.60, 237.20, $1,257.20, 1,001.40; PICK 3s $1,863, 2,214.

Comments and Analysis: In the fifth race on Friday's card the System tabbed the 4 horse, Grassy, with the Best Late Pace of an astounding 120. This was an excellent example of the ability of the FHH System to pull out of the form a long shot that the morning line setter and the betting public have overlooked or ignored for whatever reason. This was a marathon race at a mile and three quarters, making the variable of Best Late Pace doubly important. There were four foreign horses in the race, each carrying from 6 to 14 pounds less than in their last race. After deciphering the foreign chart writer's comments, it appeared that the 6 horse, Calidoscopio, was a monster closer with post time odds of 17/1. The System called for a bet to win and twice as much to place on both the 4 and 6, then to box the 4 and 6 in exactas. The 6 wins in a driving come from behind close and the 4 closes to be second.

FIFTH RACE
Santa Anita
November 2nd, 2012

1¾ MILES. (2.53^2) STAKES. Purse $500,000 *BREEDERS' CUP MARATHON (GRADE II)* FOR THREE-YEAR-OLDS AND UPWARD. Northern Hemisphere Three-Year-Olds, 122 lbs.; Older, 126 lbs.; Southern Hemisphere Three-Year-Olds, 115 lbs.; Older 126 lbs. All Fillies and Mares allowed 3 lbs.; $5,000 to pre-enter, $10,000 to enter, with guaranteed $5 00,000 purse including nominator awards of which 54% to the owner of the winner, 18% to second, 9.9% to third, 6% to fourth and 3% to fifth; plus stallion nominator awards of 3% to the winner, 1% to the second and 0.55% to third and foal nominator awardeo f 3% to the winner, 1% to second and 0.55% to third. (Clear 71)

Value of Race: $464,500 Winner $270,000; second $90,000; third $49,500; fourth $30,000; fifth $15,000. Mutuel Pool $1,872,779 Pick 3 Pool $256,103 Pick 5 Pool $745,442 Daily Double Pool $218,074 Exacta Pool $1,361,208 Superfecta Pool $848,520 Trifecta Pool $939,279

Last Raced	# Horse	M/Eqt.	A/S	Wt	PP	½	1m	1¼	1½	Str	Fin	Jockey	Odds $1
23Jun12 ^{9}HAR^1	6 Calidoscopio (ARG)	L	9H	126	6	13	12^{hd}	$10^{3\frac{1}{2}}$	$5^{1\frac{1}{2}}$	2½	$1^{4\frac{1}{4}}$	Gryder A T	17.20
30Sep12 ^{9}SA^4	4 Grassy	L	6H	126	4	7^{hd}	5^{hd}	4½	3^1	$4^{1\frac{1}{2}}$	2½	Gomez G K	13.90
29Sep12 ^{10}Bel^4	1 Atigun	L	3C	122	1	3½	$2^{1\frac{1}{2}}$	1^1	1^1	1^1	$3^{5\frac{3}{4}}$	Smith M E	3.10
14Oct12 ^{9}Fno^2	14 Juniper Pass	L	5G	126	13	$4^{1\frac{1}{2}}$	$4^{2\frac{1}{2}}$	2½	2^1	3^{hd}	$4^{1\frac{1}{2}}$	Dettori L	14.70
06Oct12 ^{10}Lrl^1	7 Not Abroad	L b	5H	126	7	$12^{7\frac{1}{2}}$	9^{hd}	7½	4^2	5^5	5^1	Petro N J	8.00
29Sep12 ^{10}SA^9	3 Balladry	L	4C	126	3	$8^{2\frac{1}{2}}$	6½	9^2	8^1	$8^{11\frac{1}{2}}$	$6^{1\frac{1}{4}}$	Graham J	47.30
06Oct12 ^{8}Haw^3	10 Eldaafer	L b	7G	126	10	9^1	$8^{1\frac{1}{2}}$	8^1	7^2	7^1	7½	Santana, Jr. R	9.80
07Oct12 ^{9}SA^3	8 Romp (ARG)	L	8G	126	8	$10^{1\frac{1}{2}}$	7^1	6½	6^1	6½	$8^{30\frac{1}{4}}$	Rosario J	52.90
06Oct12 ^{8}Hst^1	11 Commander	L	4G	126	11	$2^{1\frac{1}{2}}$	3^2	5^1	9^6	$9^{5\frac{1}{2}}$	$9^{2\frac{1}{4}}$	Gutierrez M	6.40
25May12 ^{13}SI^3	9 Almudena (PER)	L f	5M	123	9	11^3	$10^{3\frac{1}{2}}$	11^{14}	$11^{30\frac{1}{2}}$	11	10^1	Valdivia, Jr. J	27.30
21Oct12 ^{3}SA^3	5 Jaycito	L bf	4C	126	5	1½	1½	3½	10^5	$10^{3\frac{1}{2}}$	11	Talamo J	10.40
08Sep12 CUR^{10}	13 Sense of Purpose (IRE)	L	5M	123	12	5^{hd}	13	$12^{6\frac{1}{2}}$	12	12	12	Smullen P J	21.40
20Oct12 ASC^5	2 Fame And Glory (GB)	L b	6H	126	2	6½	11^1	13	13	13	13	Spencer J P	3.60

BEST LATE!

OFF AT 1:52 Start Good. Won driving. Track Fast.

TIME $:47^4$, 1:12, $1:38^1$, $2:04^2$, $2:30^2$, $2:57^1$ (:47.85, 1:12.00, 1:38.25, 2:04.53, 2:30.55, 2:57.25)

$2 Mutuel Prices:				
	6- CALIDOSCOPIO (ARG)	36.40	16.00	9.80
	4- GRASSY		12.40	7.60
	1- ATIGUN			3.40

$1 EXACTA 6-4 PAID $252.50 $1 CONSOLATION PICK 3 5-4-6 PAID $114.20 3 Correct
$1 SUPERFECTA 6-4-1-14 PAID $15,281.50 $1 TRIFECTA 6-4-1 PAID $1,133.80

Bay Horse, (Sep), by Luhuk - Calderona (ARG) by Lefty. Trainer Frankel Guillermo. Bred by Haras La Quebrada(ARG).

CALIDOSCOPIO (ARG) broke a step slow, lagged well back through the opening seven furlongs, commenced a run off the rail leaving the three quarter pole, advanced between rivals leaving the far turn, swung out six wide straightening for the wire, closed determinedly under stout left handed pressure, overtook ATIGUN approaching the sixteenth marker, had his rider switch to the right stick and eagerly kicked away. GRASSY , taken to rate early while off the rail, angled wider past the five eighths pole, gave chase under a hard ride exiting the far turn, gained ground nearing the lane, could not go with the winner but did continue willingly to get up for the place in the final yards. ATIGUN moved up inside rivals around the first turn to gain a forward spot, angled out and moved four to five wide to engage JAYCITO with about seven furlongs to go, briefly alternated with that one before edging clear mid way down the backstretch, took pressure into the lane, was overtaken nearing the sixteenth marker and gave way grudgingly. JUNIPER PASS , in range while removed from the inside, took closer order when given his cue leaving the five eighths pole, collared ATIGUN departing the far turn, pressed that one into the stretch then faded in the final furlong. NOT ABROAD settled off the early pace, gained ground working between foes near the far turn, dropped in to the rail and gained past the three furlong marker, chased into the stretch then flattened out. BALLADRY saved ground in range early, swung out wide in upper stretch and had some belated action. ELDAAFER , four to five wide, had a mild gain near the half mile marker, raced under a hard drive around the final turn then gave way. ROMP (ARG) saved ground early, angled wide approaching the five eighths pole, gave chase around the far turn then weakened. COMMANDER took over soon after the break while about four wide, rated back off of JAYCITO when that one rushed up around the initial turn, tracked while remaining well off the rail into the backstretch, came under a hard ride on the far turn, failed to kick on and faltered. ALMUDENA (PER) , four wide, faltered and was eased. JAYCITO broke a step slow, rushed up inside foes into the first turn and took over, set the pace three wide, was joined by ATIGUN around the second turn, dueled briefly with that one, chased past the five eighths pole, stopped with three furlongs to go and was eased. SENSE OF PURPOSE (IRE) , wide, faltered and was eased. FAME AND GLORY (GB) , under a drive while five wide into the second turn, failed to kick in, faltered and was eased. The opening quarter mile was run in 23.89. Also, a black trash bag blew into the center of the track as the horses neared the wire the first time but none of the runners appeared to be affected.

Owners- 6, Stud Dona Pancha ; 4, Button Stable, Hicker, George and Jones, Gary F. ; 1, Shortleaf Stable, Inc. ; 14, Irvin, Betty and Robert G. ; 7, Cunningham Timothy ; 3, Godolphin Racing, LLC Lessee ; 10, E-Racing.Com and Jacobsen, Kevin ; 8, Sisters in Racing Stable and Siskin, Jeff ; 11, North American Thoroughbred Racing Comp., Inc. ; 9, Stud Manning ; 5, Zayat Stables, LLC ; 13, Moyglare Stud Farm, Ltd. ; 2, Hay, Mrs. Fitriani, Smith, Derrick, Magnier, Mrs. John and Tabor, Michael, B.

Trainers- 6, Frankel Guillermo ; 4, Jones Martin F. ; 1, McPeek Kenneth G.; 14, Ball, II Thomas Ray; 7, Petro Michael P.; 3, Harty Eoin G.; 10, Alvarado Diane ; 8, Mulhall Kristin ; 11, Taylor Troy ; 9, Suarez Juan V.; 5, Baffert Bob ; 13, Weld Dermot K.; 2, O'Brien Aiden P.

Breeders- 6, Haras La Quebrada (ARG); 4, Claiborne Farm & Adele B. Dilschneider (KY); 1, Brereton C. Jones (KY); 14, Brookdale Thoroughbreds LLC (KY); 7, Bowman & Higgins Stable, Thomas Sutton& Huckleberry Farm LLC (MD); 3, Darley (KY); 10, Shadwell Farm, LLC (KY); 8, John T. Behrendt (ARG); 11, Paragon Farms, LLC (KY); 9, El Catorce (PER); 5, Runnymede Farm Inc. & Catesby W. Clay (KY); 13, Moyglare Stud Farm Ltd (IRE); 2, Ptarmigan Bloodstock and Miss K. Rausing (GB)

Scratched- Worth Repeating(23Sep12 ^{11}Fpx^1)

$2 Daily Double (1-6) Paid $580.40; Daily Double Pool $218,074.

4 Grassy - Best Late Pace 120'

COPYRIGHT 2012 BLOODSTOCK RESEARCH INFORMATION SERVICES

The race comes 6, 4, 1, 14.

The winner pays **$36.40 16.00 9.60; $2 exacta $505.00.**

In the Classic my key horse was the #1 system contender, the 11, Mucho Macho Man. I was also interested in Flat Out, the 2, that had been trained by my last trainer, Charles "Scooter" Dickey, who trained the horse to its Jockey Gold Cup Win, then lost the horse to Bill Mott in February of 2012. Word from Scooter was that Flat Out had soft pads and needed a wet track for his best effort. In this race he was the system's #3 contender tied.

I used the 2 and the 11 to hit the board; betting 2, 11 with 2, 11, with all; all with 2, 11 with 2, 11; and 2, 11 with all with 2, 11. I then ran the 11 up and back with the field in exactas. Caught a nice $125.40 exacta and a trifecta of $613.80 and salvaged out on my win and twice as much to place on the 11 when the race comes 4, 11, 1, 10.

The Santa Anita track handicapper couldn't restrain himself from touting the failed favorite, Game On Dude: "I guarantee you Game On Dude will win. There is no way that he can lose this race!"

Evidently he had never seen a horse stumble out of the gate. Like most track handicapping "experts" their main assignment appears to be the constant touting of the morning line favorite. Apparently the track handicapper had not studied the form which clearly showed that if Game on Dude didn't break on top he wasn't going to pass many horses in the stretch. I thought the horse was

TWELVETH RACE
Santa Anita
November 3rd, 2012

1⅛ MILES. (1.574) STAKES. Purse $5,000,000 *BREEDERS' CUP CLASSIC (GRADE I)* FOR THREE-YEAR-OLDS AND UPWARD. Northern Hemisphere Three-Year-Olds, 122 lbs.; Older, 126 lbs.; Southern Hemisphere Three-Year-Olds, 117 lbs.; Older, 126 lbs. All Fillies and Mares allowed 3 lbs. $50,000 to pre-enter, $100,000 to enter, with guaranteed $5 million purse including nominator awards of which 54% to the owner of the winner, 18% to second, 9.9% to third, 6% to fourth and 3% to fifth; plus stallion nominator awards of 3% to the winner, 1% to second and 0.55% to third and foal nominator awards of 3% to the winner, 1% to second and 0.55% to third. (Clear 77)

Value of Race: $4,545,000 Winner $2,700,000; second $900,000; third $495,000; fourth $300,000; fifth $150,000. Mutuel Pool $6,086,309 Pick 3 Pool $1,342,861 Pick 4 Pool $3,418,043 Pick 6 Pool $3,138,394 Daily Double Pool $958,997 Daily Double Pool $391,821 Exacta Pool $3,531,722 Superfecta Pool $1,929,440 Super High Five Pool $257,286 Trifecta Pool $3,208,736

Last Raced	# Horse	M/Eqt.	A/S	Wt	PP	¼	½	¾	1m	Str	Fin	Jockey	Odds $1
29Sep12 10Bel3	4 Fort Larned	L bf	4C	126	4	$1\frac{1}{2}$	$1\frac{1}{2}$	$1^{2\frac{1}{2}}$	$1^{1\frac{1}{2}}$	$1\frac{1}{2}$	$1\frac{1}{2}$	Hernandez, Jr. B J	9.40
01Sep12 10Sar2	11 Mucho Macho Man	L	4C	126	11	$2\frac{1}{2}$	$2\frac{1}{2}$	$2^{1\frac{1}{2}}$	2^{4}	2^{7}	$2^{6\frac{1}{2}}$	Smith M E	6.30
29Sep12 10Bel1	2 Flat Out	L	6H	126	2	$9^{4\frac{1}{2}}$	$9^{5\frac{1}{2}}$	$9^{2\frac{1}{2}}$	$5\frac{1}{2}$	$3^{2\frac{1}{2}}$	$3\frac{3}{4}$	Rosario J	6.20
29Sep12 10Bel6	10 Ron the Greek	L	5H	126	10	$10^{1\frac{1}{2}}$	$10^{2\frac{1}{2}}$	$10^{1\frac{1}{2}}$	8^{1}	$5\frac{1}{2}$	4^{nk}	Lezcano J	8.80
29Sep12 10SA3	9 Richard's Kid	L b	7H	126	9	12	12	12	$7\frac{1}{2}$	$7^{2\frac{1}{2}}$	$5^{2\frac{3}{4}}$	Gomez G K	16.10
29Sep12 10SA2	8 Nonios	L	3C	122	8	6^{hd}	$8^{2\frac{1}{2}}$	6^{1}	4^{hd}	$4\frac{1}{2}$	$6^{4\frac{1}{2}}$	Pedroza M A	21.00
29Sep12 10SA1	5 Game On Dude	L b	5G	126	5	7^{1}	6^{1}	$5\frac{1}{2}$	$3^{3\frac{1}{2}}$	6^{hd}	$7^{2\frac{1}{2}}$	Bejarano R	1.30
06Oct12 8Haw1	1 Pool Play	L	7H	126	1	11^{3}	11^{3}	$11^{1\frac{1}{2}}$	$9^{1\frac{1}{2}}$	9^{6}	$8^{3\frac{1}{4}}$	Mena M	38.70
22Sep12 11Prx1	7 Handsome Mike	L b	3C	122	7	4^{hd}	5^{1}	$4\frac{1}{2}$	6^{2}	8^{1}	$9^{14\frac{1}{4}}$	Gutierrez M	25.10
29Sep12 8Bel4	12 To Honor and Serve	L	4C	126	12	3^{hd}	3^{1}	$3\frac{1}{2}$	$10^{1\frac{1}{2}}$	10^{2}	$10^{2\frac{1}{4}}$	Velazquez J R	16.10
08Sep12 3Bel3	6 Brilliant Speed	L b	4C	126	6	8^{3}	$7\frac{1}{2}$	$8^{2\frac{1}{2}}$	11^{1}	11^{6}	$11^{7\frac{1}{4}}$	Alvarado J	45.40
22Sep12 11Prx6	3 Alpha	L	3C	122	3	5^{1}	4^{hd}	7^{hd}	12	12	12	Dominguez R A	23.50

ANNOUNCER'S GUARANTEED WINNER!
DOUBLE CONFIRM
FALSE FAVORITE

OFF AT 5:43 Start Good. Won driving. Track Fast.
TIME :23¹, :46², 1:10, 1:34³, 2:00 (:23.20, :46.50, 1:10.12, 1:34.66, 2:00.11)

$2 Mutuel Prices:

4- FORT LARNED	20.80	9.80	6.80
11- MUCHO MACHO MAN		6.60	4.60
2- FLAT OUT			5.20

$1 EXACTA 4-11 PAID $62.70 $1 SUPERFECTA 4-11-2-10 PAID $1,763.30
$1 SUPER HIGH FIVE 4-11-2-10-9 PAID $14,024.60 $1 TRIFECTA 4-11-2 PAID $306.90

Bay Colt, (4yr), by E Dubai - Arlucea by Broad Brush. Trainer Wilkes R. Ian. Bred by Janis R. Whitham(KY).

FORT LARNED disputed the early pace under rating outside ALPHA, dropped in towards the rail to establish command nearing the first turn, took some pressure while within himself, edged away nearing the half mile marker, came under left handed urging entering the stretch, was confronted by MUCHO MACHO MAN in the vicinity of the eighth pole, kept on tenaciously under continued left handed urging and fended off that rival. MUCHO MACHO MAN, forwardly placed between rivals into the first turn, patiently tracked the winner down the backstretch, was given his cue to go on leaving the far turn, steadily cut into the margin approaching the lane, drew alongside the winner in mid stretch, dueled gamely but could not get by. FLAT OUT settled well off the early pace while towards the inside, swung out nearing the half mile marker, commenced a five wide run leaving the far turn and into the lane, drifted in past the furlong grounds and failed to seriously sustain. RON THE GREEK, away a bit awkwardly, dropped in passing the stands the first time and lagged back, angled out to start a four wide run exiting the three eighths pole, continued progress into the stretch but could only gain slightly in the last eighth. RICHARD'S KID, three wide early while well off the pace, split foes making a nice run nearing the five sixteenths marker, angled in soon after, shifted back out in upper stretch, moved up between rivals nearing the eighth pole as his rider lost his whip, drifted in some late and flattened out. NONIOS brushed with GAME ON DUDE and was floated out five wide near the seven eighths pole, edged closer off the rail after six furlongs, gave pursuit between horses nearing the lane, angled in but failed to kick on. GAME ON DUDE lightly steadied soon after the break and angled in to rate behind rivals, brushed with NONIOS when working outward for a clear path into the first turn, steadied off the heels of TO HONOR AND SERVE nearing the backstretch, shifted out and stalked four wide, made a brief but sharp move leaving the far turn, flattened out under pressure past the five sixteenths pole, drifted in and gave way through the drive. POOL PLAY lacked speed saving some ground, swung five wide around the final turn but lacked a rally. HANDSOME MIKE, up close between rivals around the first turn, dropped in a bit and rated close into the far turn, came under pressure soon after, brushed with RICHARD'S KID nearing the stretch then gave way. TO HONOR AND SERVE, four to five wide early, angled in to about the three path around the first turn to attend the pace, steadied off the heels of GAME ON DUDE into the second turn, faltered soon after and was being eased late. BRILLIANT SPEED steadied repeatedly when difficult to settle behind rivals the entire first turn, chased off the rail and angled out leaving the second turn, gave way and was eased. ALPHA, sent from the gate to get a brief early lead, rated back along the rail to stalk the winner into the backstretch, had nothing when called upon near the half mile marker, stopped abruptly leaving the three eighths marker and was eased through the final three sixteenths.

Owners- 4, Whitham Janis R.; 11, Reeves Thoroughbred Racing ; 2, Preston Stables LLC ; 10, Brous Stable, Wachtel Stable and Hammer, Jack, T. ; 9, Kenney, D., Triple B Farms , Westside Rentals.com, et al ; 8, Smith, Jr. Green B.; 5, Diamond Pride LLC, Lanni Family Trust, Mercedes Stable LLC and Schiappa, B. ; 1, Farish, Jr. W.S. ; 7, Reddam Racing LLC ; 12, Live Oak Plantation ; 6, Live Oak Plantation ; 3, Godolphin Racing, LLC Lessee

Trainers- 4, Wilkes Ian R.; 11, Ritvo Katherine ; 2, Mott William I.; 10, Mott William I.; 9, O'Neill Doug F.; 8, Hollendorfer Jerry ; 5, Baffert Bob ; 1, Casse Mark E.; 7, O'Neill Doug F.; 12, Mott William I.; 6, Albertrani Thomas ; 3, McLaughlin Kiaran P.

Breeders- 4, Janis R. Whitham (KY); 11, John D Rio & Carole A Rio (FL); 2, Nikolaus Bock (FL); 10, Jack T. Hammer (FL); 9, Fitzhugh, LLC (MD); 8, Hermitage Farm LLC (KY); 5, Adena Springs (KY); 1, Windfields Farm (ON); 7, John Liviakis (KY); 12, Twin Creeks Farm, Larry Ross & RanchoSan Miguel (KY); 6, Live Oak Stud (FL); 3, Darley (KY).

11 - Double Confirmed - Best Start, Best Mid-pace

COPYRIGHT 2012 BLOODSTOCK RESEARCH INFORMATION SERVICES

clearly suspect at this distance, having failed in four of his last five tries at the Cup distance of a mile and a quarter. Considering that he was shamelessly over touted, I only used the horse as an insurance bet. It's interesting to note that in the 15 Cup races there were only four winning favorites. The track handicapper touted most of them. Game on Dude has surely found his way back to his barn by the time you read this recap. No word of apology from the track's handicapper tout has yet been heard.

Those of us who have been at this game for awhile have learned that no two races are exactly alike, or even close to being exactly alike; each race is a puzzle, a story unto itself. The perceptive handicapper must learn to read that story in order to solve the puzzle of selecting the likely winner. If the likely winner is obvious, the payoff will be small. Since Finding the Hidden Horse punters are looking for a decent price, they must be patient in deciding which races appear to be playable for that purpose. One of the class of races that have proven to be particularly rewarding for the System players has been any race written for horses that have not won two races; no matter the purse or distance.

An example was the sixth race at Gulfstream Park on Thursday, 1/3/2013; a five furlong race on the turf for four year olds and up, non-winners of two races: 50k claimers. The FHH interface screen presented the 2, Forest Station, as the #2 contender tied. The morning line setter opened the odds at 20/1; naturally, the betting public followed suit, letting the odds float up to 35/1 at post. Closer examination of Forest Station's three lifetime races told an interesting story.

HIDDEN HORSES FOUND!

The horse had raced all of three times in two years after breaking its maiden at first try as the 2.3/1 favorite in a 47k maiden special at 6 furlongs at Keeneland on 10/28/2010. Obviously sustaining a serious injury, Forest Station returned to the track on 10/27/2012 at Keeneland in a six furlong 52k Allowance for non-winners of two races. In contention to the half mile, he was caught six wide on the home turn and faltered. He next ran at CD on 11/16/2012 in a 50k claiming race for non-winners of two races, breaking slowly and never in contention. If that had been the only information to be pulled from the form, the horse would have and should have been ignored by hidden horse hunters. However, there was more to this story when you examined the FHH numbers and the pattern of workouts for Forest Station.

How could this horse on the above record be rated the #2 contender tied by the FHH System? The answer was in the numbers: he had the second Best Work of the field with a 4 furlong work on 12/10/2012 of :48 3/5 followed by the work on 12/29/2012 for 4 furlongs in the same :48 3/5. This was only five days before the current race. He had been put back in training from his nearly two year layoff on 8/12/2012 and had worked a dozen times since. Clearly, Forest Station was in condition for a big try. Additionally, the interface screen also revealed that the horse had a decent start of 95 and the second Best Late Pace of the field, notwithstanding the fact that this was a 5 furlong turf sprint. (It's surprising how often five and five and a half furlong sprints are won by a late pace horse, especially on the grass; it's a counter intuitive bet, often paying a generous price because the general betting public will generally favor the front runners in this type of race.)

The race comes 2, 4, 3, 6.

Winner pays **$73.60 24.60 9.20.**

Boxing the 2 with the favorite paid an exacta of $289.40.

The moral of the story of this race is: Play fewer races so that you have the time to thoroughly examine the interface screen of the FHH program and the past performances of each horse in the race. Pay particular attention to the workouts of a layoff horse.

FHH TABS $259.60 WINNER, $2,490 EXACTA IN 9TH AT REMINGTON PARK ON 12/9/2012!!

Screen presented:

TELLS	M/L	POST
2 = 9	7/2	1.6/1
11 = 5	9/2	3.7/1
3 = 4	12/1	11.9/1
4 = 4	8/1	13.6/1
8 = 4	20/1	128.8/1
9 = 4	9/2	11.9/1

BEST IN CATEGORY

Work=8	4 fur :47.2
Start= 2	97
Mid= 2	101
Late = 2	106

SIXTH RACE
Gulfstream
January 3rd, 2013

5 FURLONGS. (Turf) (.53³) CLAIMING. Purse $33,100 (Includes $6,600 FOA - Florida Owners Awards) FOR FOUR YEAR OLDS AND UPWARD WHICH HAVE NEVER WON TWO RACES. Weight, 123 lbs. Non-winners Of A Race Since December 3, 2012 Allowed 3 lbs. Claiming Price $50,000, For Each $5,000 To $40,000 2 lbs. (Condition Eligibility). (If deemed inadvisable to run thi s race over the turf course, it will be run on the main track at Five Furlongs) (Rail at 96 feet). (Clear 80)

Value of Race: $26,500 ($6,600 reverts) Winner $16,900; second $5,300; third $2,650; fourth $1,325; fifth $265; sixth $265; seventh $265; eighth $265; ninth $265. Mutuel Pool $222,719 Pick 3 Pool $56,300 Daily Double Pool $44,205 Exacta Pool $204,290 Superfecta Pool $83,196 Trifecta Pool $138,989

Last Raced	#	Horse	M/Eqt.	A/S	Wt	PP	St	3/16	3/8	Str	Fin	Jockey	Cl'g Pr	Odds $1
16Nov12 ⁷CD⁹	2	Forest Station	L	5H	116	2	3	2hd	2½	1½	1¹	Lopez P	40000	35.80
13Dec12 ⁸GP⁴	4	Core Inflation	L b	4C	120	4	5	5½	4½	3½	2¹¾	Rosario J	50000	1.80
25Nov12 ⁸Aqu³	3	Western Tryst	L	4G	120	3	9	9	8½	5hd	3¹¼	Lezcano J	50000	1.70
15Dec12 ³GP⁹	6	Visionandaprayer	L b	4G	116	5	1	3hd	1hd	2¹½	4½	Saez L	40000	10.50
21Dec12 ⁹GP³	8	Big Red Talent	L f	4G	116	7	7	7½	9	8³	5nk	Alvarez J L	40000	10.60
09Nov12 ⁸Crc⁷	1	Big Bentley	L b	5H	117	1	6	8²½	6¹½	6¹	6²¼	Desormeaux K J	40000	16.50
05Dec12 ⁹GP¹	7	Chosen Heir	L	4C	123	6	2	1½	3¹½	4²	7¹¾	Trujillo E	50000	13.90
28Apr12 ⁵Crc²	9	Riojano	L b	4C	116	8	4	4¹½	5¹½	7½	8⁴½	Torres F C	40000	6.90
14Nov12 ⁴Crc⁶	10	Harry the Hawk	L bf	5H	117	9	8	6¹	7hd	9	9	Cruz M R	40000	46.90

2ND BEST LATE PAC

OFF AT 3:09 Start Good. Won driving. Track Firm (Rail at 96 ft).
TIME :21⁴, :44³, :56⁴ (:21.98, :44.72, :56.81)

$2 Mutuel Prices:				
	2- FOREST STATION	73.60	24.60	9.20
	4- CORE INFLATION		3.80	2.60
	3- WESTERN TRYST			2.60

$2 EXACTA 2-4 PAID $289.40 $1 SUPERFECTA 2-4-3-6 PAID $1,942.70
$1 TRIFECTA 2-4-3 PAID $280.00

Chestnut Horse, (Mar), by Forest Wildcat - Wayward Susie by Way West (FR). Trainer Hamm E. Timothy. Bred by Whisper Hill Farm LLC(KY).

FOREST STATION urged up along inside an vied for early lead, continued to match strides with VISIONANDAPRAYER at top of the lane, shook free midstretch and continued clear. CORE INFLATION saved ground along inside in opening stages, began to advance position along outside, drifted out slight in turn, angled back in and gained position in late drive. WESTERN TRYST reserved in early going, began to advance along outside nearing turn, raced five wide at top of the lane and steadily gained ground to the wire. VISIONANDAPRAYER urged between rivals to vie for lead, continued along outside of FOREST STATION in upper stretch and could not keep up pace in late drive. BIG RED TALENT unhurried early and settled in near the back, fanned out six wide at top of the lane, gained position but was too late to make impact. BIG BENTLEY settled in early stages, raced between rivals midstretch and lacked late needed kick in drive. CHOSEN HEIR vied between rivals in early going and steadily began to fade heading into far turn. RIOJANO raced up close within contention in opening stages and had nothing left going into far turn. HARRY THE HAWK made a brief bid in early going and failed to be a factor late.

Owners- 2, Whisper Hill Farm LLC ; 4, Klaravich Stables, Inc. and Lawrence, William H. ; 3, Moran Thomas ; 6, Piedra Amaury J.; 8, Maragh Ricko ; 1, Morrow Jimmy L.; 7, Andrew Farm and EBG Stable ; 9, Calabrese Frank Carl; 10, Balsamo Joseph J.

Trainers- 2, Hamm Timothy E.; 4, Pompay Teresa M.; 3, Serpe Philip M.; 6, Fawkes David ; 8, Maragh Aubrey A.; 1, Shaw John E.; 7, Gray Elizabeth ; 9, Ziadie Kirk ; 10, Azpurua, Jr. Leo

Breeders- 2, Whisper Hill Farm LLC (KY); 4, JMJ Racing Stables, LLC (PA); 3, Flying Zee Stables (NY); 6, Tom Dushas (NY); 8, Sam-Son Farm (KY); 1, Lane Bloodstock, Pagel Bloodstock,Churchtown Bloodstock et al (KY); 7, Luis de Hechavarria (FL); 9, Eduardo Azpurua Sr. (FL); 10, Brad Gay & Shirley Gay (FL)

Western Tryst was claimed by Dubb Michael ; trainer, Brown Chad C.

Scratched- Kananyen(25Nov12 ¹¹Crc⁵)

$2 Daily Double (1-2) Paid $1,606.00; Daily Double Pool $44,205.
$1 Pick Three (2-1-2) Paid $3,756.20; Pick Three Pool $56,300.

Data provided or compiled by Equibase Company, which includes data from The Jockey Club, generally is accurate but occasionally errors and omissions occur as a result of incorrect data received by others, mistakes in processing and other causes. Equibase Company and Bloodstock Research Information Services, Inc. and Thoroughbred Sports Network disclaim responsibility for the consequences, if any, of such errors, but would appreciate being called to their attention. Copyright 2013

Winner 2 - #2 FHH Contender tied. 2nd Best Late Pace

COPYRIGHT 2013 BLOODSTOCK RESEARCH INFORMATION SERVICES

What jumps out at you as you look at the program's screen? For me it was, of course, the 8! Wow! Does that horse really have a prayer in this 300k Stakes for two year olds going a flat mile? No matter how he looked in the form I was going to put a few bucks on him. When I examined his past performances in the form I was determined to put some serious money on his overlooked nose. You don't encounter a race that set up like this one very often; you have to reach for the lightning when you do.

The first thing - after the odds - that caught my attention was the sensational work of :47 1/5 just eight days before the race. I knew that was the best work of the entire meet because I keep track of that and I assure you that 47 and 1 for four furlongs is running a hole in the wind at Remington Park.

Since there were 4 horses tied in tell points for third and fourth contenders, I attempted to break the ties with the "total pace figure" rule but couldn't because three of the four tied were too close in their total pace numbers to throw and even though the 8 would have been thrown in just using the total pace figures; for breaking ties the rule is: "Never throw a 'confirmed' horse."

Texas Bling had contested nine races; five at Lone Star Park, three at Remington Park, and one – his previous race – at Retama. It had taken the horse seven tries before he broke his maiden in a 28k maiden special race on the turf at Remington at 7 and 1/2 furlongs. His last race was in a 75k Stakes at Retama in which he finished sixth, but was just 3 and 3/4 lengths behind the winner. The chart writer's comment was: Pressed pace; rail trip. In addition to the noted sensational work, there was the angle of turf to dirt as his last four races were on the grass. I also thought the 3, Will Take

Charge, had a shot as another overlooked horse: he was cutting back to a mile from a mile and one-sixteenth Grade 2 Stakes at Churchill Downs.

Meanwhile, the 2, Exploring, was being bet down to favoritism at 1.6/1; after all, he was triple confirmed with Best Start, Best Mid, and Best Late numbers. At that price the only way I was going to use him was as an "insurance" bet.

The System bet was to bet the 8 to win and twice as much to place: then to run the 8 up and back in exactas with the remaining "screen" horses – the 2, 3, 4, 9, 11. Then to run the 2 over the 3, 4, 8, 9, 11 in exactas as a salvage bet.

The race comes 8, 3, 7, 5.

Winner pays **$259.60 122.00 29.80; $2 exacta $2,490.00!**

The chart writer's comments accurately told the story: "TEXAS BLING well back after a half, came three wide when making bid into the stretch, altered course mid stretch, split foes in late going, took command and drew clear in final yards..." Actually, the race fell apart in the last hundred yards as the 3, 5, and 7 were clearly running on empty. The favorite, the morning line setter and the track handicapper's "sure thing" bet, was never in the race; finally crawling across the finish line, a beaten tenth in a field of twelve.

When you encounter a race that sets up like this one, take a shot; don't be shy about putting some money on a 100/1 shot. The track handicappers and or the morning line setters are notorious chalk chasers and too often lead the novice punter down the prim-

NINTH RACE
Remington
December 9th, 2012

1 MILE. (1.354) STAKES. Purse $300,000 *REMINGTON SPRINGBOARD MILE S.* FOR TWO-YEAR-OLDS. No nomination fee. $1,250 to pass the entry box. Starters to pay $1,250 additional with $300,000 Guaranteed. The guaranteed monies to be divided 60% to the winner, 20% to second, 11% to third, 6% to fourth and 3% to fifth. Weights, Colt s and Geldings, 120 lbs.; Fillies, 117 lbs. The top three finishers in the Springboard Mile will get an automatic nomination to the Oklahoma Derby in 2013. The winner will receive an all fees paid entry into the Oklahoma Derby in 2013. This race will be l imited to 12 starters. Preference: Stakes winning or stake-placed horses in graded/group stakes (in order I,II,III), then lifetime earnings. Lifetime earnings will be determined according to statistics provided by Equibase. Trophy to the winning owner. Cl osed Friday, November 30th with (48) nominations. (Cloudy 46)

Value of Race: $300,000 ($30,000 reverts) Winner $180,000; second $60,000; third $33,000; fourth $18,000; fifth $9,000. Mutuel Pool $65,435 Pick 3 Pool $2,999 Exacta Pool $42,556 Superfecta Pool $24,845 Trifecta Pool $24,793

Last Raced	#	Horse	M/Eqt.	A/S	Wt	PP	St	¼	½	¾	Str	Fin	Jockey	Odds $1
10Nov12 ^{5}Ret^{6}	8	Texas Bling	L f	2C	120	9	2	8^{1}	7^{1}	$5\frac{1}{2}$	4^{1}	$1^{1\frac{3}{4}}$	McNeil E	128.80
24Nov12 ^{11}CD^{13}	3	Will Take Charge	L b	2C	120	3	7	1^{hd}	1^{3}	$1\frac{1}{2}$	2^{hd}	$2\frac{1}{2}$	Lebron V	11.90
10Nov12 ^{5}Ret^{2}	7	Worldventurer	L b	2G	120	8	3	4^{1}	$3\frac{1}{2}$	$3\frac{1}{2}$	1^{hd}	$3^{2\frac{1}{4}}$	Berry M C	19.90
09Nov12 ^{8}RP^{3}	5	Best of Birdstone	L	2C	120	6	4	2^{hd}	2^{2}	2^{hd}	$3\frac{1}{2}$	4no	Quinonez L S	7.70
09Nov12 ^{8}RP^{1}	11	King Henny	L	2C	120	12	1	6^{hd}	6^{hd}	$4\frac{1}{2}$	$5\frac{1}{2}$	5^{1}	Theriot J	3.70
31Oct12 ^{2}RP^{1}	1A	Smack Jack	L	2G	120	4	6	7^{1}	5^{hd}	$7\frac{1}{2}$	6^{5}	6^{2}	Compton P	a - 8.50
09Nov12 ^{8}RP^{2}	4	Backstreet Hero	L	2G	120	5	5	$10\frac{1}{2}$	11^{5}	11^{10}	7^{3}	$7^{6\frac{3}{4}}$	Wade L	13.60
10Nov12 ^{6}Crc^{2}	10	Hardrock Eleven	L	2G	120	11	11	9^{1}	$9\frac{1}{2}$	8^{2}	8^{2}	$8^{1\frac{1}{4}}$	Clark K D	7.30
09Nov12 ^{8}RP^{5}	1	Steelman Run	L	2G	120	1	8	3^{1}	$4\frac{1}{2}$	6^{hd}	$9\frac{1}{2}$	9^{1}	Corbett G W	a - 8.50
28Oct12 ^{9}CD^{3}	2	Exploring	L	2C	120	2	10	5^{hd}	8^{hd}	9^{hd}	$10^{2\frac{1}{2}}$	10^{1}	Murphy G	1.60
30Nov12 ^{3}RP^{1}	6	Hornet	L	2C	120	7	9	11^{5}	10^{2}	10^{1}	11^{1}	$11^{1\frac{1}{4}}$	Birzer A	65.70
24Nov12 ^{12}CD^{1}	9	Channel Isle	L b	2C	120	10	12	12	12	12	12	12	Court J K	11.90

BEST LATE!

a - Coupled:Smack Jack and Steelman Run

OFF AT 5:19 Start Good. Won driving. Track Fast.

TIME :23^{3}, :48^{4}, 1:14^{2}, 1:27^{1}, 1:39^{4} (:23.67, :48.81, 1:14.56, 1:27.37, 1:39.96)

$2 Mutuel Prices:

8- TEXAS BLING	259.60	122.00	29.80
3- WILL TAKE CHARGE		15.40	9.20
7- WORLDVENTURER			9.40

$2 EXACTA 8-3 PAID $2,490.00 $2 SUPERFECTA 8-3-7-5 PAID $94,384.40
$2 TRIFECTA 8-3-ALL PAID $18,827.20

Dark Bay or Brown Colt, (Mr), by Too Much Bling - Anythingmore by Country Pine. Trainer Durham Danele. Bred by Hall's Family Trust(TX).

TEXAS BLING well back after a half, came three wide when making bid into stretch, altered course mid stretch, split foes in late going, took command and drew clear in final stages. WILL TAKE CHARGE broke to front, rated well with narrow lead into stretch, went gamely while under pressure throughout stretch drive only to be outfinished in the end. WORLDVENTURER within striking distance outside from outset, came three wide when making bid into stretch, gained narrow nad mid stretch, went gamely under pressure before tiring. BEST OF BIRDSTONE chased pace from outset, held gamely to mid stretch, tired. KING HENNY came four wide from middle of pack into stretch, lacked response in drive. SMACK JACK raced ;in middle of pack, failed to menace. BACKSTREET HERO well back into stretch, passed tiring foes. HARDROCK ELEVEN was never a factor. STEELMAN RUN stalked leaders along rail for half, faded. EXPLORING was never a serious threat along inside. HORNET was outrun. CHANNEL ISLE was never close.

Owners- 8, Hall's Family Trust ; 3, Horton Willis D.; 7, Melcher Wesley ; 5, Hogue, Jr. Richard P.; 11, Woolsey, Erv and Asmussen, Keith ; 1A, Dream Walkin Farms, Inc. ; 4, Foster Dennis E.; 10, Lazenby, Virginia B. and Farm D'Allie Racing Stables ; 1, Dream Walkin Farms, Inc. ; 2, Oxley John C.; 6, Winchell Ron ; 9, Bluegrass Hall LLC

Trainers- 8, Durham Danele ; 3, Lukas D. Wayne; 7, Calhoun W. Bret; 5, Von Hemel Donnie K.; 11, Asmussen Steven M.; 1A, Von Hemel Don ; 4, Pish Danny ; 10, Banks David P.; 1, Von Hemel Kelly R.; 2, Casse Mark E.; 6, Asmussen Steven M.; 9, Lukas D. Wayne

Breeders- 8, Hall's Family Trust (TX); 3, Eaton (KY); 7, Clarence Scharbauer Jr. (TX); 5, Richard P. Hogue Jr. (AR); 11, Betz/Kidder/Lamantia/J. Betz (KY); 1A, Dream Walkin' Farms Inc. (KY); 4, Trackside Farm & Robert P. Evans (KY); 10, Farm III Enterprises & Off The HookPartners LLC (FL); 1, Dream Walkin' Farms Inc. (KY); 2, James T. Gottwald (KY); 6, Ron Winchell (KY); 9, Bluegrass Hall, LLC (KY)

$2 Pick Three (5-7-8) 2 Correct Paid $59.00; Pick Three Pool $2,999.

Winner 8 - #3 FHH Contender tied. Best Late

COPYRIGHT 2012 BLOODSTOCK RESEARCH INFORMATION SERVICES

rose path. The horse can't read the odds board. If the System says the horse has a shot, believe the System. Believe the Tells. They will light your way to Finding a Hidden Horse!

FHH SOFTWARE NAILS $684 EXACTA IN 8TH AT GULF-STREAM ON 1/5/2012; SYSTEM'S #1 CONTENDER, DOUBLE CONFIRMED, PLACES AT 59/1 FOR $42.40!

Screen presented:

TELLS	M/L	POST
10 = 7	21/1	59/1
9 = 5	15/1	7.4/1
5 = 4	10/1	4.7/1
12 = 4	10/1	9.9/1

BEST IN CATEGORY

Work= 5	4 fur :47
Start= 10, 11	99
Mid= 10	98
Late= 12	106

What jumps out at you as you look at the program's screen? The 10, of course; the #1 contender, double confirmed by being tied for the Best Start and having the Best Middle Pace. The horse had earned seven points in the system: it was a three point cutback because in its previous race at a mile and sixteenth Hansel Tazwell had led the race to the top of the stretch, where he was soon third, just a length from the front. He faded in the stretch to finish sixth, just three and three-quarter lengths back of the winner. Theoretically he would have been the winner or thereabout if that race had been a sixteenth mile shorter. At the current race distance of a flat mile, Hansel was *cutting back* and under the rules of the FHH System, was awarded three "tell" points. He also earned two points for his tie for Best Start and another two points for his Best Middle Pace number.

The general betting public and the morning line setters and expert track handicappers seem to have a great deal of difficulty in understanding this important variable in handicapping a race. Generally, the public doesn't want any part of a horse that has shortened stride in its last race, no matter the relative distance of that race to the current one. More's the better for the hidden horse hunter, for this type of horse often leaves the gate at juicy odds as in the race being reviewed.

The second thing I noted was that the 5 was live on the board, a 50% underlay. The horse was tied for #3 contender in additon to being confirmed with the Best Work of the field, a solid four furlongs in :47 flat. Accordingly, the System play was to bet the 10 to win and twice as much to place. Then to run the 5 up and back with the screen horses 9, 10, 12 in exactas.

HIDDEN HORSES FOUND!

The race comes 5, 10, 3, 6.

Winner pays $11.40 7.20 5.60; System's #1 contender places: pays 42.40 22.00; $2 exacta $684.20

When you see points awarded in the "Cutback" column of the interface screen, take the time to examine carefully that horse's last race. It will pay dividends as that type of horse generally leaves the gate at generous odds and often wins or hits the board at a decent price.

When you see one of the top four System's contenders at long morning line odds, believe the "tells," the variable or variables that the morning line setter has either ignored or just plain overlooked, but that the eagle eyes of the System have identified as a probable long shot condidate. The morning line setter is not required by the track or the state racing commission to have even a modicum of bona fides. Believe the *tells* of the system. Don't be led down the primrose path. Set your own morning line. Ignore the ramblings of the track announcers. They will generally tell the punter to bet the favorite. That is a losing bet over time, for – historically – favorites lose two out of three races. The chalk chasers have to get at least 2/1 just to break even.

As Jonathan Winters would probably have put it: "What the hell kind of a deal is that?"

Chapter 7

THE MORNING LINE: WHAT GOOD IS IT?

"'Tis with our judgements as our watches: none
Go just alike, yet each believes his own."
ALEXANDER POPE

When as a neophyte punter I first heard the phrase *morning line*, I was puzzled: after some 40 years of playing this magnificent game that never seems to lose its edge, I hesitate to admit that I am puzzled still. Most novice thoroughbred horse race handicappers come to the game wide-eyed and credulous, myself included. It was only after several years of betting and losing on the morning line favorites that I asked the queston: "The morning line, what good is it?" In spite of many years of research, I've been unable to unearth a credible explanation or justification for its universal use.

The *Merriam-Webster* dictionary defines "morning line" as: *a bookmaker's list of entries for a race meet and the probable odds on each* *that is printed or posted before the betting begins...*and they go on to note that the first known use of the phrase "morning line" was in 1935. Some thoroughbred race historians allege that the morning line first originated with British bookmakers, who before the race would post the odds at which they would take bets on any horse in the race. This practice, however, is not analogous to the present day use of the term "morning line," because no track in the country is willing to stand behind its morning line setter's picks by booking a bet at their posted odds. What then is the purpose of setting a morning line and publishing it in their race programs and the past performance printings by the *Daily Racing Form* and *Brisnet?*

The UltimateCapper.com blog tells us: "...morning line oddsmakers are up against it from the start, *having to predict what the public will bet on each horse in each race* up to 48 hours prior to post..." Yes, let's pity the poor morning line oddsmakers who so often get it wrong, then apologize to no one for their more egregious misses. A perfect example was the Santa Anita announcer's unabashed touting of Game on Dude in the 2012 Breeders' Cup Classic: "I guarantee you there is NO way Game on Dude can lose this race!!" It was ridiculous that the morning line (set five days before the race) was 9/5 on a horse that had failed in four of five tries at the Classic's distance of a mile and a quarter. Anyone with minimal handicapping experience could see that if the Dude didn't make it to the lead early, his chances of closing on this field were slim, indeed. It's easy to make guarantees when the penalty paid by the guarantor for a loss is *nada*. In the Classic Game on Dude was bucking the law of probabilities and the theorem of *regression to the mean*. A lot of bettors lost a lot of money following the track announcer's guarantee.

THE MORNING LINE: WHAT GOOD IS IT?

Show me a consistent chalk chaser, and I'll show you a consistent loser.

The first question to be asked in examining the history of the universal use of a morning line is: What is its purpose? How does it assist the public bettor, from whom track management receives its sustenance? The next question is: Who sets the morning line and by what authority?

The authority, of course, is track management which delegates the duty to just about anyone, no matter their qualifications or lack thereof. Apparently, the State Racing Commissions have no say in this matter that is of such importance to the public bettor. Many morning line setters are race office employees and track announcers who double as "expert" handicappers; others are newspaper handicappers, and still others are public relations pretenders. Unfortunately, the average punter accepts the morning line practice at face vaue on the general supposition that the setter has some expertise in the process. They no doubt would be as surprised as I to learn first hand from a reliable source that some years back at a midwestern bush track, a stable hand set the morning line. It appears that he would often hang generous odds on a horse that should have been the first or second favorite, touting the public off. After the public bit, he would place a nice bet on the horse. Rumor was that the stable boy drove around town in a new Mercedes-Benz.

Granted that the job of setting the morning line is a thankless duty, for those people have to produce it a couple of days before late workouts or scratches are determined; you would think that track management would take care to let its bettors know the bona fides of the track's morning line producer. Yet in my long stint as an unabashed *aficionado* for the Sport of Kings, I've not seen nor have

I heard of any track giving the public the qualifications, if any, of the person it has chosen to set their morning line. The State Racing Commissions don't require it; more's the pity for the two dollar grunts and the Social Security players who play such an important part in the production of track revenue.

It gives me pause to realize that for some 40 years I have been laboring under the mistaken impression that such an important duty was solely the job of the track's Racing Secretary. I was recently disabused of that notion by a former track official. Apparently, track management justifies the setting of the morning line by asserting that it's an aid to the bettor, giving punters a frame of reference with which to begin their handicapping of a race. They further make the rather odd assumption that the morning line is not the *setter's pick* of a winner, but only the morning line setter's *estimates of what the general betting public will do*. Their position is that the morning line setter is capable of putting himself in the shoes of average bettors and thus able to predict what the general public bettor will do. It's sort of like the eternal question: Which came first, the chicken or the egg? In practice the results have been nothing to write home about. In the 75 years since the first morning line was set, favorites have lost two of every three races; a losing proposition by any measure.

Generally, there are three spheres of influence that materially affect and pressure the morning line setters. The first is track management; the group that authorized them. Neither track management nor its horse owners like to see odds of 99/1 posted on any horse: it discourages the bettor and upsets the owner of the horse. Neither is the posting of 2/5 or 3/5 morning line odds on any horse met with approval by track management or the owners. This explains

THE MORNING LINE: WHAT GOOD IS IT?

why the posting of morning line odds of less than 4/5 on a favorite are as rare as the posting of odds of over 50/1 on a long shot.

The second group of people who influence the morning line setters are the newspaper handicappers, who are also inclined to tout the apparent favorites in the form and are particularly fond of touting horses that have won their last race. They have little time or inclination to dig deep into the many variables that point to long shot winners. That's why you seldom see a long shot winner tabbed by the track announcers, their handicappers, or the fourth estate touts and tipsters of the newspapers. They are all form players.

The third group of people who influence the morning line setters are the track insiders: owners, trainers, jockeys, jockey agents, and exercise riders. These insiders frequently give out a "hot tip" that spreads like wildfire throughout the track. That's why you will sometimes see a horse that looks like it should be 50/1 or more bet down to a ridiculous underlay. A bet on this type of horse seldom returns a profit. So pay no attention to the morning line setters or the track announcer, or handicapper, or the newpaper handicappers, or the so-called inside information tips that are always floating around at any track. If you are betting online, turn the sound down, and figure out the race for yourself; practice setting your own morning line. Try covering up the morning lines as printed in the form and making your own estimate of what *you* think the public will do after reviewing the past performances. Then scan the FHH interface screen. For example, if your estimate of what the morning line should be on a horse is 6/1, and that horse is one of the top four System contenders, and the track's morning line setter has tabbed that horse at 20/1, you may very well (and probably have) located a promising long shot. Everything you need is there, nowhere else. Everything you need to know is in the form, where the past performances tell the story of each race. The FHH program has examined the form with a microscopic eye to separate the wheat from the chaff. The answer to the handicapping puzzle is in the numbers, for handicapping a thoroughbred horse race is basically a mathematical problem.

The following examples demonstrate the general lack of efficacy of most morning line setters. Readers can and may disagree at the margins, but most of these examples represent the most egregious of the track controlled handicapper's efforts at setting morning lines that all too often lead the betting public down the primrose path.

In the eighth race at Gulfstream Park on January 10, 2013, the morning line favorite was the 7, Angel Dreams, entered in a six furlong Optional 25k Claimer for a purse of 54k for fillies and mares four years old and upward which have never won $7,500 other than maiden, claiming, starter, or state bred or which have never won two races or claiming price of $25,000. Whew! What a puzzle to determine the qualifiers for that race.

Angel Dreams was the morning line favorite at 5/2; the betting herd duly noted what was, in effect, the morning line setter's recommendation, notwithstanding track management's protestation to the contrary – that it was *not* the track handicapper's pick; it was only what *he thought the crowd would do* on reviewing the horse's past performances in her eleven starts over the past year. Of course. Which came first, the chicken or the egg? The betters took the bait, driving Angel Dreams down to 1.5/1 at post. As you can see, it didn't take long for the crowd's hope to be dashed as Angel turned out to be lead footed early; breaking fifth, at the quarter pole was seventh, then finished seventh by eight and one quarter lengths, never improving her first call position.

The question arises: Why did the morning line setter make the judgement that the public would make Angel Dreams the prohibitive favorite? Was it because the horse had hit the board in six of her last eight races? That may very well have been the reason the public piled in behind the morning line setter that touted the looks-good-at-first-glance horse. Keeping in mind the caution that habitually betting the obvious has proven to be a losing proposition, an experienced handicapper required further examination. Such a review revealed that in her last eight races she gave up substantial ground in the stretch after being in contention at the last turn. In her last race she was second, just two lengths back at the head of the stretch, then gave up two and a quarter lengths, finishing third by four and a quarter lengths. The chart writer's comment was: "Bid 3 wide; weakened." In her second race back Angel was just two lengths back in third on entering the stretch, then gave up three lengths to finish third, five lengths back of the winner. The chart writer's comment was: "Outfinished for place."

In six of her last seven races Angel Dreams had given up ground after being in contention at the head of the stretch. In her last seven races, five were six furlong sprints; one was at five and one half and one was at five furlongs. It seems to me that any experienced handicapper – which the morning line setters profess to be – would recognize from examining this horse's published past performances that she was probably short. Was there anything in the form to suggest otherwise, perhaps a recent exceptional workout? Angel was a layoff horse, having been away from the track since October 7, 2012. She had worked four times since December 14, 2012: three furlongs at :37 3/5 on 12/14; four furlongs at :49 1/5 on 12/21; five furlongs at 1:02 3/5 on 12/28, and 4 furlongs at :52 1/5 on January 4, 2013. All of these works were at Calder; none of them were particularly distinguished. A fair question to ask the morning line setter and or track handicapper is: What was the rationale for tabbing Angel Dreams as the favorite? Was it a hot tip from the backside of the track? Or did the morning line setter just assume that the credulous crowd wouldn't see that the record pointed to this horse being consistently faint of heart in the final furlong of the stretch?

In examining the interface screen of the FHH program, the seven was tied for best mid pace and had the best late pace in a field that had unusually low late pace numbers. The 7, however, was not one of the system's top four contenders or ties for it had only 5 tell points. The #1 contender tied was Magical Cat, the 2, with 7 tell points; and as it turned out, a $24 winner. The morning line setter thought she should be about 12/1. She had last raced in a 52k Allowance for non-winners of a race other than maiden, claiming, or starter. She was third, two and a half lengths back at the head of the stretch in a seven furlong race before quitting in the stretch. The chart writer's comment was: "Steadied inside early." The system gave her a point for a troubled previous race and three points for the cutback. Just two races back, Magical Cat had broken her maiden at seven and one half furlongs in a 40k Maiden Special. I thought her morning line should have been about 5/1 and the favorite's line 12/1. Serious handicappers should set their own morning lines: It will often pay generous dividends to the hidden horse hunter, for frequently the morning line setter unwittingly plays a large part in hiding the hidden horse.

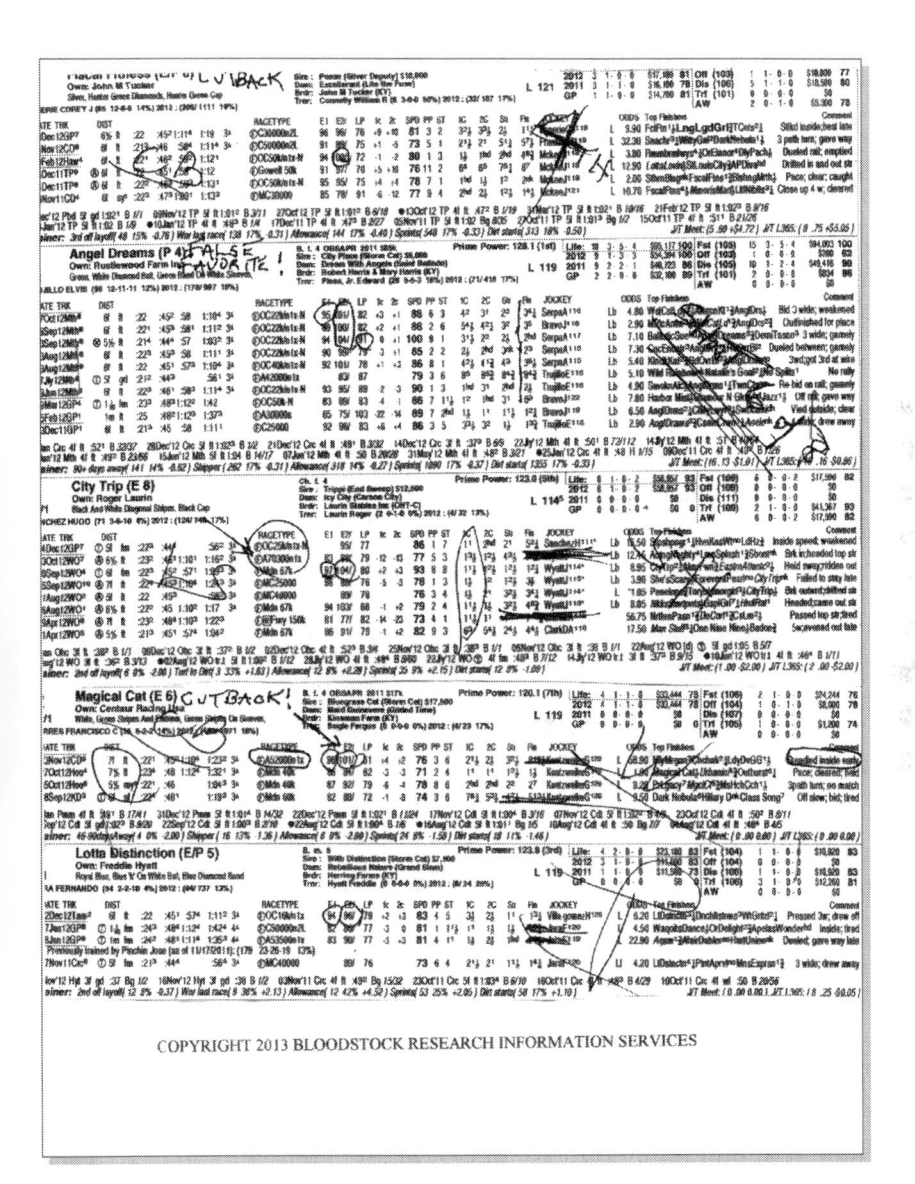

THE MORNING LINE: WHAT GOOD IS IT? 93

RUNNING A HOLE IN THE WIND: HIDDEN HORSES FOUND

[Race chart from Gulfstream, Eighth Race, January 10th, 2013 — 6 Furlongs Allowance Optional Claiming for Fillies and Mares Four Years Old and Upward. Handwritten annotations on the chart: "#2 FHH CONTENDER" next to Magical Cat (11.00 odds); "ANNOUNCER'S TOUT" pointing to Colormesaichi; "FALSE FAVORITE!" next to Angel Dreams (1.50 odds).]

Winner 2 - #2 FHH Contender. 3rd Best Start, 3rd Best Mid-Pace, 2 point cutback, troubled last race.

COPYRIGHT 2013 BLOODSTOCK RESEARCH INFORMATION SERVICES

THE MORNING LINE: WHAT GOOD IS IT?

The seventh race at Gulfstream on January 12, 2013, is a good example of what track management means regarding the duty of the morning line setter to estimate what he or she thinks the betting public will do. The race was a five and one-half furlong 15k claimer for three year olds with a purse of $26,200.

Who could argue with the morning line setter's decision to make the 2, Move Over, the 9/5 morning line favorite? The crowd saw in the form that the horse had won three of its last four races and was two for two in its last two runs. The horse was running at class; Joel Rosario was up and the trainer was a 19% winner. This race was Move Over's first start with new connections. Additionally, the horse was cutting back from his last race distance of six furlongs. The horse looked great, but as far as I was concerned he looked too good to be true. In the current race he would be bucking the law of probabilities and the theorem of regression to the mean.

What do you think the odds are of any horse winning two races in a row? I assure you, not very good. And if that is the case, the odds of winning three consecutive races is rarer still. Yet the public, and the morning line setters will always bite and hammer a horse like Move Over down to a price that no experienced handicapper should accept. In this case, the morning line setter got it right: the public would salivate over that horse. And so they did, hammering its odds down to 1.1/1. Unfortunately, Move Over regressed to the mean. He was ninth at the first quarter, ninth at three-eighths, finishing fifth, two and three-quarter lengths from the winner. His efforts earned the owner a purse of $210. Let the chalk chasers have a race like that. If a horse's form looks too good to be true, pass the race; look for value elsewhere.

SEVENTH RACE
Gulfstream
January 12th, 2013

5½ FURLONGS. (1.02^{1}) CLAIMING. Purse $26,200 (includes $5,200 FOA - Florida Owners Awards) FOR THREE YEAR OLDS. Weight, 122 lbs. Non-winners Of A Race Since December 12, 2012 Allowed 2 lbs. A Race Since November 12, 2012 Allowed 4 lbs. Claiming Price $15,000 (Races where entered for $12,500 or less not considered). (Clear 79)

Value of Race: $26,200 Winner $16,240; second $5,240; third $2,620; fourth $1,050; fifth $210; sixth $210; seventh $210; eighth $210; ninth $210. Mutuel Pool $339,707 Pick 3 Pool $63,864 Daily Double Pool $59,751 Exacta Pool $276,256 Superfecta Pool $115,918 Trifecta Pool $181,605

Last Raced	#	Horse	M/Eqt.	A/S	Wt	PP	St	¼	½	Str	Fin	Jockey	Cl'g Pr	Odds $1
26Dec12 ^{4}GP^{3}	6	Starship Titan	L b	3C	118	6	5	3½	3½	1½	1¾	Castellano J	15000	2.60
14Dec12 ^{8}GP^{3}	5	Billos Boy	L b	3C	118	5	2	6^{1}	5^{hd}	5½	2½	Jara F	15000	11.90
14Dec12 ^{8}GP^{4}	4	Tiz a Par	L bf	3C	118	4	8	8½	8^{3}	$6^{3½}$	3½	Trujillo E	15000	54.20
20Dec12 ^{8}GP^{8}	8	Trip N Run	L b	3C	118	8	7	$4^{2½}$	4^{4}	3^{1}	4½	Alvarez J L	15000	5.20
26Dec12 ^{4}GP^{1}	2	Move Over	L	3C	122	2	3	9	9	7^{1}	5½	Rosario J	15000	1.10
26Dec12 ^{4}GP^{8}	9	My Daddy's Dollars	L b	3C	113	9	4	2½	1^{hd}	2^{3}	$6^{8½}$	Chamafi J	15000	7.30
26Dec12 ^{4}GP^{6}	3	Rock Star Mia	L f	3G	113	3	1	1^{1}	2^{2}	4^{1}	$7^{11¾}$	Sanchez H	15000	24.50
21Dec12 ^{2}GP^{7}	1	Sharp Deal	L b	3C	120	1	6	5^{hd}	$6^{1½}$	8^{3}	$8^{1¼}$	Lezcano J	15000	41.60
02Jan13 ^{8}Tam^{3}	7	Richard Croy	L b	3G	118	7	9	7^{3}	7^{1}	9	9	Cruz M R	15000	57.20

BEST WORK!

OFF AT 3:38 Start Good. Won driving. Track Fast.
TIME :22^{1}, :45^{3}, :58^{3}, 1:05^{3} (:22.24, :45.63, :58.67, 1:05.74)

$2 Mutuel Prices:

6- STARSHIP TITAN	7.20	4.20	3.00
5- BILLOS BOY		8.40	4.60
4- TIZ A PAR			16.60

$2 EXACTA 6-5 PAID $68.80 $1 SUPERFECTA 6-5-4-8 PAID $2,100.30
$1 TRIFECTA 6-5-4 PAID $428.70

Bay Colt, (Mar), by City Place - Cope Lady by Copelan. Trainer Ness Jamie. Bred by Gary M. Pickel & Margie M. Webb(FL).

STARSHIP TITAN chased the pace just off inside in opening quarter, slightly settled in and stalked pacesetter nearing turn, advanced position up to lead, vied along outside of MY DADDY'S DOLLARS in upper stretch, took command midstretch and remained clear. BILLOS BOY stalked along outside of rival in backstretch, made a bid heading into turn, angled out three wide at top of the lane, angled back in upper stretch and gained place in late drive. TIZ A PAR was reserved in opening stages settled in near the back of rivals, steadily gained position along outside in backstretch, raced four wide into lane and steadily gained ground in stretch. TRIP N RUN pulled in opening stages, continued to stalk the pace, angled out slightly at top of lane, gained position in upper stretch and flattened out in late drive. MOVE OVER raced in the back of the pack in early stages, swung out three wide at top of lane, improved position in stretch but was too late to make impact. MY DADDY'S DOLLARS raced just off pacesetter in opening stages, edged up to lead going into turn, briefly vied for lead, could not match strides in upper stretch and weakened. ROCK STAR MIA flashed quick speed and rushed up to lead, challenged by MY DADDY'S DOLLARS, lost lead and began to falter. SHARP DEAL stalked the front runners along inside and began to weaken in middle of backstretch. RICHARD CROY allowed to settle in early stages, asked for response in the backstretch and failed to rally in stretch.

Owners- 6, Midwest Thoroughbreds, Inc. ; 5, Landaeta, Juan Francisco and Tabraue, Brenda ; 4, Monarch Stables, Inc. ; 8, Maragh Ricko ; 2, Hess, Jr. Robert B.; 9, Plesa Laurie ; 3, Maver Mario ; 1, De Luca and Sons Stable ; 7, Lady Luck Stable

Trainers- 6, Ness Jamie ; 5, Bezara Agustin C.; 4, Vivian David A.; 8, Maragh Aubrey A.; 2, Hess, Jr. Robert B.; 9, Plesa, Jr. Edward ; 3, Maver Mario ; 1, Garcia Rodolfo ; 7, Gatis Christos

Breeders- 6, Gary M. Pickel & Margie M. Webb (FL); 5, Helen Marie Napolitano (FL); 4, Monarch Stables (FL); 8, Cavendish Investing LTD. (FL); 2, Polo Green Stable, Cesar Nieves &Yoichi Aoyama (KY); 9, Laurie Plesa (FL); 3, James Mann (ON); 1, Nuckols Farm, Inc. (KY); 7, Don F Kulik (FL)

Move Over was claimed by GB & KAR Stables Corp. ; trainer, Brandonisio Giuseppe ,
Starship Titan was claimed by Calabrese Frank Carl; trainer, Ziadie Kirk
Scratched- Nighlowl Earlybird(02Jan13 ^{8}Tam^{7})

$2 Daily Double (10-6) Paid $41.60; Daily Double Pool $59,751.
$1 Pick Three (5-10-6) Paid $83.90; Pick Three Pool $63,864.

Data provided or compiled by Equibase Company, which includes data from The Jockey Club, generally is accurate but occasionally errors and omissions occur as a result of incorrect data received by others, mistakes in processing and other causes. Equibase Company and Bloodstock Research Information Services, Inc. and Thoroughbred Sports Network disclaim responsibility for the consequences, if any, of such errors, but would appreciate being called to their attention. Copyright 2013.

2 was false favorite, obviously faint of heart in stretch: Chalkers chased!
4 - 54/1 Show horse had Best Work.

COPYRIGHT 2013 BLOODSTOCK RESEARCH INFORMATION SERVICES

THE MORNING LINE: WHAT GOOD IS IT?

Track management justifies the practice of setting a morning line on each race, asserting that the line is set not by the *picks* of the setter but by what the setter *thinks* the betting public will do after perusing the past performances as published by the Daily Racing Form or Brisnet. Naturally, the question arises: What criteria does the morning line setter use in setting the morning line on horses that have yet to enter a race? The only past performances that first time starters have are their workouts. You would think that workout patterns would be the sole variable to identify when judging the chances of two or three year olds first trip to the winner's circle dance.

Many handicappers are big on bloodlines when judging a first time starter, but the workouts are far more important because they are predictive by their timing: they tell the handicapper what the horse *has* done. Maiden races including first time starters are among the most productive of long shot winners. And those types of races confront the morning line setters with formidable challenges in deciding what the credulous betting public will do with first time starters. It is in this type of race that the morning line setters are making their own picks; they are tabbing their own personal predilections, not just following what they think the crowd will do. Frequently – with purpose or unwittingly – they tout the public off a clearly promising first timer by pegging its morning line at 20/1 or higher. The general betting public usually will not touch a first time starter that the morning line setter has tabbed as a long shot, no matter the speed with which such a horse has negotiated the track in its workouts. More's the better for hidden horse hunters.

An example of the above contention was the sixth race at Gulfstream on January 12, 2013; a Maiden Special 52k race at one and one-sixteenth on the turf for three year old maidens. A field of 12 went to the post, four of which were maidens. The 10, Jack Milton, and the 13, All Alex, were mild co-favorites at a morning line of 7/2 and 3/1, respectively. The 13 was a logical pick as he was coming back from a good closing second in a mile race on the turf. He was the #3 contender in the FHH system, having the second Best Start, third Best Middle-pace, and third Best Late Pace. I was concerned about his far outside post, which is generally unfavorable at Gulfstream in a route turf race.

The mild co-favorite was the 10; first timer Jack Milton, trained by Todd Pletcher, a 27% winner and ridden by John Velazquez, a 19% jock. The horse had been put in training on November 20 and worked out eight times since, booking two good tries; the first on December 4 at four furlongs in :48, the second best time of the 29 horses that worked on the same day; the second on December 31 at 5 furlongs in 1:00 2/5, second best of 32 that day. I think most experienced handicappers would agree that, on their published records, the morning line setter was correct in deciding that these two horses would attract the most attention from the general betting public. And so they did.

There were three other first timers in the race besides the 10. The 2, Middleburg, though trained by the renowned turf trainer Clement Christophe, had 10 straight mundane workouts. The 8, P V Paul, had worked 12 times since October 2 with equally undistinguished results. That left the 9, War Dancer, as the other first timer.

War Dancer had worked 12 times since June 23: two of his works were exceptional; on December 15 he went :48 for four furlongs, ninth best of 49 horses working that day; on December 29, he went five furlongs in a good 1:00 3/5, fourth best of 26 working at that track that day. Here was a first time starter tied for the best work of the field with the 10 co-favorite with the 13. Yet the morning line setter tabbed him at 12/1. It's difficult to understand what criteria the setter was using in the decision to tab the 9 a long shot. In any case, the public stayed off War Dancer, letting his odds float up to 36/1 as the gates opened. It was only after the race that I noticed that the first and second place finishers were half brothers out of the sire War Front, by Danzig.

The FHH program had tabbed the 9, 10, and 11 as the #4 contenders tied. It clearly noted that the 9 and 10 were tied for the best work of the field with 4 furlongs at :48. Yet, because the morning line setter gave short shrift to War Dancer, the crowd ignored the horse because they rarely dispute the assumed "expertise" of the track's tout. A cursory review of War Dancer's work pattern clearly established him as a long shot candidate to hidden horse hunters and users of the Finding the Hidden Horse software.

The race came 10, 9, 11, 13.

The winner paid $9.20 6.00 5.20. War Dancer placed at $30.40 13.40; $2 exacta $324.80 (call it the Danzig half-brother's exacta); $2 trifecta $2,645.60

Hidden horse hunters should turn the general inefficiency of the morning line settings to their advantage. Invest some time in practicing the setting of your own line, then compare it to the track handicapper's postings in the racing form. Time spent on that process has returned substantial dividends to me and should prove equally profitable to those of you who learn to set your own morning lines.

SIXTH RACE
Gulfstream
January 12th, 2013

$1\frac{1}{16}$ MILES. (Turf) (1.38) MAIDEN SPECIAL WEIGHT. Purse $52,500 (Includes $10,500 FOA - Florida Owners Awards) FOR MAIDENS, THREE YEARS OLD. Weight, 120 lbs. (Preference To Horses That Have Not Started For Less Than $30,000 In Their Last 5 Starts). (If deemed inadvisable to run this race over the turf course, it will be run on the main track at One Mile and One Si xteenth) (Rail at 12 feet). (Clear 79)

Value of Race: $42,000 ($10,500 reverts) Winner $25,200; second $7,980; third $3,780; fourth $1,680; fifth $420; sixth $420; seventh $420; eighth $420; ninth $420; tenth $420; eleventh $420; twelveth $420. Mutuel Pool $503,826 Pick 3 Pool $74,109 Daily Double Pool $60,732 Exacta Pool $412,278 Superfecta Pool $137,996 Trifecta Pool $234,760

Last Raced	#	Horse	M/Eqt.	A/S	Wt	PP	St	¼	½	¾	Str	Fin	Jockey	Odds $1
	10	Jack Milton	L	3C	120	9	9	$4\frac{1}{2}$	$3\frac{1}{2}$	$2\frac{1}{2}$	1^{1}	$1^{2\frac{1}{2}}$	Velazquez J R	3.60
	9	War Dancer		3C	120	8	3	3^{1}	$4^{1\frac{1}{2}}$	$4\frac{1}{2}$	$3^{1\frac{1}{2}}$	$2^{3\frac{1}{4}}$	Garcia A	36.00
26Oct12 ^{10}Lrl^{2}	11	Sweet Mike	L	3G	120	10	1	1^{1}	1^{1}	$1\frac{1}{2}$	$2^{2\frac{1}{2}}$	$3^{2\frac{3}{4}}$	Bravo J	9.40
13Dec12 ^{6}GP^{2}	13	All Alex	L b	3C	120	12	10	$6\frac{1}{2}$	$5^{1\frac{1}{2}}$	5^{2}	4^{1}	$4^{1\frac{1}{2}}$	Rosario J	3.50
01Dec12 ^{2}GP^{2}	12	Vespato	L b	3C	120	11	5	2^{1}	2^{1}	3^{1}	5^{1}	5^{nk}	Lanerie C J	8.10
24Nov12 ^{2}Aqu^{6}	7	Main Man Mike	L	3G	120	6	6	5^{1}	$6\frac{1}{2}$	7^{2}	6^{1}	6^{hd}	Saez L	43.60
	2	Middleburg	L	3C	120	2	2	10^{hd}	10^{hd}	10^{1}	$9\frac{1}{2}$	7^{1}	Lezcano J	4.30
	8	P V Paul	L	3C	120	7	8	9^{2}	$9^{2\frac{1}{2}}$	$8\frac{1}{2}$	$7^{1\frac{1}{2}}$	$8^{1\frac{1}{2}}$	Castellano J	10.30
23Nov12 ^{8}Aqu^{2}	4	Efficient Market	L	3C	120	3	7	$7\frac{1}{2}$	$7^{1\frac{1}{2}}$	8^{hd}	$8\frac{1}{2}$	$9^{1\frac{1}{2}}$	Cohen D	9.10
19Dec12 ^{7}GP^{7}	1	Comancheria	L	3C	120	1	11	12	12	$11^{2\frac{1}{2}}$	11^{5}	$10\frac{3}{4}$	Trujillo E	20.10
08Dec12 ^{2}GP^{6}	5	Make Your Move	L	3C	120	4	4	$8^{2\frac{1}{2}}$	$8^{1\frac{1}{2}}$	$9^{1\frac{1}{2}}$	$10^{2\frac{1}{2}}$	11^{7}	Jara F	26.70
24Nov12 ^{12}CD^{6}	6	Wildcard	L b	3C	120	5	12	$11\frac{1}{2}$	$11\frac{1}{2}$	12	12	12	Prado E S	15.80

BEST WORK TIE
BEST WORK

OFF AT 3:10 Start Good. Won driving. Track Firm (Rail at 12 ft).
TIME :23^{2}, :48^{2}, 1:11^{4}, 1:35, 1:41 (:23.43, :48.42, 1:11.91, 1:35.11, 1:41.11)

$2 Mutuel Prices:

10- JACK MILTON	9.20	6.00	5.20
9- WAR DANCER		30.40	13.40
11- SWEET MIKE			5.80

$2 EXACTA 10-9 PAID $324.80 $1 SUPERFECTA 10-9-11-13 PAID $5,098.20
$1 TRIFECTA 10-9-11 PAID $1,321.80

Dark Bay or Brown Colt, (Apr), by War Front - Preserver by Forty Niner. Trainer Pletcher A. Todd. Bred by Cherry Valley Farm, LLC(KY).

JACK MILTON tracked the pace in early stages, began to edge up to lead heading into turn, vied along outside of SWEET MIKE into upper stretch, took command and remained clear to wire. WAR DANCER stalked along inside in backstretch, saved ground racing on rail in turn and steadily gained ground in stretch. SWEET MIKE took command in opening stages, continued to set pace in backstretch, challenged by JACK MILTON heading into turn, vied along inside at top of the lane, could not match strides and slightly weakened. ALL ALEX stalked the pace two off inside in backstretch, raced three wide into lane, continued steadily in stretch and lacked final kick in drive to make impact. VESPATO raced behind the pacesetter in early stages, made a bid and steadily began to edge up to lead heading into far turn but could not sustain bid and weakened. MAIN MAN MIKE allowed to settle along rail in early stages, continued evenly heading into turn and failed to rally in stretch. MIDDLEBURG reserved in early stages racing near back of the pack, angled out slightly nearing turn, asked for response and passed tiring rivals in drive. P V PAUL was unhurried in backstretch racing near the the back of rivals, floated out five wide in the turn and lacked response in stretch. EFFICIENT MARKET stalked rivals along outside in backstretch, raced four wide into lane and failed to rally in stretch. COMANCHERIA raced evenly near back of rivals and failed to make a bid. MAKE YOUR MOVE saved ground racing along inside and had no response in the drive. WILDCARD failed to respond throughout.

Owners- 10, Barber Gary ; 9, Magdalena Racing ; 11, Red Oak Stable ; 13, Grupo Seven C Stable ; 12, Youngblood John F.; 7, Talisman Bruce N.; 2, Firestone, Mr. and Mrs. Bertram R. ; 8, Stonestreet Stables LLC ; 4, Klaravich Stables, Inc. and Lawrence, William H. ; 1, Lake Lonely Racing ; 5, Darley Stable ; 6, Lothenbach Stables, Inc.

Trainers- 10, Pletcher Todd A.; 9, McPeek Kenneth G.; 11, Sacco Gregory D.; 13, Rodriguez Rudy R.; 12, Proctor Thomas F.; 7, Hennig Mark A.; 2, Clement Christophe ; 8, Brown Chad C.; 4, Romans Dale L.; 1, Sheppard Jonathan E.; 5, McLaughlin Kiaran P.; 6, Wilkes Ian R.

Breeders- 10, Cherry Valley Farm, LLC (KY); 9, Cherry Valley Farm, LLC. & Stuart S.Janney, III LLC. (KY); 11, Michael P. Cristello (FL); 13, Dr. J. David Richardson & Mike Chipman (KY); 12, Larry G. Richardson & Joe Aflinghaus (KY); 7, Bruce Talisman (KY); 2, Mr. & Mrs. Bertram R. Firestone (VA); 8, Stonestreet Thoroughbred Holdings LLC (KY); 4, Craig B. Singer (KY); 1, Team Block (IL); 5, H. Allen Poindexter & Darley (KY); 6, G. Watts Humphrey Jr. (KY)

Scratched- Balthazar(30Apr06 ^{6}Aqu^{9}), Grad Student(13Dec12 ^{6}GP^{9}), Blu Cobalto(13Dec12 ^{6}GP^{7}), Harrythenavigator(12Dec12 ^{7}Lrl^{2})

$2 Daily Double (5-10) Paid $47.80; Daily Double Pool $60,732.
$1 Pick Three (6/9/10-5-10) Paid $73.80; Pick Three Pool $74,109.

Data provided or compiled by Equibase Company, which includes data from The Jockey Club, generally is accurate but occasionally errors and omissions occur as a result of incorrect data received by others, mistakes in processing and other causes. Equibase Company and Bloodstock Research Information Services, Inc. and Thoroughbred Sports Network disclaim responsibility for the consequences, if any, of such errors, but would appreciate being called to their attention. Copyright 2012.

Best Work horses, tied - run 1, 2 for cold exacta $324.80!

COPYRIGHT 2013 BLOODSTOCK RESEARCH INFORMATION SERVICES

Chapter 8

A NEW HORSE IN THE BARN

"If you meet the Buddha at the track, kill him."
ERIC LANGJAHR

One of the most important variables to examine in the handicapping of a race is a change in trainers since a horse's last race. The betting crowd apparently pays little attention to this important tell in a horse's past performances. Generally, such a change is made for two reasons: first, because the horse has been claimed; second, because the horse's connections are not exactly thrilled with the results or lack thereof of their current trainer. Patience is not often generously distributed to most owners of thoroughbred horses. Data base reviews reveal that "new trainer" horses win more often than many handicappers expect and are not often favorably tabbed by the morning line setters; consequently, they often bring home long odds prices.

The racing forms denote a change in trainer in two ways: first, in the case of a private transfer, by the notation at the top of the horse's past performance listing; *Previously trained by trainer name (as of date of change): (record of previous trainer);* second, when the transfer is made by a claim: *Claimed from trainer name (as of date of claim) followed by the record of the trainer from whom the horse was claimed.* The astute handicapper can often glean invaluable information from these notations. For instance; what were the respective records of the departing trainer compared to the new handler's? For example, when a horse is moved to a new barn sporting a 26% winning record from one that was a 15% winner, it probably follows that the horse has moved to stronger hands; re – the *laws of probability*.

Frequently the new horse in the new barn is a layoff horse, having been away from the track for from 60 days to a year. It's important in evaluating the chances of such a horse to carefully examine all of its published workouts. It's important to note *when* the freshened horse was put back in training. For instance, in the sixth race at Santa Anita on January 17, 2013, we see that the 6 horse, Kir, changed hands on November 11, 2013, and was returning to the track under a new trainer after a 65 day layoff. Kir had run one race – on November 11, 2012 – in a 50k Maiden Special at six furlongs on the dirt at Churchill Downs in which the colt gradually faded after the first quarter, finishing last (probably pulled up). A Bernardini (A. P. Indy) foal, Kir had attracted some support at odds of 9.7/1.

Kir returned to training on December 8, working in :36 2/5 for three furlongs followed by an impressive workout pattern: four furlongs in : 48 4/5 on 12/14; five furlongs in 1:00 4/5 on 12/21;

six furlongs in 1:14 4/5 on 1/1/2013; six furlongs in 1:14 4/5 on 1/8/2013; three furlongs in :36 on 1/14/2013, just three days before the current race: "Just greasing the wheels," as one of my trainers used to say of three furlong workouts just a few days before a race.

For once the track handicapper had it about right; Kir was a contender at a morning line of 5/1 notwithstanding his poor first race performance. The crowd, however, couldn't get past the last place finish in his first start, letting Kir's odds float up to 16.7/1 at post time resulting in a 200% overlay. Kir broke sixth, some 9 lengths back, but closed in the stretch to win at $35.40 10.60 7.80.

Another example of the first-time-with-new-trainer angle occurred in the same race. The 2, Lefty O'Doul, had been away from the track for a full year, having last raced in a first start at Santa Anita in a 56k Maiden Special at a mile on the turf. Lefty was only four lengths back at the first quarter, but lost ground by the half, finishing tenth and last. Lefty's owners then gave the horse to Jerry Hollendorfer to handle, thus going to a 20% winning trainer from a 15% handler. Lefty was not put back into training until May; indicating an injury, probably a shin buck that can take from three to six months to fully heal, and is a common injury in two and three year old colts.

On 5/14/2012 Lefty worked six furlongs in 1:13 2/5, indicating a fit horse. His works from May to November were just average, but on 12/7/2012 he worked four furlongs in :48 3/5 at Hollywood Park, followed by four workouts of six furlongs in 1:14 3/5 on 12/21/2012; 5 furlongs of 1:01 2/5 on 12/29/2012 (Ordinarily an average workout, but in this case it was the fifteenth best of 78 horses that worked that day at that track); then six furlongs at 1:14 on 1/5/2013 and six furlongs at 1:14 on 1/14/2013, just three days before the race.

Again the track handicapper got the morning line about right at 10/1. The crowd again could not get past the last place finish in Lefty O'Doul's first and only start twelve months ago, floating his odds to 34/1 as the gates opened. The horse finished third, paying a generous $10. In this race there had been two horses that had changed trainers since their last race; both had excellent workout patterns before returning to the track, producing a $35.40 winner and a $10 show horse. Sandwiched between them was the morning line favorite; the combination produced a nice exacta of $96.60 and a nice trifecta of $1,198.20.

Because it's easy to overlook the change in trainer notation, I circle it on the form in order to highlight that variable, then come back to it after I have reviewed and completed my analysis of the FHH interface screen. If the program has tabbed the "new trainer" horse; either as one of the top four contenders or ties, or that horse is confirmed as a Best in Category horse; the handicapper should spend some extra time going over that horse's past performances and the complete listing of its published workouts. Be like Sherlock Holmes; let no detail or variable bearing on the horse's ability escape you, for just "hitting the highlights" in the form and on the program's interface screen will seldom identify the kind of horse that hidden horse hunters stalk.

SIXTH RACE
Santa Anita
January 17th, 2013

About 6½ FURLONGS. (Turf) (1.11) MAIDEN SPECIAL WEIGHT. Purse $56,800 DOWNHILL TURF FOR MAIDENS, FOUR YEARS OLD AND UPWARD. Weight, 122 lbs. (Rail at 24 feet). (Clear 76)

Value of Race: $56,750 ($16,800 reverts) Winner $33,800; second $11,200; third $6,720; fourth $3,360; fifth $1,120; sixth $250; seventh $250; eighth $250. Mutuel Pool $219,575 Pick 3 Pool $49,357 Daily Double Pool $18,217 Exacta Pool $140,811 Superfecta Pool $79,850 Trifecta Pool $110,147

Last Raced	# Horse	M/Eqt.	A/S	Wt	PP	St	¼	½	Str	Fin	Jockey	Odds $1
11Nov12 ^{7}CD^{11}	6 Kir		4C	122	6	6	6^{2}	$6^{3\frac{1}{2}}$	$4\frac{1}{2}$	$1\frac{1}{2}$	Talamo J	16.70 NEW TRAINER
14Dec12 ^{3}Bhp^{2}	1 Broker Brett	L	4C	122	1	3	$5^{2\frac{1}{2}}$	$5^{1\frac{1}{2}}$	6^{4}	$2\frac{3}{4}$	Baze T	1.20
14Jan12 ^{5}SA^{10}	2 Lefty O'Doul	L b	4G	122	2	5	$3\frac{1}{2}$	$3^{1\frac{1}{2}}$	$1\frac{1}{2}$	3no	Mojica O	34.70 NEW TRAINER
29Nov12 ^{6}Bhp^{4}	5 Just Fishin	L b	4C	122	5	4	4^{3}	$4^{2\frac{1}{2}}$	$3^{1\frac{1}{2}}$	$4^{1\frac{1}{4}}$	Puglisi I	8.50
	3 Odeon	L b	4G	122	3	8	8	8	8	$5\frac{3}{4}$	Nakatani C S	14.60
20Apr12 ^{1}SA^{3}	4 Dynamize	L	5G	122	4	7	$7^{4\frac{1}{2}}$	7^{4}	$7^{3\frac{1}{2}}$	$6\frac{1}{2}$	Stevens G L	5.90
16Nov12 ^{6}Bhp^{10}	7 Exultant	L b	4C	122	7	2	$1^{1\frac{1}{2}}$	$1^{1\frac{1}{2}}$	$2^{1\frac{1}{2}}$	$7^{4\frac{3}{4}}$	Hernandez J J	2.80
20Dec12 ^{9}SA^{12}	8 World Renowned	L	5H	122	8	1	$2^{1\frac{1}{2}}$	2^{hd}	5^{hd}	8	Bisono A	12.30

OFF AT 3:34 Start Good. Won driving. Track Firm (Rail at 24 ft).
TIME :21, :42^{3}, 1:06, 1:12 (:21.00, :42.72, 1:06.00, 1:12.19)

$2 Mutuel Prices:

6- KIR	35.40	10.60	7.80
1- BROKER BRETT		3.20	2.60
2- LEFTY O'DOUL			10.00

$1 EXACTA 6-1 PAID $48.30 $1 SUPERFECTA 6-1-2-5 PAID $3,577.00
$1 TRIFECTA 6-1-2 PAID $598.10

Bay Colt, (Mar), by Bernardini - Cassis by Red Ransom. Trainer Ellis W. Ronald. Bred by Sanford R. Robertson(KY).

KIR settled off the rail then inside on the hill, came out in upper stretch, rallied under some urging and a strong hand ride between horses in the final furlong to gain the lead in deep stretch and held. BROKER BRETT saved ground chasing the pace, came out leaving the hill and into the stretch and also rallied outside horses late. LEFTY O'DOUL stalked inside, came out into the stretch, took the lead alongside a rival, drifted in a bit past the sixteenth pole and was outfinished but held third. JUST FISHIN chased outside a rival then a bit off the rail, angled in on the hill, came out in midstretch and rallied between foes. ODEON allowed to settled just off the inside, came out in the stretch and found his best stride late. DYNAMIZE unhurried a bit off the rail to the stretch, angled to the inside in the drive and lacked the needed rally. EXULTANT sped to the early lead, set the pace a bit off the rail then inside, fought back in the drive, steadied when crowded a bit just past the sixteenth pole and weakened. WORLD RENOWNED stalked off the rail then outside a rival, came three deep into the stretch and weakened. Rail on hill at 7 feet.

Owners- 6, Robertson Sanford R.; 1, Talla Michael ; 2, Ran Jan Racing, Inc. ; 5, Nichols Thomas L.; 3, Moss, Mr. and Mrs. Jerome S. ; 4, Lenner, Tom, Skyline Stables, Strauss, William, Todaro, George and Litt, Jason ; 7, C R K Stable ; 8, Cavanaugh, Michael and Stute, Gary

Trainers- 6, Ellis Ronald W.; 1, Sadler John W.; 2, Hollendorfer Jerry ; 5, Greely C. Beau; 3, Shirreffs John A.; 4, Puype Mike ; 7, Sadler John W.; 8, Stute Gary

Breeders- 6, Sanford R. Robertson (KY); 1, David M. Talla (KY); 2, Ranjan Racing, Inc. (KY); 5, Thomas L. Nichols (KY); 3, James Gottwald (KY); 4, Robert Raphaelson (KY); 7, W. D. Burris Inc. (KY); 8, Peter Vegso Racing Stable (FL)

$2 Daily Double (4-6) Paid $107.00; Daily Double Pool $18,217.
$1 Pick Three (1-4-6) Paid $1,447.60; Pick Three Pool $49,357.

Best Work horses, tied - run 1, 2 for cold exacta $324.80!

COPYRIGHT 2013 BLOODSTOCK RESEARCH INFORMATION SERVICES

Another example of the importance of examining new-trainer horses occurred on 1/19/2013 at Oaklawn Park in the ninth and last race, a 5k claimer on the dirt for four year olds and up with a purse of $15,000. There were no less than three new-trainer horses; the 2, 4, and 8.

The 2, Bourbon King, had been claimed on 11/25/2012 from a 7.5k optional claimer in which the horse's connections entered him to be claimed. Bourbon King had previously won at a mile on the turf at Remington Park in a 20k claimer for non-winners of three races. That should have raised the eyebrows of an experienced punter: Why would a trainer, having just claimed the horse for 7.5k, run him back in a 5k claiming race? Examination of Bourbon King's three workouts under the new trainer revealed them to be slow, slower, and slowest. On 12/21/2012 the horse worked three furlongs in the strolling time of :40; last of the 14 horses that worked out at that track on that day. He next worked on 1/2/2013 in :54 for four furlongs; his was the eighty-first best work of 86 working that day; his last work was on 1/11/2013 in which he walked four furlongs in : 52 3/5 breezing and improved to be the fifty-third best work of the 70 horses that worked that day. I concluded and I believe most experienced handicappers would agree that the new trainer would probably be glad to have Bourbon King taken off his hands.

The second new-trainer horse was the 4, Sleeve, claimed for 5k on 12/7/2012 from the race he had won. Sleeve also turned out to be overly fond of leisurely workouts for on 1/2/2013 he worked five furlongs in the pedestrian time of 1:04 4/5, forty-third best of

65 horses working that day. His final pre-race prep was only slightly an improvement as he worked in 1:03 1/5 for five furlongs. The FHH program awarded just one point to Sleeve and two points to Bourbon King; both were off the board.

The third new-trainer horse was the 8, Stereo in Motion; he had been trained by Steve Assmussen when on 12/6/2012 he was entered for 7.5k in a mile and seventy yard race on the dirt at Remington Park, a race that he handily won, closing some ten lengths from the first quarter pole to win going away. The previous trainer was Ronald Moquelt as of 9/28/2012. In the current race Moquelt is once again the trainer of record. Not many people take horses from Asmussen: it would be interesting to know the reason for the switch back to Moquelt. In any case, Stereo in Motion had the second best late pace number at 96; just three points back of the best late pace horse, the 10, Lotto Cat, who was also tied for the #4 contender by the FHH program.

Screen Presented:

TELL	POINTS	M/L	POST
6=	8	6/1	7/2
5=	5	10/1	11/1
9=	5	20/1	25/1
1=	4	15/1	17/1
7=	4	5/2	5/2
10=	4	6/1	7/1

BEST IN CATEGORY

Work=5	4 fur :48
Start= 7	94
Mid= 7	110
Late=10	99

The 10 had shown solid closes in his last three races and was confirmed. I thought the 5 was suspect because of his low late pace, some 16 points behind the best late number. It appeared the system bet was to tab the 10 up and back in exactas with the screen horses 1, 5, 6, 7, 9 and to include the 8 for the reasons set out above; then to bet the 10 for first and second with 1, 5, 6, 7, 8, 9 with the 1, 5, 6, 7, 8, 9 in fifty cent trifectas. Then to put the 10 in first and second with the same horses in at least dime superfectas.

Race comes 10, 8, 1, 7.

Winner pays $17.00 5.40 5.20; $2 exacta $381.80; $2 trifecta $6,012.40; Dime super $2,465.49!

The key to the huge payout was, of course, the inclusion of the new-trainer horse, the 8, that had won his last race at a 50 per cent higher claiming price than the race from which it was claimed.

NINTH RACE
Oaklawn Park
January 19th, 2013

1 MILE. (1.342) WCL . Purse $15,500 (Includes $7,750 Other Sources) FOR FOUR YEAR OLDS AND UPWARD. Weight, 122 lbs. Non-winners Of A Race Since November 19, 2012 Allowed 3 lbs. A Race Since September 19, 2012 Allowed 5 lbs. Claiming Price $5,000. (Clear 55)

Value of Race: $15,500 Winner $9,300; second $3,100; third $1,550; fourth $775; fifth $465; sixth $45; seventh $45; eighth $44; ninth $44; tenth $44; eleventh $44; twelveth $44. Mutuel Pool $168,184 Pick 3 Pool $20,577 Pick 4 Pool $44,882 Daily Double Pool $27,769 Exacta Pool $109,988 Superfecta Pool $46,993 Trifecta Pool $69,540

Last Raced	#	Horse	M/Eqt.	A/S	Wt	PP	St	¼	½	¾	Str	Fin	Jockey	Cl'g Pr	Odds $1
16Nov12 ^{7}RP^2	10	Lotto Cat	L	5G	117	10	12	12	11^{hd}	8½	3½	1½	Corbett G W	5000	7.50
06Dec12 ^{6}RP^1	8	Stereo in Motion	L b	4G	122	8	10	10^{hd}	10½	7½	2^{hd}	2½	Quinonez L S	5000	25.90
23Dec12 ^{2}TP^5	1	Gratitat	L b	5G	117	1	3	1½	1^1	$1^{2½}$	1½	3^{hd}	Vazquez R A	5000	17.60
07Dec12 ^{10}TP^7	7	D. C. Gene	L b	5H	119	7	6	8^2	7^2	4^1	4^{hd}	4½	Albarado R	5000	2.80
07Dec12 ^{5}RP^1	4	Sleeve	L	7G	122	4	1	5^{hd}	6^{hd}	5^1	$5^{3½}$	$5^{1¼}$	Mello D	5000	3.60
03Nov12 ^{10}CD^2	5	Saviano	L b	10G	117	5	5	$9^{3½}$	$9^{3½}$	10^{hd}	$7^{1½}$	6^{nk}	Thompson T J	5000	11.40
28Nov12 ^{7}RP^6	2	Bourbon King	L	4G	119	2	8	6^{hd}	8^{hd}	9^1	6^{hd}	$7^{2½}$	Wade L	5000	8.90
18Nov12 ^{7}Mnr^4	9	Dont Tell Kitten	L b	6G	117	9	11	$11^{2½}$	12	$11^{1½}$	8½	$8^{2¼}$	Loveberry J	5000	25.20
20Oct12 ^{6}Ded^9	11	Nolan's Revenge	L b	5G	117	11	9	7½	$4^{1½}$	3^1	9^4	$9^{5½}$	Birzer A	5000	18.80
07Dec12 ^{5}RP^6	12	Mae B Today	L f	5H	117	12	7	3^1	$3^{3½}$	2^{hd}	10^4	$10^{5¼}$	Gonzalez C	5000	46.60
08Dec12 ^{2}RP^9	3	Baluarte	L	4G	117	3	2	$4^{1½}$	5^{hd}	12	11^{10}	$11^{16¾}$	McKee J	5000	54.20
20Sep12 ^{8}Lad^1	6	The Bay Phantom	L b	5G	110	6	4	2^{hd}	2^{hd}	6^{hd}	12	12	Canchari A		3.70

BEST LATE
2ND BEST LATE

OFF AT 5:19 Start Good. Won driving. Track Fast.
TIME :23², :47², 1:13, 1:27, 1:40³ (:23.47, :47.40, 1:13.05, 1:27.06, 1:40.67)

$2 Mutuel Prices:

10- LOTTO CAT	17.00	5.40	5.20
8- STEREO IN MOTION		20.20	12.00
1- GRATITAT			13.60

$2 EXACTA 10-8 PAID $381.80 $1 SUPERFECTA 10-8-1-7 PAID $24,654.90
$1 TRIFECTA 10-8-1 PAID $3,006.20

Dark Bay or Brown Gelding, (Apr), by Jump Start - America's Quest by Quiet American. Trainer Prather, Jr. Henry John. Bred by Burning Sands Stable, LLC(KY).

LOTTO CAT in a bit tight at the start, advanced in some traffic second turn, came four wide into the stretch, finished with good mettle out in the strip to win going away. STEREO IN MOTION unhurried off the inside, five wide when gaining out of the final turn, challenged nearing the furlong ground, proved no match for the winner in the late going, determined for the place. GRATITAT got clear soon after the start, set a legit pace, larger lead second turn, responded when challenged upper stretch, proved stubborn in the battle for the place spot. D. C. GENE allowed the pace to go while racing outside, angled in for the drive, outkicked for the place in the late going. SLEEVE settled off the pace, enjoyed a good trip along the inside into the lane, came up empty. SAVIANO lacked early foot, improved position slightly in the drive while not a serious threat. BOURBON KING off the pace in the two path, moved inside to save ground into the stretch, lacked a late kick. DONT TELL KITTEN void of early foot, well back, passed tiring rivals. NOLAN'S REVENGE four wide in the first turn, within striking distance, weakened in the drive. MAE B TODAY forwardly placed while off the inside, gave way. BALUARTE forwardly placed in the early going, staged a steady retreat. THE BAY PHANTOM chased the early leader for five furlongs, stopped, finished far back.

Owners- 10, Greer Michael D.; 8, Southern Springs Stables ; 1, Mansfield, Sherry and Hiles, Rick ; 7, Prezocki Glenn R.; 4, Jackrabbit Thoroughbreds, LLC ; 5, Stoll, III Edward F.; 2, Caldwell Danny R.; 9, Burkholder Gene ; 11, Turner Jack ; 12, Adami Tony Lynn; 3, Mullins Jesse ; 6, Hogwild Stables LLC

Trainers- 10, Prather, Jr. John Henry; 8, Moquett Ron ; 1, Hiles Rick ; 7, Romans Dale L.; 4, Richard Chris ; 5, Bowman Carl ; 2, Villafranco Federico ; 9, Puhl Kim A.; 11, Roberts Stanley W.; 12, Williams C. Blaine; 3, Mullins Jesse ; 6, Cates Al

Breeders- 10, Burning Sands Stable, LLC (KY); 8, William Duignan, Patrick Heraty &Gabriel Duignan (KY); 1, Sherry R. Mansfield & Kay Kitchen (FL); 7, William Lamaster & Adena Springs (KY); 4, Mr. & Mrs. R. D. Randal (KY); 5, Spendthrift Farm LLC & James Brown (KY); 2, Edwin Anthony & Melissa Anthony (KY); 9, Kenneth L. Ramsey & Sarah K. Ramsey (KY); 11, Palides Investments N.V., Inc. (KY); 12, Liberation Farm (KY); 3, Anderson Farms (KY); 6, McDowell Farm (AR)

D. C. Gene was claimed by Greer Michael D.; trainer, Prather, Jr. John Henry

$2 Daily Double (7-10) Paid $42.40; Daily Double Pool $27,769.
$1 Pick Three (7-7-10) Paid $878.00; Pick Three Pool $20,577.
$1 Pick Four (4/7-7-7-10) Paid $5,064.30; Pick Four Pool $44,882.

Data provided or compiled by Equibase Company, which includes data from The Jockey Club, generally is accurate but occasionally errors and omissions occur as a result of incorrect data received by others, mistakes in processing and other causes. Equibase Company and Bloodstock Research Information Services, Inc. and Thoroughbred Sports Network disclaim responsibility for the consequences, if any, of such errors, but would appreciate being called to their attention. Copyright 2013.

Best Late, 2nd Best Late, run 1, 2 for cold straight exacta $$381.80.
Long shot place horse had new trainer.

COPYRIGHT 2013 BLOODSTOCK RESEARCH INFORMATION SERVICES

Taking the time to carefully examine the past performances of all new-trainer horses will frequently land the punter on long odds runners, otherwise hidden to the cursory look that the morning line setters and the credulous betting public too often give to this type of horse.

Another case-on-point example of a new-trainer horse long shot bringing home the bacon occurred on 1/20/2013 in the seventh race at Gulfstream Park in a six furlong race on the dirt in a 50k maiden claimer for three year old maiden fillies.

Screen presented:

TELL POINTS	M/L	POST
4=8	15/1	13.1/1
2=5	15/1	18.6/1
6=5	20/1	4.1/1
8=5	3/1	4.6/1
9=5	4/1	3.8/1

BEST IN CATEGORY

Work=12	4 fur :46.6
Start= 2	91
Mid= 4	103
Late= 9	89

A NEW HORSE IN THE BARN

The 2 and the 4 nearly jumped off the page at me for the reason that they were system long shots at juicy odds, and both were confirmed by their Best Start and Best Mid-Pace numbers, respectively. The 6 drew my attention for a different reason: it was a substantial underlay – live on the board, as they say. When I examined the Brisnet form I noted that the 2, Box Office Smash, had been claimed in her first start on 10/19/2012 for $30,000 by her present trainer, a 14 per cent winner. In that seven furlong race the horse was bet down to 10/1, finishing eighth after being just a length and a half from the front at the second call.

She was freshened for 60 days, returning to training on 12/13/2012, working four times since then. Examining those workouts was enlightening: on 12/13/2012 she worked three furlongs in a meaningless :38 1/5, just walking, really. On 12/23/2012 the newly claimed Box Office Smash woke up from her nine hum-drum works of that year by breezing four furlongs in :48 3/5, third best of 40 horses working that same day at that track – it was her best work since being put into training. She next worked on 12/31/2012 at five furlongs in a bullet work of 1:01; generally, not a work to write home about; nevertheless, the best of 27 horses that worked that day at that track. Her final work on 1/9/2013 was at five furlongs in 1:00 4/5, third best of 19. Clearly, the new trainer had managed by whatever method (perhaps known only to himself) to get Box Office Smash to work faster than she had worked for the previous trainer.

The 12, Work n Flirt, not only had the best work of the field; she had the best *works* by volume, having worked a dozen times since being put into training on 6/8/2012 – here was a trainer with extraordinary patience. The working pattern included no less than three bullet works, her best being four furlongs in :47 3/5. If she had not been on the far outside in the large field, I would have liked her for the win. The morning line setter and his followers liked her, tabbing her the favorite at 2.3/1, bet down from a morning line of 5/1 – another live-on-the-board horse.

The system bet was to win with twice as much to place on the 2 and 4. Then to run the 2 and 4 up and back with the screen horses 6, 8, 9, 12 in exactas, trifecta, and superfectas.

Race comes 2, 12, 4, 6.

Winner pays $39.20 14.20 10.00; $2 exacta $187.40; $2 tri fecta $1,668; $2 superfecta $6,782.00!

The key horse, of course, was the 2 which was the only horse in the race that had been claimed in her last race. So as a general habit – a good one, you see – the hidden horse hunter should always check and mark any new-trainer horses for extra close examination, for this type of runner frequently pays double digits for the discerning punter and user of the *Finding the Hidden Horse* thoroughbred horse race handicapping software.

Another instructive example of the new-trainer angle paying off with a long shot price was the second race at Oaklawn Park on 1/24/ 2013. Only seven horses were entered in a six furlong sprint on the dirt, an optional 25k claimer for four year olds and up which had started for a claiming price of $12,500 or less in 2012 or claiming price of $20.000.

A NEW HORSE IN THE BARN

SEVENTH RACE
Gulfstream
January 20th, 2013

6 FURLONGS. (1.08) MAIDEN CLAIMING. Purse $33,700 (includes $6,700 FOA - Florida Owners Awards) FOR MAIDENS, FILLIES THREE YEARS OLD. Weight, 122 lbs. Claiming Price $50,000, if for $45,000, allowed 2 lbs. (Clear 80)

Value of Race: $27,000 ($6,700 reverts) Winner $16,200; second $5,400; third $2,700; fourth $1,080; fifth $270; sixth $270; seventh $270; eighth $270; ninth $270; tenth $270. Mutuel Pool $260,684 Pick 3 Pool $39,353 Daily Double Pool $35,954 Exacta Pool $202,327 Superfecta Pool $77,400 Trifecta Pool $121,281

Last Raced	# Horse	M/Eqt.	A/S Wt	PP St	¼	½	Str	Fin	Jockey	Clg Pr	Odds $1
19Oct12 ²Kee⁹	2 Box Office Smash	L	3F 122	2 1	1½	1¹½	1⁴½	1⁸	Castanon J L	50000	19.60
	12 Work N Flirt	L f	3F 122	10 4	2¹½	2½	2¹	2¹½	Velazquez J R	50000	2.30
26Dec12 ³GP⁶	4 Rosie My Way	L	3F 122	3 8	7³	6³	4²	3¹½	Cruz M R	50000	13.10
20Dec12 ⁷GP⁶	6 Camille Garey	L	3F 122	5 5	5⁴	3²	3²	4¹	Lopez P	50000	4.10
	11 Gunner Gal	L f	3F 122	9 6	10	8²½	8⁴	5²¾	Saez L	50000	17.00
27Dec12 ⁷GP⁴	9 Hope's Dream	L	3F 120	7 9	8¹	10	9³	6ⁿᵏ	Castellano J	45000	3.80
	1 Lion Belle	L	3F 115	1 7	4½	5ʰᵈ	5¹	7²½	Zayas E J	50000	6.20
30Dec12 ²GP³	8 Scaleile	L b	3F 120	6 3	6½	7⁵½	7¹	8²	Lanerie C J	45000	4.50
30Dec12 ²GP⁷	5 Abeni	L f	3F 120	4 2	3ʰᵈ	4½	6²	9⁴½	Gomez D F	45000	93.40
	10 Twin Kisses	L	3F 122	8 10	9¹½	9ʰᵈ	10	10	Garcia A	50000	35.40

BEST START!
BEST WORK!
BEST MID

OFF AT 3:39 Start Good. Ridden out. Track Good.
TIME :22⁸, :46, :58¹, 1:11¹² (:22.42, :46.02, :58.35, 1:11.51)

$2 Mutuel Prices:
2 - BOX OFFICE SMASH 39.20 14.20 10.00
12 - WORK N FLIRT 4.00 3.00
4 - ROSIE MY WAY 6.00

$2 EXACTA 2-12 PAID $187.40 $1 SUPERFECTA 2-12-4-6 PAID $3,391.00
$1 TRIFECTA 2-12-4 PAID $834.00

Bay Filly, (Ap), by Dixie Union - Bees by Rahy. Trainer Cheeks Joseph. Bred by Courtlandt Farm(KY).

BOX OFFICE SMASH broke sharp and took command in opening stages, dictated the pace along the inside in the backstretch, continued clear going into the far turn and drew off in final stages. WORK N FLIRT raced behind the leader in early stages, made a bid for BOX OFFICE SMASH heading into far turn and continued to chase the winner into the lane. ROSIE MY WAY was allowed to settle in and stalk the pace in early stages, steadily gained position leaving the backstretch, angled out in the upper stretch and gained position in the stretch. CAMILLE GAREY stalked the pace in early stages, asked to pick up the pace nearing the far turn, shifted three wide into the lane and lacked a kick in the late drive. GUNNER GAL was unhurried and settled in stalking the pace in early stages, made a bid leaving the backstretch, raced three wide into the far turn and improved position in the stretch. HOPE'S DREAM was unhurried in early stages, floated out six wide into the far turn, improved position but failed to make an impact. LION BELLE tracked the pace along the rail in the backstretch and flattened out nearing the top of the lane. SCEALEILE stalked the front runners in early stages, raced four wide in the far turn and lacked response in the drive. ABENI tracked the top two leaders in opening quarter, continued to stalk the pace in the middle of the backstretch and steadily began to fade nearing the top of the lane. TWIN KISSES lacked speed in early stages, continued reserved near the back heading for home and failed to make a bid in the stretch.

Owners- 2, Cheeks, Joseph and Damasceno, Lui; 12, Kuehne Racing; 4, Paikoff Mel; 6, Garey Jack; 11, Tucker John M.; 9, Wine Debora; 1, Joseph Saffie; 8, Never Better Stables and Paddas, John; 5, Jones Monica; 10, Calvo Joseph

Trainers- 2, Cheeks Joseph; 12, Moreina Michael; 4, Orseno Joseph F.; 5, Hamm Timothy E; 11, Connelly William R.; 9, White William P.; 1, Joseph, Jr. Saffie A; 8, Baker James E.; 6, Cascallares Nestor; 10, Hills Timothy A.

Breeders- 2, Courtlandt Farm (KY); 12, Dr. John A Chandler, Jamm, LTD. & Millridge Farm, LTD. (KY); 4, Barbara Brown Ward (KY); 6, Arindel Farm LLC (KY); 11, John M. Tucker (KY); 9, Christina Latimer & Richard S. Taulman (KY); 1, Lynn Jones, Olin Gentry & Omar Trevino (KY); 8, Timber Bay Farm (FA); 5, Glencrest Farm LLC (KY); 10, Joseph A. Calvo (KY).
Scaleile was ridden by Rumsey, Kenneth L. and Sarah K.; trainer, Maker Michael J.

Scratched- With Polish, Dreaming of Lucy, Arabian Dream

$2 Daily Double (1-2) Paid $199.00; Daily Double Pool $35,954.
$1 Pick Three (6-1-2) Paid $461.90; Pick Three Pool $39,353.

Winner 2 - New trainer by claim - Best Start
Place 12 - Best Work
Show 4 - Best Mid-Pace

COPYRIGHT 2013 BLOODSTOCK RESEARCH INFORMATION SERVICES

Screen presented:

TELL POINTS	M/L	POST
5=7	5/2	1.6/1
6=7	7/2	8.5/1
1=6	8/1	9.3/1
4=6	15/1	33.9/1
7=6	9/5	1.5/1

BEST IN CATEGORY

Works=5	4 fur :47.8
Start= 7	99
Mid= 1	100
Late= 2	103

There were three new-trainer horses in the race: the 1, Lunar Fleet; the 4, Doinmysongndance; and the 6, Tangled Sheets. The 1 had been claimed on 12/6/2012 for 20k in the race in which he was beaten by a nose; however, he had not worked since that race of seven weeks before. This was a red flag to me, though otherwise the horse looked to be in good form. The 4, Doinmysongndance, piqued my interest; I thought he was the class of the race, having run in three medium stakes in his last ten races. He had the second best work and had been freshened with an eleven week layoff since the clunker he threw in his race of 11/12/2013. This new-trainer horse had changed hands after that race due to the owner's choice. The third new-trainer horse was the 6, Tangled Sheets; also changing hands due to owner's choice on 12/28/2012. The horse was cutting back in this race to six furlongs from six and one-half furlongs in which he led to the head of the stretch before mildly yielding to finish second, just a length and three-quarters back of the winner. I thought the 7, Fifth Date, was a false favorite. Last starting – and winning – on 12/6/2012 then putting two slow workouts together. The near co-favorite with the 7 was the 5, Homeboykris, that had posted a clunker in a 100k stakes on 12/1/2012, then posted two slow workouts prepping for this race.

The 4 was clearly the long shot stand-out on the interface screen. With post time odds of 33/1, I reasoned that if he came first or second, the payoff would be large. The system bet was to win and twice as much to place on the 4; then to run the 4 up and back with the field in exactas and trifectas. A $1 exacta for the 4 up and back with the field would have cost all of $12; a fifty cent trifecta – the 4 with all with all and then all with 4 with all would have cost all of $30.

Race comes 3, 4, 6, 2.

Winner pays $88.60 35.20 13.00; Place Horse 4 pays 32.40 11.00; $2 exacta $879.80; 50 cent trifecta $1,781.65

The first and second favorites finished last and next to last. *Caveat emptor* once again of the morning line setter's unfortunate touts. Of the three new-trainer horses in the field, one placed and one showed, proving again that the change-in-trainer angle since a horse's last race is a variable well worth following.

SECOND RACE
Oaklawn Park
January 24th, 2013

6 FURLONGS. (1.074) SOC . Purse $24,000 (Includes $12,000 Other Sources) FOR FOUR YEAR OLDS AND UPWARD WHICH HAVE STARTED FOR A CLAIMING PRICE OF $12,500 OR LESS IN 2012 OR CLAIMING PRICE $20,000. Weight, 124 lbs. Non-winners Of Two Races Since October 24, 2012 Allowed 4 lbs. Two Races Since June 24, 2012 Allowed 8 lbs. Claimi ng Price $20,000 (Races Where Entered For $12,500 Or Less Not Considered). (Cloudy 43)

Value of Race: $24,000 Winner $14,400; second $4,800; third $2,400; fourth $1,200; fifth $720; sixth $240; seventh $240. Mutuel Pool $51,336 Daily Double Pool $24,352 Exacta Pool $36,756 Trifecta Pool $36,225

Last Raced	#	Horse	M/Eqt.	A/S	Wt	PP	St	¼	½	Str	Fin	Jockey	Cl'g Pr	Odds $1
27Sep12 ^{5}Pid^{4}	3	Pocket Medal	L b	6G	116	3	5	4½	2^{hd}	1½	1¾	Loveberry J	20000	43.30
18Nov12 ^{9}CD^{10}	4	Doinmysongndance	L b	5G	118	4	1	1½	1^{hd}	2½	2^{1}	Wade L	20000	33.90 BEST WORK
28Dec12 ^{9}TP^{2}	6	Tangled Sheets	L b	7H	116	6	3	3^{2}	4^{2}	3^{1}	3^{nk}	Homeister, Jr. R B	20000	8.50
06Dec12 ^{7}RP^{3}	2	Lee's South	L	5G	116	2	4	5^{2}	5^{1}	$4^{1\frac{1}{2}}$	$4^{2\frac{3}{4}}$	Quinonez L S		4.40
06Dec12 ^{8}TP^{2}	1	Lunar Fleet	L f	7G	120	1	6	7	7	6½	5^{nk}	Thompson T J		9.30
01Dec12 ^{6}GP^{6}	5	Homeboykris	L bf	6G	120	5	7	6½	6^{hd}	7	6¾	Albarado R		1.60
06Dec12 ^{7}RP^{1}	7	Fifth Date	L f	9G	124	7	2	2^{1}	3^{1}	$5^{2\frac{1}{2}}$	7	Birzer A		1.50

OFF AT 1:58 Start Good. Won driving. Track Fast.
TIME :22, :45^{3}, :58^{1}, 1:10^{4} (:22.14, :45.77, :58.20, 1:10.87)

$2 Mutuel Prices:

3- POCKET MEDAL	88.60	35.20	13.00
4- DOINMYSONGNDANCE		32.40	11.00
6- TANGLED SHEETS			5.00

$2 EXACTA 3-4 PAID $879.80 $1 TRIFECTA 3-4-6 PAID $3,563.30

Bay Gelding, (Feb), by Medallist - Pocket Brush by Broad Brush. Trainer Martin R. Joseph. Bred by Dr. K. K. Jayaraman &Dr. Vilasini Jayaraman(KY).

POCKET MEDAL off the pace, four wide advance in the turn, engaged the leader when straightened for home, wore that foe down under firm handling. DOINMYSONGNDANCE broke on top, set the pace inside, responded when the winner challenged upper stretch, gave ground grudgingly. TANGLED SHEETS within striking distance off the inside while under firm restraint, lacked a winning kick in the drive. LEE'S SOUTH forwardly placed toward the inside early, fell back into the turn, went evenly in the drive. LUNAR FLEET fell back to trail, picked off a couple of tiring rivals while not a factor. HOMEBOYKRIS last to leave, raced back in showing little. FIFTH DATE pressured the pace while off the inside, gave way.

Owners- 3, Jayaraman, Dr. K. K. and Jayaraman, Dr. Vilasini D. ; 4, Alan Booge Racing, Inc. ; 6, Clark, Rick and Brent W. ; 2, Estate of Lee R. Jones ; 1, Diamond F Racing, LLC ; 5, Hui Michael M.; 7, Caldwell Danny R.

Trainers- 3, Martin Joseph R.; 4, Padilla Tim P.; 6, Kopp Glenn ; 2, Petalino Joseph ; 1, Tomlinson Michael A.; 5, Moquett Ron ; 7, Villafranco Federico

Breeders- 3, Dr. K. K. Jayaraman &Dr. Vilasini Jayaraman (KY); 4, Gulf Coast Farms, LLC (KY); 6, Ralph Stroope (KY); 2, Lee R. Jones (TX); 1, Brass Oaks Farm (KY); 5, Dark Hollow Farm & William Paca Beatson (MD); 7, Al J. Horton (OK)

Tangled Sheets was claimed by Pollard Carl F.; trainer, Vance David R.

$2 Daily Double (8-3) Paid $287.00; Daily Double Pool $24,352.

Data provided or compiled by Equibase Company, which includes data from The Jockey Club, generally is accurate but occasionally errors and omissions occur as a result of incorrect data received by others, mistakes in processing and other causes. Equibase Company and Bloodstock Research Information Services, Inc. and Thoroughbred Sports Network disclaim responsibility for the consequences, if any, of such errors, but would appreciate being called to their attention. Copyright 2013.

4 - 33.9/1 long shot place - Best Work

COPYRIGHT 2013 BLOODSTOCK RESEARCH INFORMATION SERVICES

A NEW HORSE IN THE BARN

The tenth race at Tampa Bay on 1/26/2013 was a nearly perfect example of new-trainer horses that were ready to give a top effort for their new handlers. The race was a 75k stake for fillies and mares, four years old and up going 5 furlongs on the turf. In the field of 10, there were two new-trainer horses: the 8, Trippin' Along, (handled by Wayne Catalano by the owner's decision); and the 10, Smartys Emperoress.

The 8 had not raced for 59 days, but had worked four times since 12/11/2012; two of these works were exceptional: on 12/11/2012 Trippin' Along worked four furlongs handily in :47 1/5, followed by a four furlong work of :47 3/5 breezing on 1/3/2013. The filly had won her last race on 11/28/2012 at Calder in a five furlong turf race for 25k Optional Claimers.

The 10, Smartys Emperoress, had last raced on 12/19/2012 at the Fairgrounds in a 62.5k optional claimer at 5 1/2 furlongs on the turf, turning in a sub-par effort after being in the mix until the second call. At Churchill Downs on 5/12/2012 she had placed in a 5 furlong turf 68k stakes, finishing just one and one-quarter lengths behind the winner. After changing trainers, the filly worked twice: her work of :48 4/5 on 1/9/2013 showed that she was fit. This race was her second race after an eight month layoff, no doubt from a serious injury. All variables pointed to a top effort from her in today's race. The crowd, however, could not get past her last race in which she stopped badly. Her morning line was 5/1; she left the gate at 16/1. For once the morning line setter was close to right and the crowd was completely wrong.

The system bet was to bet the 10 to win and twice as much to place; then to box the 8, 10 in exactas; then to bet trifectas using the 8, 10 over the 8, 10 with all. (The cost of the exacta and trifecta bets was $36 using a $2 betting unit; the straight bet would have cost $6, for a total investment in the race of $42.)

Race comes 10, 8, 2, 9.

Winner pays $34.60 13.20 9.00; $2 exacta $233.20; $2 tri fecta $2,951.20! (A $42 investment returned $3,245.20.)

The two new-trainer horses in the race ran one, two. The discerning punter should *always* search in the past performances for horses with this variable. As we have demonstrated, such horses hit the board with surprising regularity.

Another instructive example demonstrating the value of tabbing new-trainer horses occurred on 1/24/2013 in the ninth race at Oaklawn; a 15k claimer for maidens, fillies and mares four years old and up going six furlongs on the dirt.

The sole new-trainer horse in the race was the 11, Motokiks Dancer; an owner-trainer change. The horse had run one race on 9/13/2012, a five and one half furlong 5k maiden claimer at Louisiana Downs, finishing seventh in a field of 10. Although the chart writer's comment was "never dangerous," the form

TENTH RACE
Tampa Bay
January 26th, 2013

6 FURLONGS. (Turf) (.544) STAKES. Purse $75,000 *LIGHTNING CITY S.* FOR FILLIES AND MARES FOUR YEARS OLD AND UPWARD. By subscription of $50 each which should accompany the nomination, $350 to pass the entry box and $350 additional to start with $75,000 Guaranteed with 60% to the winner, 20% to second, 10% to third, 5% to fourth, 3% to fifth and 2% to sixth. Weights: 122 lbs. Non-winners of a Sweepstakes on the turf since September 1, 2012, 2 lbs.; $42,000 on the turf since then, 4 lbs.; three races other than maiden, claiming or starter in 2012-2013, 6 lbs. (Maiden, Claiming and Starter races not considered in estimating weight allowances). Starters and riders to be named through the entry box by the usual time of closing. This field will be limited to twelve starters. In the event more than twelve pass through the entry box, the twelve starters will be determined with preference given to Grade I, II or III Stakes winners in that order, then those that have accumulated the highest earnings in 2012-13. For those that enter and are eliminated under these conditions , the nomination and entry fees will be refunded. SUPPLEMENTARY NOMINATIONS OF $2,000 EACH (which include entry and starting fees) DUE BY THE USUAL TIME OF CLOSING. CLOSED SATURDAY, JANUARY 12, 2013 WITH 22 NOMINATIONS. (Rail at 22 feet). (Clear 73)

Value of Race: $75,000 Winner $45,000; second $15,000; third $7,500; fourth $3,750; fifth $2,250; sixth $1,500. Mutuel Pool $225,192 Pick 3 Pool $10,058 Daily Double Pool $16,215 Exacta Pool $108,562 Superfecta Pool $91,957 Trifecta Pool $143,271

Last Raced	#	Horse	M/Eqt.	A/S	Wt	PP	St	3/16	%	Str	Fin	Jockey	Odds $1
19Dec12 ^{8}FG^{7}	10	Smartys Emperoress	L	5M	116	10	5	$6\frac{1}{2}$	$5\frac{1}{2}$	$3\frac{1}{2}$	1no	Serpa A	16.30
28Nov12 ^{10}Crc^{1}	8	Trippin' Along	L b	4F	116	8	10	10	10	10	2no	Bridgmohan J V	5.10
11Jan13 ^{10}Tam^{2}	2	Christina d'Oro	L	5M	116	2	8	$7^{1\frac{1}{2}}$	$7^{1\frac{1}{2}}$	7^{1}	3^{nk}	Villa-Gomez H	20.70
08Dec12 ^{9}GP^{5}	9	Honey Chile	L	5M	119	9	2	$5\frac{1}{2}$	$6^{1\frac{1}{2}}$	6^{hd}	4^{nk}	Sanchez J	6.80
27Dec12 ^{3}GP^{2}	5	Madame Giry	L	4F	122	5	6	$3\frac{1}{2}$	$3\frac{1}{2}$	2^{1}	$5\frac{1}{2}$	Castro E	0.70
19Jan13 ^{5}GP^{6}	7	Becauseimworthit	L b	5M	116	7	7	$1^{1\frac{1}{2}}$	1^{3}	1^{2}	6^{nk}	Gallardo A A	20.90
04Jan13 ^{7}Tam^{4}	3	Brinca	L b	7M	116	3	3	$8\frac{1}{2}$	9^{1}	8^{1}	7^{hd}	Garcia J A	21.80
01Dec12 ^{10}TP^{2}	6	Queen's Award	L	6M	116	6	4	9^{1}	$8\frac{1}{2}$	9^{hd}	$8^{1\frac{1}{2}}$	Pedroza M	9.80
05Jan13 ^{9}Tam^{7}	1	Hard Truth	L b	7M	116	1	9	$4^{1\frac{1}{2}}$	4^{1}	5^{hd}	9^{nk}	Spieth S	73.70
20Oct12 ^{8}Kee^{2}	4	Standing By	L f	5M	116	4	1	2^{3}	$2\frac{1}{2}$	$4\frac{1}{2}$	10	Allen, Jr. R D	19.00

NEW TRAINER
BEST WORK!

OFF AT 5:00 Start Good. Won driving. Track Firm.
TIME :20^{4}, :43^{3}, :56^{2} (:20.98, :43.66, :55.50)

$2 Mutuel Prices:

10- SMARTYS EMPERORESS	34.60	13.20	9.00
8- TRIPPIN' ALONG		5.60	4.20
2- CHRISTINA D'ORO			9.20

$2 EXACTA 10-8 PAID $233.20 $1 SUPERFECTA 10-8-2-9 PAID $8,522.40
$2 TRIFECTA 10-8-2 PAID $2,951.20

Bay Mare, (Apr), by Holy Roman Emperor (IRE) - I'll Get Along by Smile. Trainer Spicknall L James. Bred by Gaines-Gentry Thoroughbreds(KY).

SMARTYS EMPERORESS made a middle move, fanned five wide,closed with a rush to gain a short lead and just last over TRIPPIN' ALONG late. TRIPPIN' ALONG steadied inside into the turn, fanned seven wide for the drive then closed along the far outside to just miss. CHRISTINA D'ORO also made a middle move, split rivals six wide then also just missed. HONEY CHILE split rivals into the final furlong and was gaining late. MADAME GIRY stalked the pace early, bid down the middle of the course but was outkicked. BECAUSEIMWORTHIT vied early, drew off through the turn into the stretch then just hung. BRINCA was slowly gaining in traffic. QUEEN'S AWARD was no factor. HARD TRUTH chased into the stretch then faded. STANDING BY stopped.

Owners- 10, Jamgotchian Jerry ; 8, Polivka Equine Holdings LLC ; 2, R. J. Nappi Stables ; 9, Miller James F.; 5, Nutmeg Stable ; 7, Ups and Downs Racing ; 3, World Thoroughbred Racing, Inc. and Stewart, Chad J. ; 6, Coudelaria Jessica, Inc. ; 1, Cooper, Brittany and Murphy, Linda A. ; 4, Corrado, Mark and Inez

Trainers- 10, Spicknall James L; 8, Catalano Wayne M.; 2, Tebbutt John ; 9, Catalano Wayne M.; 5, Gambolati Cam M.; 7, Thomas Monte R.; 3, Stewart Chad J.; 6, Caramori Eduardo ; 1, Williams Edward L.; 4, Caramori Eduardo

Breeders- 10, Gaines-Gentry Thoroughbreds (KY); 8, Adam J. Parker & Suzette Parker (FL); 2, Liberation Farm & Stonewall Farm (KY); 9, Peachtree Stable (FL); 5, Raintree Thoroughbred Farm, Inc. (MD); 7, Ups and Downs Farm (FL); 3, Gene Phelps, Chad Stewart &Laurie Stewart (FL); 6, Carl Hurst, Fred Bradley &William Bradley (KY); 1, Thomas J. Cooper (FL); 4, Cynthia Knight (KY)

Scratched- Double the Energy(27Dec12 ^{3}GP^{1})

$2 Daily Double (2-10) Paid $165.20; Daily Double Pool $16,215.
$2 Pick Three (4-2-10) Paid $684.40; Pick Three Pool $10,058.

[illegible]

Winner 10, Place 8, had new trainers. 8 had Best Work. $233.20 exacta.

COPYRIGHT 2013 BLOODSTOCK RESEARCH INFORMATION SERVICES

revealed that the horse had closed some five and one-half lengths from the head of the stretch to the finish. That race was followed by a 97 day layoff, probably due to an injury sustained in her first maiden try. Motokiks Dancer then worked nine times under the new trainer's hands; eight of the nine works were undistinguished. Suddenly, on 1/19/2012 – just five days before the current race – she woke up with a :48 3/5 breeze for four furlongs, the best of the current race field. The morning line setter thought a morning line of 30/1 should be just about right for her and the crowd dutifully followed by ignoring her chances, sending her off at 37.2/1.

In examining the FHH interface screen I noted that the 3, Smarty Carol, was the system's #2 contender and was confirmed with a Best Late Pace number of 102, seven points better than the next best late pace horse, so I concurred with the morning line setter's judgement that the crowd would probably make Smarty Carol the favorite.

The System bet was to bet the 11 to win and twice as much to place; then to box the 3 and 11 in exactas, and to put the 3, 11 with 3, 11 with all in trifectas (this bet would have cost all of $14 for a $1 betting unit). The Dancer broke dead last and was a good 15 lengths back in the early going, but caught the field entering the stretch and closed some 10 lengths to just get up for place, following the easy winner, the favorite, Smarty Carol.

Race comes 3, 11, 8, 10.

Motokiks Dancer placed at $19.00 9.00; $2 exacta $96.80; $2 trifecta $1,329.80! (A $38 investment returned $1,426.60.)

A NEW HORSE IN THE BARN

NINTH RACE — 6 FURLONGS. (1.074) MAIDEN CLAIMING. Purse $15,500 (Includes $7,750 Other Sources) FOR MAIDENS, FILLIES AND MARES FOUR YEARS OLD AND UPWARD. Weight, 121 lbs. Claiming Price $15,000. (Cloudy 43)
Oaklawn Park
January 24th, 2013

Value of Race: $15,500 Winner $9,300; second $3,100; third $1,550; fourth $775; fifth $465; sixth $78; seventh $78; eighth $77; ninth $77. Mutuel Pool $70,952 Pick 3 Pool $13,218 Pick 4 Pool $26,814 Daily Double Pool $19,262 Exacta Pool $48,134 Superfecta Pool $29,324 Trifecta Pool $40,500

Last Raced	#	Horse	M/Eqt	A/S	Wt	PP	St	¼	½	Str	Fin	Jockey	Cl'g Pr	Odds $1
04Jan13 9FG3	3	Smarty Carol	L	4F	121	2	4	4½	4³	1½	1¹	Berry M C	15000	0.90
13Sep12 10Lad7	11	Motokiks Dancer	L b	4F	116	9	9	9	9	4½	2nd	Shino K A	15000	37.20 BEST WORK
30Dec12 10TP9	8	Stormy Commandress	L b	4F	121	6	1	3½	2hd	2²	3²¾	Ocampo I	15000	33.00
11Jan13 4OP5	10	Littlebitcranky	L bf	4F	121	8	8	8⁹	8½	6½	4½	Court J K	15000	5.90
11Jan13 4OP7	9	Glowing Review	L	4F	116	7	5	6½	5³½	5½	5⁴½	Canchari A	15000	12.00
	4	Genie M	L	4F	121	3	3	2hd	1hd	3³½	6³	Albarado R	15000	3.20
16Nov12 7RP2	7	Cactusa	L b	4F	121	5	2	1hd	3½	7⁶	7³½	Laviolette S	15000	5.90
10Oct12 9RP11	5	Carrie the Cowgirl	L	4F	121	4	6	5¹	8⁵½	8²	8⁵	Quinonez B	15000	50.50
05Jan13 3Ded8	1	T Byrd Too	L	4F	122	1	7	7¹	7hd	9	9	Pizarro R	15000	73.10

OFF AT 5:14 Start Good. Won driving. Track Fast.
TIME :22¹, :47¹, 1:00², 1:14 (:22.33, :47.29, 1:00.55, 1:14.05)

$2 Mutuel Prices:
3-SMARTY CAROL 3.80 3.00 2.80
11- MOTOKIKS DANCER 19.00 9.00
6- STORMY COMMANDRESS 6.80

$2 EXACTA 3-11 PAID $96.80 $1 SUPERFECTA 3-11-8-10 PAID $2,891.00
$1 TRIFECTA 3-11-6 PAID $664.90

Chestnut Filly, (Ap), by Smarty Jones - Distinct Manner by Distinctive Pro. Trainer Milligan Allen. Bred by Parrish Hill Farm & Whodat Racing LLC(KY).

SMARTY CAROL brushed at the start, stalked the pace off the inside, ranged up four wide to challenge turning for home, edged clear late. MOTOKIKS DANCER sluggish for almost a half, swung out to be five wide turning for home when beginning to advanced, finished fast to be in time for the place. STORMY COMMANDRESS vied up front while three wide, raced on equal terms with the winner past the furlong marker, could not match the winner the final sixteenth, nipped in the final stride for the place. LITTLEBITCRANKY lacked early foot, improved position while never dangerous. GLOWING REVIEW evenly paced off the inside, roused for the drive, continued one paced to the wire. GENIE M broke in, brushed with the winner, quickly recovered to vie up front closest to the inside, weakened in the drive. CACTUSA set or forced the pace for a half while between rivals, gave way in the drive. CARRIE THE COWGIRL lacked speed, carried out to be six wide turning for home, lacked a late kick while well out in the strip. T BYRD TOO saved ground to no avail, trailed home.

Owners- 3, Keene Danny ; 11, Davis Jeff J.; 8, Pordes, Richard, Esposito, Robert and Lynda ; 10, Trammell, Joyce, Scalberg, Bonnie and Terry ; 9, Margaux Farm LLC and Lauer, Penny S. ; 4, Logan, Andrew, Reppa, S. and McKellar, Joseph P. ; 7, Dream Walkin Farms, Inc. ; 5, Double M Stables ; 1, Kyzer Alicia S.

Trainers- 3, Milligan Allen ; 11, Oliver Barry E.; 8, Hellman Leroy ; 10, Medrano Marcos G.; 9, Lauer Michael E.; 4, Wiggins Lon ; 7, Smith Kenny P.; 5, Burwell Tom C.; 1, Wakeland David

Breeders- 3, Parrish Hill Farm & Whodat Racing LLC (KY); 11, Jeff J Davis (AR); 8, Ronald Clark (CA); 10, Stacy Lane Hendry (FL); 9, Margaux Farm LLC (KY); 4, Joe McKellar (TX); 7, Dream Walkin' Farms, Inc.Prime Time Racing (KY); 5, Chris Duncan (OK); 1, Matthews Thoroughbred Farm (LA)

Scratched- Value Your Song(03Dec12 6Mnr2), Lady Spencer(19Feb12 9FG2), Sandy's Snow Day(19Feb12 9FG4)

$2 Daily Double (1-3) Paid $25.80; Daily Double Pool $19,262.
$1 Pick Three (6-1-2/3/6/12) Paid $119.30; Pick Three Pool $13,218.
$1 Pick Four (6/7/11-5-1-2/3/6/12) Paid $276.60; Pick Four Pool $26,814.

11 - Place at 37.2/1 had new trainer by owner decision - Best Work

COPYRIGHT 2013 BLOODSTOCK RESEARCH INFORMATION SERVICES

A last but not least race demonstrating the variables pointing to a top performance from a new-trainer horse occurred in the first race at Santa Anita on 1/27/2013 in a one and one-sixteenth mile maiden special race for fillies three years old for a purse of $56,000.

There was one new-trainer horse in the race: the 2, Lady Assano, having been claimed from her first start in a maiden claimer for 75k on 11/29/2012 at Hollywood. This was an unusual event in itself; I can assure the reader that not many horses entered in a 75k maiden claiming race are in any danger of someone haltering them – before they have run their first race – and for that kind of money. My conclusion was that the claiming trainer and connections were extremely high on the fillies' bloodlines. John Sadler is an experienced trainer; a 19 per cent winner, having an excellent reputation for being an acute judge of horseflesh. $75,000 is a lot of cash to be spending on a horse that had yet to run her first race.

After the claim, Lady Assano had been away from the track for 59 days, though she worked seven times since 12/7/2012. Three of these works were exceptional; on 12/7/2012 she worked four furlongs in :48 4/5 handily, followed by a five furlong workout on 12/23/2012 of 1:00 handily. On 1/17/2013 she worked seven furlongs in 1:28 3/5. Seven workouts in 51 days are exceptional; obviously, the claiming trainer was pointing to this specific race.

Sadler's record is impressive: a 19 per cent winner with 46-90 day layoffs; a 32 per cent winner with first after a claim, a 30 per cent winner with first try at a route; a 22 per cent winner with a horse's second career win, and a 23 per cent winner when he takes the blinkers off (as he did in the current race).

Screen presented:

TELL POINTS M/L POST

3=8	3/1	5.4/1
1=7	6/1	5.9/1
4=5	6/5	1.1/1
2=4	15/1	19.9/1
5=4	5/2	2.6/1
6=4	6/1	8.1/1

BEST IN CATEGORY

Work=3	5 fur :59.8
Start= 1	92
Mid= 1	94
Late= 4	91

The FHH screen was telling the user that the stand-out long shot was, of course, the 2. The system bet was to win and twice as much to place on the 2, then to run the 2 up and back with the field in exactas and trifectas.

Race comes 2, 5, 1, 3.

Winner pays $41.80 12.60 8.20;$2 exacta $175.40; $2 trifecta $908.80.

RUNNING A HOLE IN THE WIND: HIDDEN HORSES FOUND

FIRST RACE
Santa Anita
January 27th, 2013

1 1/16 MILES. (1.39) MAIDEN SPECIAL WEIGHT. Purse $56,000 FOR MAIDENS, FILLIES THREE YEARS OLD. Weight, 121 lbs. (Cloudy 57)

Value of Race: $56,250 ($16,800 reverts) Winner $33,600; second $11,200; third $6,720; fourth $3,360; fifth $1,120; sixth $280.
Mutuel Pool $179,116 Exacta Pool $114,093 Superfecta Pool $45,774 Trifecta Pool $70,399

Last Raced	# Horse	M/Eqt.	A/S	Wt	PP	St	1/4	1/2	3/4	Str	Fin	Jockey	Odds $1	
29Nov12 8Hol8	2 Lady Asano	L c	3F	121	2	2	6	6	5½	1²½	1⁷¼	Lezcano J R	19.90	NEW TRAINER
12Jan13 1SA3	5 Iconic Spirit	L c	3F	121	5	4	3hd	5³	6	4½	2nk	Smith M E	2.60	
04Nov12 8CD7	1 Temptress	L	3F	121	1	6	1¹	1¹	1½	2²½	3²¾	Nakatani C S	5.90	
04Jan13 4SA2	3 Miss Derek	L b	3F	121	3	1	2½	2½	2²	3²¾	4³½	Valdivia, Jr. J	5.40	
04Jan13 4SA2	4 Black Witch	L	3F	121	4	3	4¹	4hd	3½	5³	5³½	Garcia M	1.10	
04Jan13 4SA4	6 Humming Beethoven	L b	3F	121	5	5	5½	3¹	4½	6	6	Maldonado E A	8.10	

OFF AT 12:30 Start Good. Ridden out. Track Wet Fast (sealed).
TIME :23¹, :47³, 1:12³, 1:38¹, 1:44⁴   (:23.27, :47.70, 1:12.64, 1:38.27, 1:44.91)

$2 Mutuel Prices:
2- LADY ASANO 41.80 12.60 8.20
5- ICONIC SPIRIT 4.20 4.00
1- TEMPTRESS 7.20

$1 EXACTA 2-5 PAID $87.70 $1 SUPERFECTA 2-5-1-3 PAID $1,244.90
$1 TRIFECTA 2-5-1 PAID $454.40

Bay Filly, (Mr.), by Teuflesberg - Golden Tour by Lac Ouimet. Trainer Sadler W. John. Bred by Sherry R. Mansfield & Kenneth H. Davis(FL).

LADY ASANO rank and steadied between horses passing the finish line the first time around, raced unhurried down the backstretch, moved up three deep around the second turn, bid for the lead three wide entering the stretch, left one tap from the whip leaving the furlong marker, drew clear and was under a long hold nearing the wire. ICONIC SPIRIT was caught three wide into the first turn, stalked between horses on the backstretch, angled over to save ground around the second turn, angled back out late to gain the place on the wire. TEMPTRESS sped to the lead on the inside into the first turn, set the pace a bit off the rail to the stretch, weakened on the inside in the final furlong and lost the place on the wire. MISS DEREK stalked outside the pacesetter down the backstretch and into the second turn, came into the lane between horses and weakened in the final furlong. BLACK WITCH went into the first turn between horses, angled to the rail around the turn, stalked on the inside down the backstretch and around the second turn, came out for the drive and did not rally. HUMMING BEETHOVEN was four wide into the first turn, stalked the pace three deep on the backstretch and outside a rival into the second turn and failed to make an impact in the lane. LADY ASANO and ICONIC SPIRIT wore calks.

Owners- 2, Hronis Racing LLC ; 5, Desert Sun Stables ; 1, Winchell Thoroughbreds LLC ; 3, Peacock Cecil N.; 4, Mercedes Stables LLC ; 6, Blinkers On Racing Stable, Barker, Butler, Coons, Dante, Dante et al.

Trainers- 2, Sadler John W.; 5, Sadler John W.; 1, Asmussen Steven M.; 3, Hendricks Dan L.; 4, Baffert Bob ; 6, Puype Mike

Breeders- 2, Sherry R. Mansfield & Kenneth H. Davis (FL); 5, Castleton Lyons & Kilboy Estate (KY); 1, Patchen Wilkes Farm, LLC (KY); 3, Scott Lanier (FL); 4, T/C Stable, LLC (KY); 6, Woodford Thoroughbreds, LLC (KY)

Winner - 2 - New trainer by claim- 59 day layoff- Blinkers off

COPYRIGHT 2013 BLOODSTOCK RESEARCH INFORMATION SERVICES

Carefully and thoroughly checking the workout patterns of a horse that threw in a clunker in the race from which it was claimed will pay generous dividends, for the general betting public will not often give this type of horse more than a cursory glance; to use a trite but true observation: They can't see the forest for the trees. The hidden horse hunter must learn to separate the foliage in order to clear his or her vision. In this kind of race the money – not the devil – is in the details.

There are a number of reasons why new-trainer horses are often a good bet, aside from the fact that they often win at good prices, for the morning line setters usually tab them with generous odds. Seldom have I seen these types of horses selected as favorites; for, as we have seen, the betting crowd seldom ignores the Pied Piper songs of the "expert" track handicappers. The average punter would be better off if he or she never heard a word of the announcer's picks; better to wear earplugs than to be distracted by the track's pitch man or woman's incessant touting of the morning line favorite.

In the ten years that I was associated with the Prairie Pride Farms Racing Stable, we claimed just one horse – preferring to breed and raise our own foals, or to be buyers at the two year olds in training sales. (The Stable was always on the lookout for the Nasrullah line and the descendants of the hot blooded and frequently irascible stallion that had produced so many stakes winners. We thought we had struck gold when we located a four by four inbred Nasrullah foal.) The considerable amount of time I spent in studying thoroughbred blood lines was time well spent, not only in deciding which stallions would service our broodmares, but also in the later handicapping efforts for my own betting account.

The one horse we claimed was a fortitious accident. The promising two year old Nazrullah foal we purchased in a spring sale, Jaipur's Pride, bowed a tendon in her third race after being abused by a jockey who was ticked at our trainer for whatever reason. (Jockeys are often hot-headed and quick-tempered; but I take my hat off to them for the courage they generally display each day they mount the hot-blooded thoroughbred that out weighs them by twelve to fourteen hundred pounds, supported by spindle thin legs.)

After bringing our permanently injured horse back to the farm to become a broodmare, we looked for a replacement. We found it in a four year old and up 5k claiming race at six furlongs at Ak-Sar-Ben. The horse had won nearly $30,000 and was a shipper from Oaklawn, having been claimed from its last race for 5k. The new owners had decided to keep him "in jail," for under the claiming rules the claimant has to run the newly claimed horse at a claiming price at least 30 per cent higher than the claim if running the horse back within 30 days of the claim. Past the 30 days, the claimed horse can be entered for the amount of the claim, or less. (And sometimes it is for less than the claim, because the claiming trainer has discovered he has bought an injured horse and hopes to salvage out if he can just get the horse claimed again.) That's why the bettor should always cast a jaundiced eye toward a horse that is running back for a price less than the price for which the horse was claimed in its last race.

Between the time of our claim and the horse's first start, the barn spared no effort in getting the new horse ready. We had just spent $5,000 and were anxious to get a quick dividend for our investment. The horse had finished a steady second in the race from which he was claimed and his works for our barn told us he was ready for a big effort, so we entered him in a 7.5k claimer. To our surprise, the morning line setter pegged him at 16/1; probably because we were moving the horse up in class. To make a long story short, he won. Our share of the purse was $3,000; our Stable bet of $200 to win and $300 to place returned $5,980 – a profit of $5,380 for the bet. Yes, we often bet on our own horses, especially when we could get decent odds. I have heard many trainers say: "We don't bet on our own horses; we run for the purse." Yeah, sure. And trainers don't mess with the minds of other trainers. And bears don't relieve themselves in the woods.

Generally, the main reason a barn claims a horse is that their trainer has spotted something about the prospective claim that leads him or her to believe that the horse is a bargain. Implicit in that perception is the claimer's conviction that he can get more out of the horse than its present trainer has produced. The stories are legend about horses being claimed for a modest amount, then being moved up to – and winning – allowance, handicap, and even graded stakes. That is the romance of the game. The indomitable but obstreperous John Henry (best known in his early years for his habit of ripping tubs and buckets from his stall wall and stomping them flat) was purchased by a junk dealer for $25,000 – his sire, Old Bob Bowers, was sold as a stallion for $900; two years later it was surprising that the owner who sold John Henry did not take a header off a high bridge over deep waters, for the legendary little hard driving horse went on to win over six and a half million dollars in purses, winning 39 races before being retired at nine from a serious injury. It is one of thoroughbred racing's tragedies that John Henry had to be gelded, foreclosing the continuance of his blood line. Artificial insemination is illegal when it comes to thoroughbred horses, as every horseman knows: the mare must be bred by a stallion mounting, and that's that. But what a shame in John Henry's case that his bloodline was buried with him.

The perceptive handicapper should always mark the new-trainer horses entered in a race that he or she is handicapping, and they should do that first. The *Finding the Hidden Horse* thoroughbred handicapping software user should always examine the interface screen before going to the printed racing form listing the past performances of each horse in the race. Each new-trainer horse's past performances should be thoroughly examined and if such a horse is marked on the interface screen as one of the race's top four contenders and ties, and/or is one of the Best in Categories, that horse should be given substantial consideration for making a solid bet, unless such a horse is the favorite or near favorite. The new-trainer angle is too often overlooked, even by experienced punters. From my own experience I can assure you that a horse's new connections will move heaven and earth to get the newly aquired steed ready for a big try in its first time out.

Chapter 9

THEIR FIRST DANCE

"Better keep yourself clean and bright; you are the window through which you must see the world."
GEORGE BERNARD SHAW

In Michael Pizzolla's excellent book *Handicapping Magic,* he asserts that he wouldn't touch most two year old races "filled with first time starters, with a ten-foot pole. There's usually nothing to go on except rumors or the latest breeding fad." Until I got into the game as an owner and breeder, I felt the same way; what was there to go on? Today, I consider two year old races filled with first time starters (and all maiden races, for that matter) a promising betting opportunity.

Of all the classes of races, one of the most promising in which to identify hidden horse long shots are maiden contests for two, three, or four year olds and up. It appears that the betting public has been sold the bill of goods that "there is nothing to go on with first time starters." Consequently, the unsophisticated punter usually takes the morning line setter's tabs at first glance. That's why so many long shot winners come in two and three year old races filled with half a dozen or more first timers. To dig those long odds horses out of those kinds of races requires particular attention to what little there is to go on when analyzing a first time starter.

One of the first variables to examine is the actual age of the horse. I hear the rejoinder: "What do you mean – the two year old is two years old." That is the definition by regulation; by the calendar none of them have reached their second birthday. For instance, a foal born in April is only 20 months or so of age when the registration officials declare the horse to be a two year old. You don't see many April or May foals entered in the two year old maiden races for the reason that there is a good possibility that their knees are not yet fully closed. Impatient owners are the cause of many two year old breakdowns on the track. So it's a good idea to check the month in which the foal was dropped, with the optimum being January. Most thoroughbred foals emerge in mid to late springtime. So the "older" the two year old the better. I would have some reservations about betting on a May foal; fortunately, due to the planning of the breeding, there are not that many two year old May foals to bet on. This variable is the reason why so many owner-breeders wait until their horses are three years old by regulation definition. The above may be getting farther into the "weeds" than the average punter wants to venture, but if you are a serious handicapper it's a variable that you should note.

The lineage of the horse is also important; that's the sole variable many handicappers use in selecting first time starter contenders. At the big league tracks, however, nearly all of the first timers are equally well-bred. Many punters are strictly followers of first time starter trainers with the best records, but long shot winners do not often come from hot trainer barns. It is not often profitable over time to bet on favorites in two year old races loaded with first time starters.

Experience has taught me that the most important variable to analyze in a first time starter race for any age is the horse's workout pattern. For instance, when was the horse put into training? Some trainers will work their first timers a dozen times before sending them to their first dance. More impatient ones will only give the horse two or three works before its first start. An on point example occurred in the tenth race at Tampa Bay Downs on 2/2/2013, a six furlong 25k maiden claimer for three year olds. After scratches there remained four first timers in a field of nine.

The 3, Revere's Ride, out of a Mr. Prospector stallion, was trained by a 10 per cent handler. A March foal, it had been worked only twice; on 1/11/2013 at three furlongs in :37 4/5, and on 1/27/2013 in a meaningless 1:03 1/5 for five furlongs. In examining the field for the best works, it was surprising that Revere's Ride's work of 1/11/2013 was the third best work of the field. While that work earned no points from the FHH program, it was important to note his sire was out of the legendary Mr. Prospector, one of Nasrullah's most prolific producers of stakes winners.

The 8, Quiquinho, another first-timer, had a best work of :50 2/5: his trainer was a five percent first time starter winner, and his sire was a nondescript stallion. So it was no go on Quiquinho. The 9, Jimmy's Repete, was trained by a twelve per cent trainer and was tied for carrying the low weight of the field at 113 pounds;

however, at six furlongs low weight is not ordinarily an important variable. In examining his five workouts I noted that they were slow, slower, and slowest – his "best" work was a leisurely four furlongs in :51 2/5. The 11, Gargamellow, was handled by a 17 per cent trainer and was out of an Elusive Quality stallion. The horse had worked three times; its best was on 12/9/2012 when it breezed from the gate in :37 for three furlongs; tied for the best work of the field.

The morning line on the two more promising first time starters – the 3 and 11 – was 12/1 on Revere's Ride and 10/1 on Gargamellow. The 3 left the gate at 19.7/1 and the 11 went off at 15.5/1; both were substantial overlays. The system bet was to win and twice as much to place on the 3, then to run the 3 up and back with the FHH screen horses – the 1, 5, 6, 7 plus the 11 in exactas, trifectas and supers.

Race comes 3, 5, 1, 11.

Winner pays $41.40 13.80 6.80; $2 exacta $275. $2 tri fecta 1,179.80; $2 super $13,183.00!!

If you are going to play maiden races that include first time starters in the field, take the time to thoroughly analyze their workout patterns. The extra time spent will frequently pay generous dividends, for the betting crowd rarely spends much time on the first-timers, usually deferring to the morning line setters

THEIR FIRST DANCE 133

TENTH RACE 6 FURLONGS. (1.08) MAIDEN CLAIMING. Purse $14,000 (Includes $1,500 FOA - Florida Owners Awards) FOR MAIDENS, THREE YEARS OLD. Weight, 120 lbs. Claiming Price $25,000. If for $20,000, allowed 2 lbs. (Clear 71)
Tampa Bay
February 2nd, 2013
Value of Race: $14,000 Winner $8,300; second $2,800; third $1,400; fourth $700; fifth $125; sixth $125; seventh $125; eighth $125; ninth $125; tenth $125. Mutuel Pool $227,406 Pick 3 Pool $12,929 Daily Double Pool $15,099 Exacta Pool $172,722 Superfecta Pool $66,736 Trifecta Pool $113,896

Last Raced	#	Horse	M/Eqt.	A/S	Wt	PP	St	¼	½	Str	Fin	Jockey	Cl'g Pr	Odds $1	
	3	Revere's Ride	L bf	3C	120	2	10	8³½	8⁴	5¹	1ⁿᵒ	Gallardo A A	25000	19.70	3rd BEST WORK
26Jan13 ⁵Tam⁸	5	Jackpotkidd	L b	3G	120	4	3	1¹	1¹	1½	2¹½	Clemente A	25000	3.80	
04Jan13 ⁴Tam⁷	1	T. V. Plasma		3G	113	1	5	6²	7ʰᵈ	7³	3½	Zayas E J	25000	5.50	
	11	Gargamellow	L bf	3G	118	10	7	4½	4½	4ʰᵈ	4¹½	Villa-Gomez H	20000	15.50	
13Jan13 ¹⁰Tam⁹	6	Il Cannone	L b	3G	115	5	1	2¹½	2¹	2ʰᵈ	5³	Mejias R	25000	21.20	
	8	Quiquinho	L bf	3C	120	7	9	7¹½	6¼	5ʰᵈ	6³	Cedeno C	25000	10.20	
18Jan13 ⁵Tam⁴	7	Checkered Cab	L b	3G	120	6	4	3²½	3⁴	3²	7ⁿᵏ	Spieth S	25000	2.10	
	4	Wilko's Bullet	L	3C	120	3	8	9½	9⁶½	8¹	8⁸½	Coraloto R	25000	26.40	
21Sep12 ¹¹Crc⁹	10	Duppyzapper	L b	3C	120	9	2	5²	5ʰᵈ	9⁷½	9¹½	Espinoza J L	25000	3.20	
	9	Jimmy's Repete		3C	113	8	6	10	10	10	10	Cardoso M	25000	64.20	

OFF AT 5:01 Start Good. Won driving. Track Fast.
TIME :22², :46², :59³, 1:13² (:22.45, :46.43, :59.67, 1:13.43)

$2 Mutuel Prices:
3 - REVERE'S RIDE 41.40 13.80 6.80
5 - JACKPOTKIDD 6.00 4.00
1 - T. V. PLASMA 4.60

$2 EXACTA 3-5 PAID $275.00 $1 SUPERFECTA 3-5-1-11 PAID $6,591.50
$2 TRIFECTA 3-5-1 PAID $1,179.80

Gray or Roan Colt, (Mr), by Strategic Mission - Icy Warning by Caveat. Trainer Thomas R. Monte. Bred by James F. Webb(FL).
REVERE'S RIDE made a middle move, angled out five wide in the drive then ran down the leader in the final stride. JACKPOTKIDD set a moderate pace, held on gamely through a long drive and just failed to last. T. V. PLASMA made a middle move, got through along the rail in the drive and was gaining late. GARGAMELLOW was boxed and lacked room into the final furlong then was gaining once clear. IL CANNONE chased to mid stretch then weakened. QUIQUINHO failed to menace. CHECKERED CAB chased three wide into the stretch then gave way. WILKO'S BULLET was no factor. DUPPYZAPPER was through after a half. JIMMY'S REPETE trailed.
Owners- 3, Webb James ; 5, L and D Farm ; 1, Rontos Racing Stable Corp. ; 11, Big Lick Farm ; 6, Roulston Allison Hill; 8, Degwitz Luisa ; 7, Hayford-Quinones Jennifer A.; 4, Diaz Frank ; 10, Bishop Chester A.; 9, Thomas Jim
Trainers- 3, Thomas Monte R.; 5, Camilo Juan ; 1, Azpurua Manuel J.; 11, Nagle Reid ; 6, O'Connell Kathleen ; 8, Sano Antonio ; 7, Hayford- Quinones Jennifer A.; 4, Griffith Gregory A.; 10, Passley Mark ; 9, Gatis Christos
Breeders- 3, James F. Webb (FL); 5, L & D Farms, Inc. (FL); 1, Lambholm & Colts Neck Stable (FL); 11, Dr. D. W. Frazier (FL); 6, Allison Hill Roulston (FL); 8, Luisa Degwitz (FL); 7, Jennifer Hayford (FL); 4, John Lewis Wallace (FL); 10, Chester A Bishop (FL); 9, Jim Thomas (FL)
Scratched- Desire to Acquire

$2 Daily Double (4-3) Paid $175.60; Daily Double Pool $15,099.
$2 Pick Three (9-4-3) Paid $556.60; Pick Three Pool $12,929.

Winner - 3 - 3ʳᵈ Best Work - Pattern of Works

COPYRIGHT 2013 BLOODSTOCK RESEARCH INFORMATION SERVICES

A particularly instructive example of how to evaluate first time starters was in the sixth race at Gulfstream on 1/12/2013; a mile and sixteenth 52.5k maiden special turf race for three year olds.

Screen presented:

TELL POINTS	M/L	POST
5= 7	12/1	26.7/1
12= 6	4/1	8.1/1
13= 4	3/1	3.5/1
7= 4	15/1	43.6/1
9= 3	12/1	3.6/1
10= 3	7/2	3.6/1
11= 3	6/1	9.4/1

BEST IN CATEGORY

Work= 9,10	4 furlongs :48
Start= 12	92
Mid= 7	98
Late= 5	89

After scratches, there were four first timers in the race. The 2, Middleburg, was trained by the redoubtable grass handler, Christophe Clement; but after noting the workout pattern of the horse, it was clear that Christophe was unable to get a decent work out of Middleburg in no less than ten works dating back to 10/23/2012; the horse's best try was a leisurely :49 for four furlongs on 12/4/2012.

The 8, P V Paul, had worked a dozen times since being put into training on 10/2/2012; his "best" try was a match to Middleburg's four furlongs in :49 in spite of his well bred sire – Dynaformer – whose stud fee was 150k.

The 9 was War Dancer, whose grandsire was Danzig, and was purchased for 220k at the FTS auction in August of 2011, then put into training on 06/23/2012. His trainer was a 15 per cent winner with maiden special first time starters. War Dancer worked a dozen times before his start; he was tied with his half-brother, Jack Milton, the 10, for the best work of the field – 4 furlongs in :48. The only negative I could find on War Dancer was that he was a May foal, and that was mitigated by the fact that he stayed sound through the rigors of no less than 12 workouts.

Jack Milton was trained by Todd Pletcher, a 27 per cent winner with an amazing record of winning at a 24 per cent rate with first time starters. His horse was the second morning line favorite; deservedly so, in my opinion.

In examining the breeding of each horse in the field, I noted that the 9, 10, and 13 were half brothers out of War Front – they should have named the race, "Here come the Danzigs" as each of the three had impressive breeding credentials. In fact, Jack Milton and the 13, All Alex, were co-favorites when they left the gate. The other brother, War Dancer, waspegged at a surprising 36/1; notwithstanding his tie with Jack Milton for the best work of the field, the public let him leave the gate at a 200 per cent overlay.

The system bet was to win and twice as much to place on the 9, War Dancer. Then to run the 10, Jack Milton, up and back with

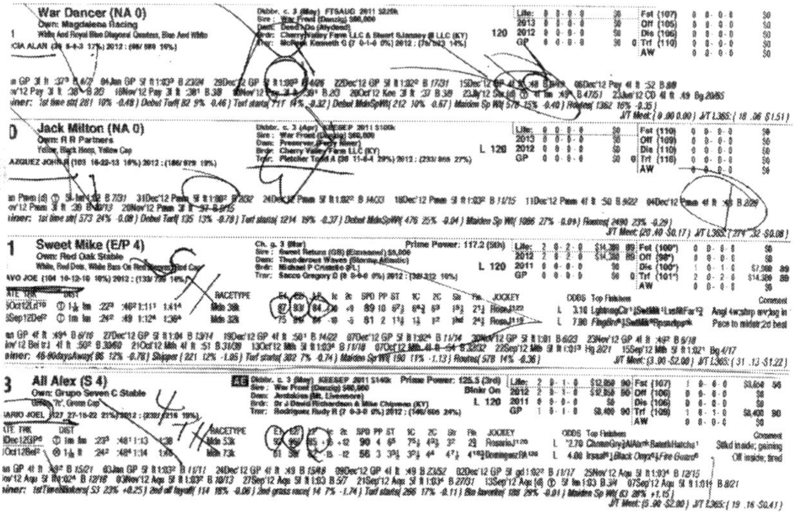

War Dancer (NA 0)
Own: Magdalena Racing
White And Royal Blue Diagonal Quarters, Blue And White
120
Life: 0 0 - 0 - 0 $0 | Fst (107) 0 0 - 0 - 0 $0
2013 0 0 - 0 - 0 $0 | Off (105) 0 0 - 0 - 0 $0
2012 0 0 - 0 - 0 $0 | Dis (106) 0 0 - 0 - 0 $0
GP 0 0 - 0 - 0 $0 0 | Trf (110) 0 0 - 0 - 0 $0
AW 0 0 - 0 - 0 $0

Jack Milton (NA 0)
Own: R R Partners
Yellow, Black Hoop, Yellow Cap
L 120
Life: 0 0 - 0 - 0 $0 | Fst (110) 0 0 - 0 - 0 $0
2013 0 0 - 0 - 0 $0 | Off (109) 0 0 - 0 - 0 $0
2012 0 0 - 0 - 0 $0 | Dis (110) 0 0 - 0 - 0 $0
GP 0 0 - 0 - 0 $0 0 | Trf (118) 0 0 - 0 - 0 $0
AW 0 0 - 0 - 0 $0

Sweet Mike (E/P 4)
Own: Red Oak Stable
Prime Power: 117.2 (5th)
L 120
Comment: Angl 4w;stmp aw;bg in
Comment: Pace to midstr;2d best

All Alex (S 4)
Own: Grupo Seven C Stable
Prime Power: 125.5 (3rd)
Blinkr On
L 120
Comment: Stkd inside; gaining
Comment: Off inside; tired

SIXTH RACE
Gulfstream
January 12th, 2013

$1\frac{1}{16}$ MILES. (Turf) (1.38) MAIDEN SPECIAL WEIGHT. Purse $52,500 (Includes $10,500 FOA - Florida Owners Awards) FOR MAIDENS, THREE YEARS OLD. Weight, 120 lbs. (Preference To Horses That Have Not Started For Less Than $30,000 In Their Last 5 Starts). (If deemed inadvisable to run this race over the turf course, it will be run on the main track at One Mile and One Si xteenth) (Rail at 12 feet). (Clear 79)

Value of Race: $42,000 ($10,500 reverts) Winner $25,200; second $7,980; third $3,780; fourth $1,680; fifth $420; sixth $420; seventh $420; eighth $420; ninth $420; tenth $420; eleventh $420; twelveth $420. Mutuel Pool $503,826 Pick 3 Pool $74,109 Daily Double Pool $60,732 Exacta Pool $412,278 Superfecta Pool $137,896 Trifecta Pool $234,760

Last Raced	#	Horse	M/Eqt.	A/S	Wt	PP	St	¼	½	¾	Str	Fin	Jockey	Odds $1
	10	Jack Milton	L	3C	120	9	9	4½	3½	2½	1^{1}	$1^{2½}$	Velazquez J R	3.60
	9	War Dancer		3C	120	8	3	3^{1}	$4^{1½}$	4½	$3^{1½}$	$2^{2¾}$	Garcia A	36.00
26Oct12 ^{10}Lrl^{2}	11	Sweet Mike	L	3G	120	10	1	1^{1}	1^{1}	1½	$2^{2½}$	$3^{2¾}$	Bravo J	9.40
13Dec12 ^{6}GP^{2}	13	All Alex	L b	3C	120	12	10	6½	$5^{1½}$	5^{2}	4^{1}	$4^{1½}$	Rosario J	3.50
01Dec12 ^{2}GP^{2}	12	Vespato	L b	3C	120	11	5	2^{1}	2^{1}	3^{1}	5^{1}	5^{nk}	Lanerie C J	8.10
24Nov12 ^{2}Aqu^{6}	7	Main Man Mike	L	3G	120	6	6	5^{1}	6½	7^{2}	6^{1}	6^{hd}	Saez L	43.60
	2	Middleburg	L	3C	120	2	2	10^{hd}	10^{hd}	10^{1}	9½	7^{1}	Lezcano J	4.30
	8	P V Paul	L	3C	120	7	8	9^{2}	$9^{2½}$	8½	$7^{1½}$	$8^{1½}$	Castellano J	10.30
23Nov12 ^{6}Aqu^{2}	4	Efficient Market	L	3C	120	3	7	7½	$7^{1½}$	6^{hd}	8½	$9^{1½}$	Cohen D	8.10
19Dec12 ^{7}GP^{7}	1	Comancheria	L	3C	120	1	11	12	12	$11^{2½}$	11^{5}	10¾	Trujillo E	20.10
08Dec12 ^{2}GP^{6}	5	Make Your Move	L	3C	120	4	4	$8^{2½}$	$8^{1½}$	$9^{1½}$	$10^{2½}$	11^{7}	Jara F	26.70
24Nov12 ^{12}CD^{6}	6	Wildcard	L b	3C	120	5	12	11½	11½	12	12	12	Prado E S	15.80

BEST WORK } TIE
BEST WORK

OFF AT 3:10 Start Good. Won driving. Track Firm (Rail at 12 ft).
TIME :23^{2}, :48^{2}, 1:11^{4}, 1:35, 1:41 (:23.43, :48.42, 1:11.91, 1:35.11, 1:41.11)

$2 Mutuel Prices:

10- JACK MILTON	9.20	6.00	5.20
9- WAR DANCER		30.40	13.40
11- SWEET MIKE			5.80

$2 EXACTA 10-9 PAID $324.80 $1 SUPERFECTA 10-9-11-13 PAID $5,098.20
$1 TRIFECTA 10-9-11 PAID $1,321.80

Dark Bay or Brown Colt, (Ap), by War Front - Preserver by Forty Niner. Trainer Pletcher A. Todd. Bred by Cherry Valley Farm, LLC(KY).

JACK MILTON tracked the pace in early stages, began to edge up to lead heading into turn, vied along outside of SWEET MIKE into upper stretch, took command and remained clear to wire. WAR DANCER stalked along inside in backstretch, saved ground racing on rail in turn and steadily gained ground in stretch. SWEET MIKE took command in opening stages, continued to set pace in backstretch, challenged by JACK MILTON heading into turn, vied along inside at top of the lane, could not match strides and slightly weakened. ALL ALEX stalked the pace two off inside in backstretch, raced three wide into lane, continued steadily in stretch and lacked final kick in drive to make impact. VESPATO raced behind the pacesetter in early stages, made a bid and steadily began to edge up to lead heading into far turn but could not sustain bid and weakened. MAIN MAN MIKE allowed to settle along rail in early stages, continued evenly heading into turn and failed to rally in stretch. MIDDLEBURG reserved in early stages racing near back of the pack, angled out slightly nearing turn, asked for response and passed tiring rivals in drive. P V PAUL was unhurried in backstretch racing near the the back of rivals, floated out five wide in the turn and lacked response in stretch. EFFICIENT MARKET stalked rivals along outside in backstretch, raced four wide into lane and failed to rally in stretch. COMANCHERIA raced evenly near back of rivals and failed to make a bid. MAKE YOUR MOVE saved ground racing along inside and had no response in the drive. WILDCARD failed to respond throughout.

Owners- 10, Barber Gary ; 9, Magdalena Racing ; 11, Red Oak Stable ; 13, Grupo Seven C Stable ; 12, Youngblood John F.; 7, Talisman Bruce N.; 2, Firestone, Mr. and Mrs. Bertram R. ; 8, Stonestreet Stables LLC ; 4, Klaravich Stables, Inc. and Lawrence, William H. ; 1, Lake Lonely Racing ; 5, Darley Stable ; 6, Lothenbach Stables, Inc.

Trainers- 10, Pletcher Todd A.; 9, McPeek Kenneth G.; 11, Sacco Gregory D.; 13, Rodriguez Rudy R.; 12, Proctor Thomas F.; 7, Hennig Mark A.; 2, Clement Christophe ; 8, Brown Chad C.; 4, Romans Dale L.; 1, Sheppard Jonathan E.; 5, McLaughlin Kiaran P.; 6, Wilkes Ian R.

Breeders- 10, Cherry Valley Farm, LLC (KY); 9, Cherry Valley Farm, LLC. & Stuart S.Janney, III LLC. (KY); 11, Michael P. Cristello (FL); 13, Dr. J. David Richardson & Mike Chipman (KY); 12, Larry G. Richardson & Joe Aflinghaus (KY); 7, Bruce Talisman (KY); 2, Mr. & Mrs. Bertram R. Firestone (VA); 8, Stonestreet Thoroughbred Holdings LLC (KY); 4, Craig B. Singer (KY); 1, Team Block (IL); 5, H. Allen Poindexter & Darley (KY); 6, G. Watts Humphrey Jr. (KY)

Scratched- Balthazar(30Apr06 ^{4}Aqu^{6}), Grad Student(13Dec12 ^{6}GP^{9}), Blu Caballo(13Dec12 ^{6}GP^{7}), Harrythenavigator(12Dec12 ^{7}Lrl^{2})

$2 Daily Double (5-10) Paid $47.80; Daily Double Pool $60,732.
$1 Pick Three (6/9/10-5-10) Paid $73.80; Pick Three Pool $74,109.

Data provided or compiled by Equibase Company, which includes data from The Jockey Club, generally is accurate but occasionally errors and omissions occur as a result of incorrect data received by others, mistakes in processing and other causes. Equibase Company and Bloodstock Research Information Services, Inc. and Thoroughbred Sports Network disclaim responsibility for the consequences, if any, of such errors, but would appreciate being called to their attention. Copyright 2013.

Winner - 10 - Place - 9 - Tied for Best Work. $324.80 exacta

COPYRIGHT 2013 BLOODSTOCK RESEARCH INFORMATION SERVICES

the screen horses 5, 7, 9, 11, 12, 13 in exactas and trifectas and as many dime supers as affordable.

Race comes 10, 9, 11, 13.

Winner pays $9.20 6.00 5.20; place pays $30.40 13.40; $2 ex acta $324.80; $2 trifecta $2,343.60; dime super $509.82!!

The war Dancer/Danzig's three half brothers placed first, second, and fourth; sometimes breeding really does count, especially when that superior lineage produces the best works and second best start figures on the FHH interface screen.

A further example of a maiden race that included no less than six first timers, but in which there were considerable variables pointing to probable contenders, occurred on 11/9/2012 with the tenth at Churchill Downs; a 6 1/2 furlong race on the dirt for fillies and mares three and up in a maiden 35k claimer.

Five of the first timers were in the 1 through 5 posts; the sixth was in the 11 hole. The 1, Just Shut Up, had worked 11 times since 6/15/2012, without producing a single distinguished work. The 2, Miss C C, had the second best work of the field; four furongs in :48 on 10/14/2012, followed by the slow work of :50 4/5 four days before the race. The 3, Gravitate, had the third best work; breezing four furlongs at :48 1/5, just six days before the race.

The 4, Slammin Rose, caught my attention with her two exceptional works at four furlongs of :47 2/5 and :47 3/5 – both works were by far the best of the field. Her trainer was a 15 per cent winner with maiden claimers. It is perplexing that the morning line setter tabbed Slammin Rose's morning line at 30/1. (I remember thinking, "What a gift!") How could an experienced handicapper ignore those two exceptional works? Apparently, he or she was overly susceptible to the latest breeding fad.

My Girl Sherri, the 5, was handled by Dale Romans, a 20 per cent maiden claimer winner. While the horse did not exactly burn up the track in her dozen works since being put into training on 7/16/2012, she did have three decent works in :49 and change. The other first timer, the 11, Alex's Gold, with 11 mundane works and just an average trainer.

The tepid favorite was the 6, Maiden Warrior, tabbed at a morning line of 4/1. Her trainer was Cecil Borel, an 18 per cent winner; his jockey was nephew Calvin Borel. The Warrior miss was returning from a 47 day layoff; dropping into this race from a maiden special 23k in which she was second, just two and one-half lengths out. The chart writer's comment was "4w 1/4 out, game second." Maiden Warrior had the best start and the second best mid-pace numbers on the FHH screen and was tied for the #2 contender in tell points. She appeared to be the legitimate favorite. The FHH program gave the hidden horse hunter the 6 and the 4 on the interface screen.

The sytem play was to bet the 4 (whose post time odds ballooned to 54.5/1) to win and twice as much to place, then to run the 6 up and back with four of the six first time starters – the 2, 3, 4, 5 – in exactas and trifecas and as many dime supers as affordable.

Races comes 6, 4, 3, 5.

Winner pays $8.60 5.40 4.60; place on the 4 $38.00 17.00; $2 exacta $359.20; $2 trifecta $4,339.20; dime superfecta $3,594.80!!

The "something to go on" in this race that included half the field as first time starters, was their workout patterns. The works "tell" is one of the most valuable variables in the formula the FHH uses to find hidden horses that frequently leave the gate as long shots, ignored or overlooked by the general betting public and the track handicapping "experts." What possible logical reason was there for the 4, with the two best workouts of the field by far, to be tabbed with a morning line of 30/1? In fairness, hidden horse hunters should not complain; the track handicapper did them a favor.

The ninth race at Aqueduct on 11/14/2012 produced a remarkable result in which the FHH program nailed a boxcar odds winner, posting it as the #1 contender (tied with the favorite) on the interface screen. The race was for two year old New York Breds going a mile and one-sixteenth on the turf in a maiden special 57k contest.

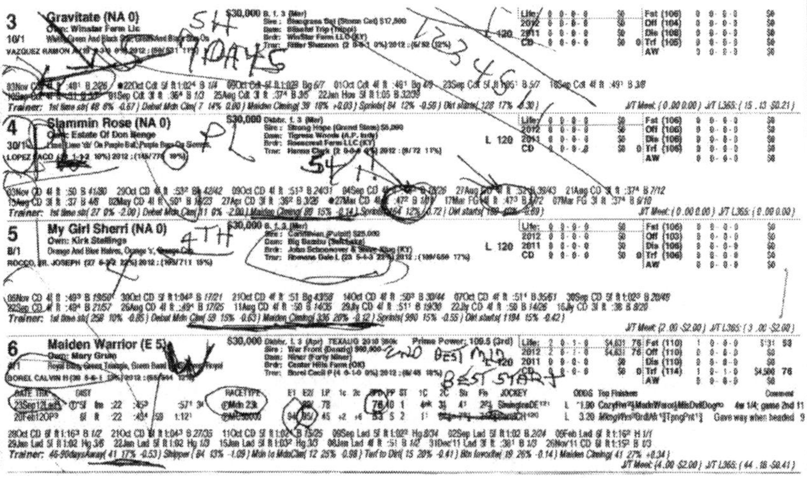
3 Gravitate (NA 0) $30,000
Own: Winstar Farm Llc
10/1
VAZQUEZ RAMON
Trainer: 1st time str(48 6% -0.67) Debut Mdn Clm(7 14% 0.00) Maiden Claiming(39 10% +0.03) Sprints(84 12% -0.58)
4 Slammin Rose (NA 0) $30,000
Own: Estate Of Don Benge
30/1
LOPEZ PACO
Trainer: 1st time str(27 0% -2.00) Debut Mdn Clm(11 0% -2.00) Maiden Claiming(85 15% -0.14)
5 My Girl Sherri (NA 0) $30,000
Own: Kirk Stallings
8/1 Orange And Blue Halves, Orange 's'
ROCCO, JR. JOSEPH
Trainer: 1st time str(258 10% -0.85) Debut Mdn Clm(59 15% -0.63) Maiden Claiming(336 20% -0.12) Sprints(990 15% -0.55) Dirt starts(1194 15% -0.42)
6 Maiden Warrior (E 5) $30,000 Prime Power: 109.5 (3rd)
Own: Mary Grum
BOREL CALVIN H
Sire: War Front (Danzig)
Trnr: Borel Cecil P
Trainer: 46-90daysAway(41 17% -0.53) Shipper(84 13% -1.09) Mdn to MdnClm(12 25% 0.98) Turf to Dirt(15 20% -0.41) Btn favorite(19 26% -0.14) Maiden Claiming(41 27% +0.34)

COPYRIGHT 2013 BLOODSTOCK RESEARCH INFORMATION SERVICES

TENTH RACE
Churchill
November 9th, 2012

6½ FURLONGS. (1.14^{1}) MAIDEN CLAIMING. Purse $19,000 FOR MAIDENS, FILLIES AND MARES THREE YEARS OLD AND UPWARD. Three Year Olds, 120 lbs.; Older, 122 lbs. Claiming Price $30,000, For Each $2,500 To $25,000 1 lb. (Clear 51)

Value of Race: $19,285 Winner $11,400; second $3,800; third $1,900; fourth $950; fifth $570; sixth $95; seventh $95; eighth $95; ninth $95; tenth $95; eleventh $95; twelveth $95. Mutuel Pool $145,655 Pick 3 Pool $57,144 Pick 4 Pool $107,354 Pick 5 Pool $46,968 Pick 6 Pool $6,448 Daily Double Pool $37,347 Exacta Pool $129,322 Superfecta Pool $83,847 Super High Five Pool $7,229 Trifecta Pool $88,236

Last Raced	#	Horse	M/Eqt.	A/S	Wt	PP	St	¼	½	Str	Fin	Jockey	Cl'g Pr	Odds $1	
23Sep12 ^{4}Lad^{2}	6	Maiden Warrior	L	3F	120	6	1	2½	1½	$1^{2\frac{1}{2}}$	1^{hd}	Borel C H	30000	3.30	BEST START
	4	Slammin Rose	L	3F	120	4	10	9½	6^{hd}	3^{3}	$2^{1\frac{3}{4}}$	Albarado R	30000	54.50	BEST WORK
	3	Gravitate	L	3F	120	3	3	3^{1}	3^{2}	2^{2}	$3^{7\frac{3}{4}}$	Vazquez R A	30000	14.40	2ND BEST WORK
	5	My Girl Sherri	L	3F	120	5	7	$8^{2\frac{1}{2}}$	$8^{2\frac{1}{2}}$	4½	$4^{2\frac{3}{4}}$	Rocco, Jr. J	30000	9.20	
	2	Miss C C	L	3F	120	2	5	6^{1}	7^{hd}	6^{3}	5½	Bridgmohan S	30000	9.80	
14Jun12 ^{1}CD^{2}	9	Love Numbers	L	3F	120	9	6	10^{hd}	$10^{3\frac{1}{2}}$	7^{hd}	$6^{3\frac{1}{2}}$	Gonzalez, Jr. S	30000	4.20	
	11	Alex's Gold	L f	3F	120	11	11	11^{7}	$11^{8\frac{1}{2}}$	$10^{4\frac{1}{2}}$	$7^{1\frac{1}{2}}$	Mena M	30000	14.20	
17Oct12 ^{7}Hoo^{8}	8	Dancingovertheline	L	3F	118	8	2	$1^{1\frac{1}{2}}$	2½	5^{1}	$8^{5\frac{1}{2}}$	Kuntzweiler G	25000	96.90	
27May12 ^{8}CD^{6}	10	Highway Girl	L	3F	120	10	9	5^{2}	5^{1}	9^{2}	9¾	Court J K	30000	7.70	
10Jun12 ^{3}Mth^{3}	7	Love On Line	L	3F	120	7	4	4^{hd}	4^{1}	8½	$10^{8\frac{3}{4}}$	Lanerie C J	30000	3.90	
	1	Just Shut Up		3F	120	1	12	12	12	12	11no	Lebron V	30000	25.20	
19Oct12 ^{3}Kee^{7}	12	Simply Dashing	L bf	3F	120	12	8	7^{1}	$9^{1\frac{1}{2}}$	11^{9}	12	Hernandez, Jr. B J	30000	13.80	

OFF AT 5:04 Start Good. Won driving. Track Fast.
TIME :22^{3}, :46^{4}, 1:12^{1}, 1:18^{4} (:22.72, :46.94, 1:12.23, 1:18.84)

$2 Mutuel Prices:

6- MAIDEN WARRIOR	8.60	5.40	4.60
4- SLAMMIN ROSE		38.00	17.00
3- GRAVITATE			9.00

$2 EXACTA 6-4 PAID $359.20 $2 SUPERFECTA 6-4-3-5 PAID $71,897.00
$1 SUPER HIGH FIVE 6-4-3-5-2 PAID $0.00 Carryover Pool $5,853 $2 TRIFECTA 6-4-3 PAID $4,339.20

Dark Bay or Brown Filly, (Ap), by War Front - Miner by Forty Niner. Trainer Borel P. Cecil. Bred by Center Hills Farm(OK).

MAIDEN WARRIOR close up along the inside, challenged from the rail on the turn, drew clear into the stretch and lasted late. SLAMMIN ROSE broke slowly, was outrun early, made a good middle move off the rail then closed fast to miss. GRAVITATE forwardly placed, challenged three wide on the turn, dropped back a bit into the stretch then lacked a solid late bid. MY GIRL SHERRI outsprinted early, saved ground on the turn and was no late threat. MISS C C within striking distance three wide, tired. LOVE NUMBERS outrun early, raced off the inside on the turn, angled out for the drive but could not threaten. ALEX'S GOLD was outrun in the three path. DANCINGOVERTHELINE set the pace off the inside, held on well to the stretch and faded. HIGHWAY GIRL within reach five wide, faded. LOVE ON LINE within striking distance in the four path, faded. JUST SHUT UP broke slowly and was outrun. SIMPLY DASHING was through early.

Owners- 6, Grum Mary ; 4, Estate of Don Benge ; 3, WinStar Farm LLC ; 5, Stallings Kirk ; 2, River Bend Farm ; 9, Ward Wesley A.; 11, Deegan Joseph ; 8, Britton Chris ; 10, Stonecrest Farm ; 7, American Equistock Racing, Inc. ; 1, Lewis, Kevin, Lindsey, Dennis and Rennekamp, Nick J. ; 12, Jim Tafel LLC

Trainers- 6, Borel Cecil P.; 4, Hanna Clark ; 3, Ritter Shannon ; 5, Romans Dale L.; 2, Carroll David M.; 9, Ward Wesley A.; 11, Deegan Joseph ; 8, Engler Jeff ; 10, Morse Randy L.; 7, Walsh Brendan P.; 1, Rennekamp Nick J.; 12, Nafzger Carl A.

Breeders- 6, Center Hills Farm (OK); 4, Rosecrest Farm LLC (KY); 3, WinStar Farm, LLC (KY); 5, John Schoonover & Steve Klug (KY); 2, River Bend Farm, Inc. (KY); 9, W. S. Farish & Skara Glen Stables (KY); 11, Gainesway Thoroughbreds Ltd. (KY); 8, Juliana Whittenburg, Gary Elletracht, William Steele & Eleanor Steele (FL); 10, Dr. William A Reed (KY); 7, Mrs. C. Oliver Iselin III (VA); 1, William C. Chaudoin (KY); 12, Jim Tafel, LLC (KY)

Scratched- Bay Kohinor(18Aug12 ^{9}Elp^{8}), Nearctic Edge(18Aug12 ^{9}Elp^{8}), Izalu(18Aug12 ^{9}Elp^{8}), Malibu Mudslide(01Oct12 ^{3}Del^{4})

$2 Daily Double (12-6) Paid $33.00; Daily Double Pool $37,347.
$2 Pick Three (3-12-6) Paid $108.60; Pick Three Pool $57,144.
$2 Pick Four (6-3-1/3/4/8/11/12/14-6) Paid $1,264.40; Pick Four Pool $107,354.
i 3-6-3-1/3/4/8/11/12/14-6 PAID $2,536.15 $2 Pick Six (4-3-6-3-1/3/4/8/11/12/14-6) 5 Correct Paid $130.40; Pick Six Poc
$2 Pick Six (4-3-6-3-1/3/4/8/11/12/14-6) Paid $13,207.60; Pick Six Pool $6,448.

[illegible]

Winner - 6 - Best Start Place 4 at 54.5/1 Best Work

COPYRIGHT 2012 BLOODSTOCK RESEARCH INFORMATION SERVICES

Screen presented:

TELL POINTS	M/L	POST
2=7	30/1	54.75/1
5=7	3/1	3.5/1
7=5	7/2	3.2/1
8=5	8/1	5.1/1

BEST IN CATEGORY

Work=5	4 furlongs :48.3
Start= 2	82
Mid = 7, 8	80
Late= 1	88

There were two first timers in the race; the 3, Disaster Relief, and the 9, Charity Reins. Disaster Relief had only worked four times since being put into training on 10/10/2012. He was out of a nondescript mare and an undistinguished sire; his best work was at four furlongs in :49 3/5, but his trainer was the legendary turf handler, Christophe Clement. Better to be safe than sorry, so I left him in as a contender. The other two year old (A February foal) was the 9, Charity Reins, who had been put into training on 5/5/2012, then worked a dozen times before being sent to the big dance. Two of his works were decent ones at four furlongs in :49 3/5 and :49.1, the latter, in fact, being the third best work of the field.

My key horse, of course, was the 2, Noosh's Tale. Granted that a cursory look at his three races tended to turn the punter to look elsewhere in the field for current form; nevertheless, the FHH system had tabbed him as a #1 contender tied with the favorite for most tell points at seven. Examining the details of his score revealed that he was returning from a 45 day freshener; had a good work pattern since his last race; had the best start number; was getting five pounds off from his last race, and had worked three furlongs at :36 breezing on a good track just three days before the race (just "greasing the wheels").

The system bet, of course, was to bet the 2 to win and twice as much to place; then to run the 2 up and back with the 1, 3, 5, 7, 8, 9 (at odds of 16/1 on both of the first timers, couldn't leave them out) in exactas and trifectas and as many dime supers as affordable.

Race comes 2, 9, 8, 4.

Winner pays $111.50 37.20 16.20; $2 exacta $1,458.00; $2 trifecta $13,670.00!!

In the land of first time starters, workout pattern is king.

THEIR FIRST DANCE

NINTH RACE
Aqueduct
November 14th, 2012

1 1/16 MILES. (Turf) (1.40⁴) MAIDEN SPECIAL WEIGHT. Purse $57,000 FOR MAIDENS, TWO YEARS OLD FOALED IN NEW YORK STATE AND APPROVED BY THE NEW YORK STATE-BRED REGISTRY. Weight, 120 lbs. (If the Stewards consider it inadvisable to run this race on the turf course, this race will be run at One Mile on the Main Track.) (Cloudy 47)

Value of Race: $57,000 Winner $34,200; second $11,400; third $5,700; fourth $2,850; fifth $1,710; sixth $285; seventh $285; eighth $285; ninth $285. Mutuel Pool $195,142 Pick 3 Pool $72,294 Pick 4 Pool $163,731 Pick 6 Pool $267,931 Daily Double Pool $94,876 Exacta Pool $175,347 Superfecta Pool $66,498 Trifecta Pool $107,869

Last Raced	#	Horse	M/Eqt.	A/S	Wt	PP	St	1/4	1/2	3/4	Str	Fin	Jockey	Odds $1
30Sep12 ⁶Bel⁷	2	Noosh's Tale	b	2C	115	2	2	4hd	5⁴	5¹½	2¹	1²	Coa K J	54.75
	9	Charity Reins	L	2C	120	8	4	5¹½	4hd	4²½	1¹½	2²¹	Ortiz, Jr. I	16.30
28Oct12 ¹Bel³	8	Captain Gaughen	L	2C	120	7	5	2½	2²½	2²	4²	3nk	Morales P	5.10
20Aug12 ⁷San⁶	4	Night Editor	L b	2G	115	4	1	1¹½	1¹	1½	3½	4hd	Ortiz J L	9.40
26Oct12 ²Bel⁶	10	Shortcoming	L b	2C	120	9	7	7²	6¹½	6⁴½	5²	5¹½	Silvera R	78.75
21Oct12 ⁷Bel⁵	1	Ego Friendly	L	2C	120	1	3	3¹½	3²	3hd	6¹½	6hd	Maragh R	1.90
04Oct12 ¹Bel⁷	5	M Six		2C	120	5	8	8½	7¹	7¹⁰	7⁷	7⁷½	Dominguez R A	3.85
	3	Disaster Relief		2C	113	3	6	9	8	8²⁰	8	8	Tomas P	15.90
21Oct12 ⁷Bel³	7	Gulltopper	L b	2C	120	6	9	6½	8¹	9	9^∞	9^∞	Alvarado J	3.20

OFF AT 4:13 Start Good. Won driving. Track Good.
TIME :25, :50½, 1:16², 1:41¹, 1:47¹ (:25.11, :50.76, 1:16.41, 1:41.28, 1:47.33)

$2 Mutuel Prices:
2 - NOOSH'S TALE 111.50 37.20 16.20
9 - CHARITY REINS 14.60 9.80
8 - CAPTAIN GAUGHEN 4.50

$2 EXACTA 2-9 PAID $1,458.00 $2 SUPERFECTA 2-9-8-4 PAID $86,220.00
$2 TRIFECTA 2-9-8 PAID $13,670.00

Bay Colt, (Apr), by Tale of the Cat - Upper Noosh by Red Ransom. Trainer Kelly J. Patrick. Bred by Fox Ridge Farm(NY).

NOOSH'S TALE steadied leaving the chute when CAPTAIN GAUGHEN shifted over, settled tracking in mid pack, progressed on the front nearing the quarter pole, swung four wide in upper stretch, rallied to seize command nearing the sixteenth marker, edged away under a drive to prevail. CHARITY REINS just off the inside mid pack, advanced on the front from the five-sixteenths, seized command straightening for home, dug in with good kick, got collared nearing the sixteenth pole continued on safely and second best. CAPTAIN GAUGHEN a bit keen early resisting the restraint of the rider, settled three wide in close range, came under a drive at the quarter pole, had the leader drift in a bit and altered outside sharply at the three-sixteenths, offered up a mild bid thereafter for the show honors. NIGHT EDITOR set the pace from the two path, got let out cutting the corner into the stretch when displaced straightening away, fought on to the eighth pole before weakening late on while holding for the last major share. SHORTCOMING rank early on between rivals in the two path and resisting the rating tactics of the rider, settled more professionally once backed away from in between foes, came under urging at the three-eighths pole, swung five wide for home, offered up a mild kick in the late stages while unable to make an impact. EGO FRIENDLY tracked inside just off the pace, came under prolonged urging from the seven-sixteenths, made little to no headway and weakened. M SIX hesitated at the start, settled just off the inside towards the rear, came under encouragement at the five-sixteenths, spun four wide into the stretch and never factored. DISASTER RELIEF three wide towards the rear initially, came under urging three furlongs out, cut the corner into the lane while being outrun. GULLTOPPER three wide mid pack initially faded while being taken a path or two further outside and pulling noticeably on the new side bit with his head cocked to the offside, faded from contention, was eased just approaching the five-sixteenths and subsequently walked off under his own power.

Owners- 2, Fox Ridge Farm, Inc. ; 9, Quest Realty ; 8, Generazio Patricia A. ; 4, Melvern and Janet Burroughs LLC ; 10, Callahan Peter J. ; 1, Broman, Sr., Chester and Mary ; 5, Goichman Lawrence ; 3, Delehanty Stock Farm ; 7, Philip Birsh and William Gilden

Trainers- 2, Kelly Patrick J.; 9, Cooney Susan S.; 8, Ryerson James T.; 4, Ward Wesley A.; 10, Badgett, Jr. William ; 1, Kimmel John C.; 5, Pletcher Todd A.; 3, Clement Christophe ; 7, Jerkens James A.

Breeders- 2, Fox Ridge Farm (NY); 9, Saratoga Select Broodmares LLC (NY); 8, Patricia Generazio (NY); 4, Melvern & Janet Burroughs, LLC (NY); 10, The Peter J. Callahan Revocable Trust Dated 2/28/02 (NY); 1, Chester Broman & Mary R. Broman (NY); 5, Lawrence Goichman (NY); 3, Delehanty Stock Farm (NY); 7, Philip S. Birsh & William Gilden (NY)

Scratched- Ten Ed(28Oct12 ⁶Bel⁶), Ultimate Empire(04Oct12 ¹Bel⁵), Song of Aspen(21Oct12 ⁷Bel⁵), No Nukes(24Oct12 ⁶Bel²), Siniakha(03Nov12 ⁴Aqu⁶), Face the Race(17Oct12 ⁹Del⁷), Chrisandlorieposse(04Oct12 ¹Bel⁸)

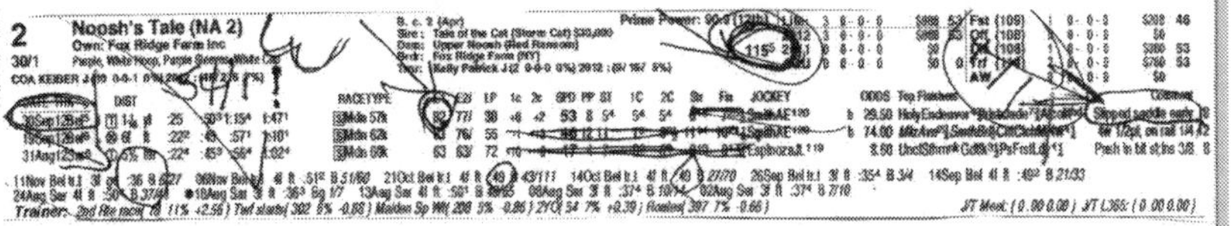

Winner - 2 - FHH #1 contender, Best Start, 45 day layoff

COPYRIGHT 2012 BLOODSTOCK RESEARCH INFORMATION SERVICES

Chapter 10

TRAINERS AND THE GAMES THEY PLAY

*"If I told you what it takes to reach the highest high,
you'd laugh and say, 'ha, nothing is that simple'."*
THE WHO, from the ROCK OPERA *TOMMY*

Once a horse breaks its maiden, its connections are faced with a difficult decision: will they move their steed up, down, or sideways in considering what class of race to enter for their winner's next race. This is not any easy call. Much depends on the trainer's evaluation of the class of the horse (or lack thereof). The decision is best left to the trainer: owners tend to believe that their horse is probably a Kentucky Derby contender. Unless the horse's connections are bona fide experts on breeding lineage, they should bow to the judgement of their trainer. That's why most trainers first start a horse in a maiden special race, even if they privately think the horse should start, for example, in a medium maiden claimer.

If the horse wins its maiden special, so much the better – but most do not. After a couple of failed tries at the top of the maiden class, the owner is usually more amenable to a trainer's decision to move down the class ladder, entering the horse in a claiming race where the trainer thinks it belongs.

Aside from lineage, how does a trainer objectively determine the "class" of a new horse in his or her barn, before the horse has raced in an actual contest? How else but workouts; how fast can the horse run three, four, five furlongs or more in the morning as the sun comes up and all you can hear is the pump, pump, pump of its hoofs as you lean on the backstretch rail, stop-watch in hand, ready to click as your hopeful hits the finish line, and you look at the time and hope that it was at least sixty seconds flat for five furlongs, and that maybe this time you've got a real "contenda," a stakes winner, or at the least a "black type" runner; that's the nature of the romance of the game that Lil and I grew to love.

Not only does the thoroughbred trainer have to master the finer points of bringing a sound horse to the track, he or she must be somewhat of a politician when dealing with the owners of his or her charges. Generally, most owners who are new to the game tend to push their trainers to overmatch their horses. A savvy trainer will insist at the beginning of his engagement that the decisions of race placements are his alone. That's why you see a lot of "trainer-shuffling" at the minor league tracks. New owners are looking for the trainer who can put some magic into their hot-blooded horse. The bottom line is: trainers have to win often enough to attract new connections to their barn. As trite as it is: nothing succeeds like success and nothing fails more than failure.

An interesting example of the problem of "where does the trainer place a horse for its first post-maiden win try" occurred on 1/16/2013 in the ninth race at Tampa Bay Downs. The 75k Optional Claiming mile race on the turf was for three year olds which had never won a race other than maiden, claiming, or starter or which had never won two races or optional claiming price of $75,000. (You would think that for this class of race the purse would have been substantially more than $21,200.)

In scrolling down the Brisnet form entries, I stopped at the 7, Balino: what was this horse doing in this race? His first start had been on 8/25/2012 at Calder in a MC25k 5 1/2 furlong race in the slop on dirt. The comments were: *hesitated, ducked in start*. Despite the green start, Balino closed some five lengths from the first call to the head of the stretch, where no doubt the jockey eased him upon finding his horse some eight lengths from the lead, and losing traction. The only interesting thing about that race was that the Calder crowd sent him off at odds of 8.6/1, indicating barn betting.

His second start was on 9/26/2012 at Calder in a 25k Maiden Claimer at six furlongs in which Balino threw in a clunker, finishing sixth in an eight horse field. No excuses were apparent. A change of trainer and a 75 day layoff ensued. Balino returned to the track on 12/14/2012, entered in a seven furlong 12.5k Maiden Claimer at Tampa Bay. He left the gate as the favorite at 2.1/1, romping home on top by a length.

Now here he was in an Optional Claiming 75k race at a mile on the turf. It was no surprise that the crowd let him go at 61/1. The surprise was that he made an easy lead, crawling the first quarter in 24 2/5; the half in :49 3/5, wiring the field to win by a nose. My guess is that the other jockeys and their trainers noted the cheap maiden win and were reasonably certain that when the real running began he would regress to the class. Since no other runner pressed Balino, there was little pace for the closers to run at.

When you see a race like this set up; that is, where it appears that a horse or horses don't belong in the race, go over their past performances with a fine tooth comb. Balino was not a hidden horse. The key to the win was the change in trainer and the 75 days in which the new trainer rounded the horse into form. Another angle was that the horse was going from dirt to turf. I knew of Bernell Rhone's reputation: he does not enter horses unless he thinks they have a real chance; he doesn't enter horses for "training purposes" only, as many trainers do

So the next time you see a race in which you think a last race maiden winner is too cheap to compete at a higher class, think again. That just might get you a $124.20 winner!

Bernell's placement of his horse in the above race was an honest play. Unfortunately, the games a few desperate trainers play are not honest, as we have seen by too many examples. Today's racing industry is ill-equipped to prevent the monkey business that is often played at tracks where the purses are relatively small, the handle meager. This is not to say that even at the major tracks sometimes a horse can only win if it: "gets a little help from its friends." Rumors persist among horsemen of a performance enhancing legendary *Argentina joy juice* that is presently undetectable by testing authorities. When doping *is* detected, too often the trainer receives a slap on the wrist and a mild rule off period by the State Racing Commission. The racing patron – the proverbial two dollar bettor - is

TRAINERS AND THE GAMES THEY PLAY

NINTH RACE
Tampa Bay
January 16th, 2013

1 MILE. (Turf) (1.33³) ALLOWANCE OPTIONAL CLAIMING. Purse $21,200 (includes $3,000 FOA - Florida Owners Awards) FOR THREE YEAR OLDS WHICH HAVE NEVER WON A RACE OTHER THAN MAIDEN, CLAIMING, OR STARTER OR WHICH HAVE NEVER WON TWO RACES OR OPTIONAL CLAIMING PRICE OF $75,000. Weight, 122 lbs. Non-winners Of A Race At A Mile Or Over Since December 16 Allowed 2 lbs. Such A Race Since November 16 Allowed 4 lbs. Claiming Price $75,000 (Claiming races for $40,000 or less not considered in weight allowances) (Condition Eligibility). (If deemed inadvisable by management to run this race over the turf course, it will be run on the main track at One Mile and Forty Yards.) (Clear 80)

Value of Race: $20,300 ($900 reverts) Winner $12,838; second $3,646; third $1,820; fourth $1,092; fifth $182; sixth $182; seventh $182; eighth $182; ninth $182. Mutuel Pool $136,138 Pick 3 Pool $14,569 Pick 4 Pool $38,121 Pick 5 Pool $14,819 Daily Double Pool $28,154 Exacta Pool $107,088 Superfecta Pool $45,129 Super High Five Pool $37,276 Trifecta Pool $71,361

Last Raced	# Horse	M/Eqt.	A/S Wt	PP St	¼	½	¾	Str	Fin	Jockey	Clg Pr	Odds $1
14Dec12 ¹Tam¹	7 Balino	L	3C 118	5 1	11½	11	1½	1²	1no	Goodwin N G		61.10
07Dec12 ⁵Tam¹	5 Fessed Up	L b	3C 118	3 7	3½	3hd	4½	2¹	2¹	Garcia L	75000	6.70
23Dec12 ¹⁰Tam¹	6 Righteous Place	L b	3C 118	5 6	7½	7¹	6¹	3½	3nk	Butler D P		9.80
08Dec12 ⁴GP⁴	2 Over and Back	L	3G 118	9 4	6¹	5½	5½	5½	4²½	Serpa A	75000	2.10
23Dec12 ⁶GP⁷	4 Tejitukitiscoach	L b	3G 118	2 9	9	9	8¹	6¹½	5nk	De La Cruz F	75000	3.90
30Dec12 ³Tam¹	3 Run to Class	L b	3C 122	1 8	8²½	8½	9	9	6¹	Lopez C C	75000	7.20
23Dec12 ⁴Tam³	8 Tori's Guy	L	3C 118	7 3	4¹	4¹	3½	4hd	7nk	Centeno D		3.40
22Dec12 ⁷Tam²	1 Pyritedan	L	3G 118	4 5	5½	6²	7¹	7½	8²	Feliciano R	75000	9.80
02Jan13 ⁸Tam⁹	9 Tiger Distinction	L	3G 118	8 2	2¹½	2¹	2½	6¹½	9	Dominguez E	75000	78.30

OFF AT 4:37 Start Good. Won driving. Track Firm (Rail at 12 ft).
TIME :24, :49², 1:13³, 1:26³, 1:37² (:24.15, :49.46, 1:13.76, 1:25.70, 1:37.54)

$2 Mutuel Prices:
7- BALINO 124.20 44.00 17.60
5- FESSED UP 7.80 5.80
6- RIGHTEOUS PLACE 7.60

$2 EXACTA 7-5 PAID $1,050.00 $1 SUPERFECTA 7-5-6-2 PAID $22,141.10
$1 SUPER HIGH FIVE 7-5-6-2-4 PAID $0.00 Carryover Pool $84,775 $2 TRIFECTA 7-5-6 PAID $5,859.20

Dark Bay or Brown Colt, (Feb), by Mr. Elway - Love That Touch by Arroyo. Trainer Rhone B. Bernell. Bred by Joe Serena & Vivi Serena(FL).

BALINO set a moderate pace, drew off a bit leaving the second turn to mid stretch then was all out to narrowly prevail. FESSED UP raced close up from the outset, was boxed through the second turn then angled off the rail in the drive and finished stoutly to just miss. RIGHTEOUS PLACE made a middle move, bid four wide in the drive but was outkicked late. OVER AND BACK was boxed in the second turn, angled inside in the drive then was gaining late. TEJITUKITISCOACH passed tiring rivals and was vanned off. RUN TO CLASS failed to menace. TORI'S GUY chased early, bid in the second turn then weakened in the drive. PYRITEDAN was no factor. TIGER DISTINCTION pressed the pace then stopped.

Owners- 7, Serena Vivi ; 5, Luel Stables ; 6, Bolen Bailey ; 2, Panic Stable LLC ; 4, Buttoglia, Lee and Divito, James P. ; 3, Edition Farm ; 8, Midwest Thoroughbreds, Inc. ; 1, Pyrito Stables ; 9, Martinez Jose Manuel

Trainers- 7, Rhone Bernell B. ; 5, Delacour Leigh ; 6, Rhone Bernell B. ; 2, Cibelli Jane ; 4, DiVito James P. ; 3, Wasiluk, Jr. Peter ; 8, Ness Jamie ; 1, Feliciano Miguel A. ; 9, Maestre Pedro

Breeders- 7, Joe Serena & Vivi Serena (FL); 5, Mr. & Mrs. M. Roy Jackson (PA); 6, Bailey Bolen (KY); 2, Darley (KY); 4, Liberation Farm & Brandywine Farm (KY); 3, Edition Farm (NY); 8, Bulldog Racing (PA); 1, Dr. D. W. Frazier (PA); 9, Carlos Victor Mompellier (FL)

Scratched- Centaur Man(22Sep12 ⁹Mth¹), Pyrlie Green(22Dec12 ⁶Tam⁴)

$2 Daily Double (1-7) Paid $584.20; Daily Double Pool $28,154.
$2 Pick Three (3-1-7) Paid $11,949.60; Pick Three Pool $14,589.
$2 Pick Four (4/9-3-1-7) Paid $41,670.40; Pick Four Pool $38,121.
$1 Pick Five (7-4/9-3-1-7) 4 Correct Paid $247.70; Pick Five Pool $14,819; Carryover Pool $9,447.

Winner - 7 - Off a 75 day layoff. "Trainer's Gambit"

COPYRIGHT 2012 BLOODSTOCK RESEARCH INFORMATION SERVICES

ill served for the steady money they can be counted on to lay down for the game most of them love. Many of them contribute a steady percentage of their Social Security checks: they deserve far more transparency than they presently receive.

Wouldn't it be great for all punters to know the following before they lay their money down?

1. When a horse returns to the track after a 45 day or more layoff, what was the reason for the layoff?
2. Was it a simple freshening?
3. Was it an injury? What was the vet's diagnosis? Such information is vital but withheld from the bettor. Unless punters are also insiders, they can only guess the reason for the layoff. Was the injury a shin-buck (similar to a sprained ankle in humans) that heals in a few weeks to six months; or was it more problematic, for example a bowed tendon?
4. How many times over the past three years has the current trainer been ruled-off because any of his horses tested positive for an outlawed performance enhancing drug?

The above information could easily be abbreviated enough so that it could be placed as a notation in the involved horse's nomenclature of the racing form. We should not hold our breath until these changes are made by the powers that presently determine the rules of the game.

While there are many ways to manipulate the outcome of a thoroughbred horse race, not all of them involve drugs. One of the more blatant ways to enhance a horse's performance involves the use of a "buzzer" judiciously applied by the jockey at strategic points in the race, usually at the head of the stretch. A perfect example occcurred at Belmont on 4/26/2013 in the sixth race, a 30k claimer for three year olds and upward which had never won two races or three olds going a mile on the dirt. I recommend that you take the time to pull up the replay, for it is highly instructive.

After two scratches, a field of six went to the post. In examining the FHH screen, I noted that the three, Tycoon Cat, was the cheapest horse in the race, having run 41 races for average earnings of $1,896 per race. The horse had yet to win his second lifetime race. He had not hit the board in his five distance races. His jockey was a five per cent winner; the trainer had won one race in 26 tries.

In this race, however, Tycoon Cat was tied for the second Best Start and second Best Mid-Pace. This earned the horse four tell points, tieing him for the FHH System's pick for third. The Cat was the longest shot in the race, as I believe in my own system I made my usual long shot bet of win and twice as much to place. The race was a substantial move up in class as eight of his last ten races were in non-winners of two for a claiming price of $12,500. It was surprising to see that he was 14.8/1 at post time.

The chart writer reported: "TYCOON CAT coaxed along on the front off the inside, inched away nearing the quarter pole, got set down at that station, dug in under challenge in the final eighth, held his nearest rival at bay being kept to task to the wire." The chart writer left out what he should (but never would) have put in: "At the head of the stretch Tycoon Cat's tail shot straight up, violently twirling at the very least a hundred rpm's as the horse was obviously being stimulated by an electronic hand held device."

The track announcer, adding insult to injury, rubbed the bettor's noses in it, for at the head of the stretch he intoned: "Tycoon Cat is still there, swishing his tail, trying to bid goodbye to the field." At the finish, the announcer exclaimed: "and Tycoon Cat wins, swishing his tail *all the way around the track* and winning it, beating the 2/5 favorite." The announcer must not have been watching the first half of the race because the Cat's tail was calm; the straight up, whirlwind twirling began at the head of the stretch, not before. I won't belabor the point: pull the replay of that race and come to your own conclusion from the evidence in plain sight. Search though I might, I couldn't find a news story regarding the New York State racing stewards taking any action to investigate the obvious use of a buzzer. In fairness to the stewards, the device must be found in the winning jockey's possession. You can be sure that it is never on his or her person in the winner's circle: one mile tracks have huge infields.

I still maintain that most thoroughbred horse races are honest tries, but it's races like this that make the motto *caveat emptor* (let the buyer beware) particularly important to the punter. The question remains: why did the announcer say that Tycoon Cat was swishing his tail *all around* the track when the film clearly shows that the horse's tail didn't go crazy until the head of the stretch?

Tycoon Cat's connections brought home a $31.60 winner for their gamble. A lot of bettors lost a lot of money on the 2/5 favorite that surely couldn't lose. After all, he was a "mortal lock," as my dog track tip-sheet-selling friend was too often prone to assert. I'm always incredulous that a rational bettor will actually put money on the nose of a 2/5 horse. (Just today at Belmont and Churchill Downs a pair of them bit the dust.)

Shertzer (P 3)
Own: Scalzione Vincent
Vee's Accolade (E/P 4)
Own: La Marca Stable
FALSE FAVORITE!
Tycoon Cat (S 3)
Own: Granville Stable
BOAT?
THE HORSE WITH THE WHIRLING TAIL!

(c) Copyright 2013 Bloodstock Research Information Services www.brisnet.com This product was created with data that were supplied by and are proprietary to Equibase Company LLC. All rights reserved. Reuse of this data is expressly prohibited.

COPYRIGHT 2013 BLOODSTOCK RESEARCH INFORMATION SERVICES

RUNNING A HOLE IN THE WIND: HIDDEN HORSES FOUND

SIXTH RACE
Belmont Park
April 26th, 2013

1 MILE. (1.33¹) CLAIMING. Purse $36,000 (UP TO $6,840 NYSBFOA) FOR THREE YEAR OLDS AND UPWARD WHICH HAVE NEVER WON TWO RACES OR THREE YEAR OLDS. Three Year Olds, 118 lbs.; Older, 124 lbs. Non-winners of a race at a mile or over since February 26 Allowed 2 lbs. Claiming Price $30,000. If for $2 5,000, allowed 2 lbs. (Races where entered for $16,000 or less not considered). (Clear 62)

Value of Race: $36,000 Winner $21,600; second $7,200; third $3,600; fourth $1,800; fifth $1,080; sixth $720. Mutuel Pool $222,501 Pick 3 Pool $31,623 Daily Double Pool $40,285 Exacta Pool $191,899 Superfecta Pool $54,385 Trifecta Pool $119,338

Last Raced	#	Horse	M/Eqt.	A/S	Wt	PP	St	¼	½	¾	Str	Fin	Jockey	Cl'g Pr	Odds $1
19Apr13 ¹Aqu²	3	Tycoon Cat	L		5G 122	3	3	1¹	1²	1²	1¹	1¹½	Camacho, Jr. S	30000	14.80
04Apr13 ³Aqu³	2	Vee's Accolade	L b		5G 122	2	1	5³½	2½	2¹½	2²	2¹	Lezcano J	30000	0.45
29Mar13 ⁷Aqu⁵	1	Shertzer	L bf		5H 122	1	6	6	5½	3⁶	3⁹	3¹¼	Ortiz, Jr. I	30000	5.90
18Apr13 ⁵Aqu²	8	In Todd We Trust	L b		3R 115	6	4	4½	4½	4⁵½	4⁵	4¹½	Castellano J	25000	3.00
07Apr13 ⁹Aqu¹⁰	4	Skyview Park	L b		5G 113	4	2	2 bd	3¹	5½	5⁴½	5¹⁰½	Franco M	25000	41.00
04Apr13 ¹Aqu⁵	6	Augie Dawgie	L bf		3C 118	5	5	3½	6	6	6	6	Cohen D	30000	27.75

OFF AT 3:25 Start Good For All But AUGIE DAWGIE. Won driving. Track Fast.
TIME :23³, :46⁴, 1:11², 1:37 (:23.62, :46.85, 1:11.56, 1:37.13)

$2 Mutuel Prices:	3- TYCOON CAT	31.60	7.90	5.30
	2- VEE'S ACCOLADE		2.80	2.20
	1- SHERTZER			3.90

$2 EXACTA 3-2 PAID $97.00 $2 SUPERFECTA 3-2-1-8 PAID $396.50
$2 TRIFECTA 3-2-1 PAID $216.50

Chestnut Gelding, (My), by Belong to Me - Valentine Kisses by Candy Stripes. Trainer Granville Pedro. Bred by Dr. Frank Ariosta & Peggy Ariosta(NY).

TYCOON CAT coaxed along on the front from just off the inside, inched away nearing the quarter pole, got set down at that station, dug in under challenge in the final eighth, held his nearest rival at bay being kept to task to the wire. VEE'S ACCOLADE tracked the pace along the inside until angled to the three path three furlongs from home, got let out at the quarter pole, offered up a mild kick to issue a challenge in the final furlong but was repulsed to the wire. SHERTZER unhurried early on, ranged up along the inside to get within aim at the three-eighths pole, shifted to be three to four wide at that juncture, spun four wide in upper stretch under a drive, offered up a mild bid in deep stretch but was outfinished by the top two while well clear of the rest. IN TODD WE TRUST three to four wide early on in pursuit from within range, faded from contention and shifted to the rail three furlongs out, cut the corner into the stretch weakening in a drive. SKYVIEW PARK two to three wide in pursuit, faded through the turn urged from the three-eighths and tired. AUGIE DAWGIE briefly steadied at the start, chased three wide within aim early on, lost position and ground on the turn urged from midway and made no impact.

Owners- 3, Granville Stable ; 2, La Marca Stable ; 1, Scalcione Vincent ; 8, Drawing Away Stable and Jacobson, David ; 4, Paradise Farms Corp. ; 5, Big Dawg Stable, Caren, Linda and Joseph

Trainers- 3, Granville Pedro ; 2, Rodriguez Rudy R. ; 1, Barbara Robert ; 8, Jacobson David ; 4, Quick Patrick J.; 6, Englehart Chris J.

Breeders- 3, Dr. Frank Ariosta & Peggy Ariosta (NY); 2, Martha Magliacane (FL); 1, Brereton C. Jones (KY); 8, Gaines-Gentry Thoroughbreds,Dearborn Stables & Tom Van Meter (KY); 4, Dennis Drazin, John C. Kimmel &Caesar P. Kimmel (KY); 6, Dewglewood Thoroughbreds Inc. (NY)

Vee's Accolade was claimed by Winning Move Stable ; trainer, Jacobson David
Scratched- Harley(22Mar13 ⁸Aqu²¹), Yo Blue(21Mar13 ³Aqu¹)

$2 Daily Double (6-3) Paid $357.00; Daily Double Pool $40,265.
$2 Pick Three (1-6-3) Paid $1,781.00; Pick Three Pool $31,623.

Winner - 3 - Watch the replay!

COPYRIGHT 2013 BLOODSTOCK RESEARCH INFORMATION SERVICES

One of the most important variables that the handicapper must master is to recognize a race in which the trainer plays the game of: "We want to sell this horse through the claiming box." In my early years of learning the game, I was easily baited into betting on this type of horse – the substantial class dropper whose past performances listed several races at a class three, four, sometimes half a dozen steps above the current race class. An example of such a horse occurred in the eleventh race at Belmont Park on 5/27/2013 in a seven furlong 20k turf race for three year olds and upward which had never won two races or three year olds. The winner's share of the purse was 18k.

Perusing the past performances of the 3, Mr Algebra, revealed that the four year old gelding had raced 18 times; winning once, placing twice, and showing once for total winnings of $51,847; an average purse share of $2,881. In Mr Algebra's last seven races he had contested in five "non-winners of two" allowance races for purses of 67k, 54k, 59K, 59k, and 62k at the big league tracks of Saratoga, Aqueduct, and Belmont. At Aqueduct on 12/1/2012 the horse was entered in an open 16k claiming race on the turf at a mile and 1/16 after finishing eighth by 5 lengths in a 59k allowance race for non-winners of two races. The crowd – with considerable encouragement from the Aqueduct morning line setter – promptly made Mr Algebra the 1.9/1 favorite in the cheap (for Aqueduct) claimer. The horse finished fourth by 4 3/4 lengths: the chart writer commented: "Rode rail to 1/4; empty." The horse was claimed for 16k by a 20 per cent winning trainer. Then ensued a five month layoff for Mr Algebra.

His workout pattern since being put back into training in March of 2013 was not encouraging. His best work of seven tries was a tepid :49 for four furlongs on 5/20/2013. The horse returned to the track on 5/4/2013 at Belmont, entered in a 62k allowance race at a mile and 1/16 on the turf for non-winners of two races. Finishing a never threatening fifth by four lengths, the chartwriter's comments were: "3-4 w turn; no kick." Similar comments had followed Mr Algebra's previous six races: "empty, no headway, mildly, no kick, mild rally, steadied 3/8."

Such was the record the horse carried into this 20k claimer. It was surprising to me that Joel Rosario accepted the mount. I thought the horse's connections would be only too happy to have Mr Algebra claimed. But at what odds do you think the morning line setter thought the crowd would send the horse to post with? An unbelievable 2/1 – the favorite. The betting public, egged on by the morning line setter, bit at the bait of: "Wow! Look at that class drop." I wasn't going to touch that horse with the proverbial ten foot pole.

The other cliff-dropping class horse in the race was the 4, Mississippi Duel, who was also dropping from a last race in a 62k allownace race for non-winners of two. That horse was the pick of the FHH system, earning six points to tie for top contender. The horse had the Best Start by seven points and was tied for the second Best Mid-Pace. Even though Mississippi Duel had been eased at the half after being close to the lead, it looked like he could get an easy lead in the current race.

As the FHH system indicated, the Mississippi Duel was on the lead at the quarter and increased it to wire the field by five lengths to win going away. Clearly, his connections were not trying to sell Mississippi Dual through the claiming box.

Mr Algebra, the morning line setter's favorite, meandered out of the gate and was never in the race. Once again the credulous betting public was led down the primrose path. Class didn't tell in this race because the back class was without current form.

The next time you are tempted to jump on a horse cliff-dropping in class, think again. And then, think some more.

The winning owner's share of the purse is generally 60 per cent, out of which the trainer and jockey receive 10 percent each, bringing the owner's net share of the overall purse down to 48 percent. In addition, a day rate for each day the horse is in training at the track is charged by the trainer. (Referred to by trainers as "the day money.")

Generally, the purse division at major tracks is paid to the first five finishers – 60, 20, 12, 5, and 3 percent. Think of it; in a million dollar stakes race the winning jockey and trainer will earn $60k each. For the jockey that's a nice payday for a two minute ride, notwithstanding the serious risk of injury they take each time they mount the hot-blooded thoroughbred ten times the rider's weight.

The bottom line is that a punter's best insurance to prevent being cheated in a monkey business race is to confine his or her bets to the major league tracks where the purses are substantial, and the stewards are strict in enforcing the rules of racing, such as they are.

Chapter 11

IN THE LAND OF LONG SHOT HUNTERS, PATIENCE IS KING

"A man is nothing but his mind; if that be out of order, all's amiss, and if that be well, the rest is at ease."
GIROLAMO CARDANO
(16th century "gambler's gambler")

Chance! Think of it! What will likely happen and what will not likely happen? Since the dawn of civilization mankind has continually asked the question: what are the chances of this or that proposition happening? What will be the outcome of some unknown posit that remains unknowm *until* it happens with the passing of time? Such as, for instance, the outcome of a thoroughbred horse race. Without numbers the predictions of experts would have to be little more than an educated guess, controlled only by the goddess of chance.

So when a morning line setter – who can apparently be anyone from the racing secretary to a stable hand – sets a morning line on a horse, say 10/1, the betting public is being told that the track management's "expert opinion" is that there is one chance in ten for that horse to win the race. Usually, the harried morning line expert has little time to go over each entry with any kind of effort that can take an inordinate amount of time; at best it's a superficial call.

The FHH system software uses a mathematical formula developed over three years by persistant algorithmic research over a large back data base to make its decisions regarding the chances of each horse to hit the board. Over the two years through May of 2013 that the software has been on the market, its formula has identified and selected hundreds of hidden horse winners. The examples that follow are typical.

FHH NAILS KENTUCKY OAKS: $79.60 WINNER; $727 EXACTA; $3,470.80 TRIFECTA!!!

Screen presented:

CONTENDER TELL POINTS

2= 6
3= 4
4= 4
6= 4
11= 4

BEST IN CATEGORY

Work=2, 11   4 FUR :47.4
Start= 3   98
Mid= 11   116
Late= 6   112

Who can fathom the minds of the morning line setters? In this 1 and 1/8 mile million dollar stakes race the horse with the Best Late and second Best Mid was tabbed with a ridiculous morning line of 20/1, leaving the gate at the more than generous odds of 38.8/1. What a gift to the hidden horse hunters! Not only was the winner tied for the number 2 contender but he was confirmed by the exellent Best Late number of 112.

Considering the above, the system bet was to win and twice as much to place on the 6, Princess Of Sylmar, then to run the 6 up and back with the screen horses in exactas and trifectas. Another play was to box the confirmed horses – 3, 6, 11 in exactas – a less expensive bet than using all of the screen horses.

Princess of Sylmar ran back to her numbers under a well judged ride by Mike Smith, lighting up the board for a $79.60 win.

Race comes 6, 3, 4, 8

Winner (6) Princess of Sylmar **$79.60 29.40 14.00**
Place (3) Beholder   9.00   5.60
Show (4) Unlimited Budget   3.80

$2 ex $727.00
$2 tri $3,460.80

ELEVENTH RACE
Churchill
May 3rd, 2013

1⅛ MILES. (1.471) STAKES. Purse \$1,000,000 *LONGINES KENTUCKY OAKS (GRADE I)* FILLIES, THREE YEARS OLD. By subscription of \$200 each on or before February 23, 2013 or \$1,500 each on or before Wednesday, April 10, 2013. A Supplemental Nomination of \$30,000 each may be made at time of entry. \$5,000 to pass the entry box; \$5,000 addit ional to start, with \$1,000,000 guaranteed. Weight: 121 lbs. (Cloudy 68)

Value of Race: \$1,000,000 Winner \$580,000; second \$190,000; third \$95,000; fourth \$47,500; fifth \$28,500; sixth \$10,000; seventh \$10,000; eighth \$10,000; ninth \$10,000; tenth \$10,000. Mutuel Pool \$4,786,114 Pick 3 Pool \$660,341 Pick 4 Pool \$1,331,616 Pick 5 Pool \$595,684 Pick 6 Pool \$503,880 Daily Double Pool \$380,360 Exacta Pool \$2,686,893 Superfecta Pool \$915,337 Super High Five Pool \$92,288 Trifecta Pool \$2,288,898

Last Raced	#	Horse	M/Eq.	A/S	Wt	PP	St	¼	½	¾	Str	Fin	Jockey	Odds \$1
06Apr13 ^{8}Aqu^{2}	6	Princess of Sylmar	L	3F	121	6	8	$9^{3\frac{1}{2}}$	$9^{6\frac{1}{2}}$	$4\frac{1}{2}$	$3\frac{1}{2}$	$1\frac{1}{2}$	Smith M E	38.80
06Apr13 ^{6}SA^{1}	3	Beholder	L	3F	121	3	9	2^{1}	2^{1}	$2\frac{1}{2}$	1^{2}	2^{2}	Gomez G K	9.00
30Mar13 ^{7}FG^{1}	4	Unlimited Budget	L	3F	121	4	2	3^{hd}	4^{2}	$3^{1\frac{1}{2}}$	$2\frac{1}{2}$	3^{hd}	Castellano J	4.40
30Mar13 ^{8}GP^{1}	8	Dreaming of Julia	L	3F	121	8	6	$8^{2\frac{1}{2}}$	$6\frac{1}{2}$	$7\frac{1}{2}$	$5^{4\frac{1}{2}}$	$4^{6\frac{1}{2}}$	Velazquez J R	1.50
24Mar13 ^{10}Sun^{1}	2	Midnight Lucky	L	3F	121	2	5	1^{1}	$1^{1\frac{1}{2}}$	$1\frac{1}{2}$	4^{2}	$5^{1\frac{1}{2}}$	Bejarano R	3.40
20Apr13 ^{9}Kee^{7}	7	Pure Fun	L	3F	121	7	7	10	10	10	8^{hd}	6^{nk}	Leparoux J R	20.20
06Apr13 ^{8}Aqu^{1}	11	Close Hatches	L	3F	121	10	4	$7^{2\frac{1}{2}}$	8^{1}	8^{1}	7^{1}	7^{nk}	Rosario J	7.70
10Apr13 ^{8}OP^{1}	9	Rose to Gold	L	3F	121	9	10	$6^{1\frac{1}{2}}$	$7\frac{1}{2}$	$9^{2\frac{1}{2}}$	$6^{1\frac{1}{2}}$	$8^{3\frac{3}{4}}$	Borel C H	15.90
30Mar13 ^{7}FG^{3}	5	Seaneen Girl	L	3F	121	5	1	5^{hd}	$5^{1\frac{1}{2}}$	6^{1}	$9^{5\frac{1}{2}}$	$9^{20\frac{1}{4}}$	Napravnik R	30.80
23Mar13 ^{9}TP^{1}	1	Silsita	L	3F	121	1	3	4^{2}	3^{hd}	5^{1}	10	10	Stevens G L	48.70

BEST LATE!

OFF AT 5:46 Start Poor For All. Won driving. Track Fast.
TIME :22^{4}, :46^{3}, 1:11^{1}, 1:36, 1:49 (:22.84, :46.79, 1:11.34, 1:36.11, 1:49.17)

\$2 Mutuel Prices:

6- PRINCESS OF SYLMAR	79.60	29.40	14.00
3- BEHOLDER		9.00	5.60
4- UNLIMITED BUDGET			3.80

\$2 EXACTA 6-3 PAID \$727.00 \$2 SUPERFECTA 6-3-4-8 PAID \$12,445.00
\$1 SUPER HIGH FIVE 6-3-4-8-2 PAID \$18,863.90 \$2 TRIFECTA 6-3-4 PAID \$3,470.80

Chestnut Filly, (Mar), by Majestic Warrior - Storm Dixie by Catienus. Trainer Pletcher A. Todd. Bred by Ed Stanco(PA).

PRINCESS OF SYLMAR was roughed up between horses at the start, settled off of the inside, advanced between horses after the opening half, continued the advance four wide through the second turn and wore down the leaders in the final yards. BEHOLDER was fractious in the post, unseated her jockey and was off her feet briefly, broke outwardly bumping UNLIMITED BUDGET at the start, recovered quickly and tracked the pace three wide, came to level terms with a quarter to run, shook clear and continued on well but was unable to resist the winner. UNLIMITED BUDGET was bumped at the start, pulled to contention four wide, loomed a danger entering the stretch but went evenly through the drive and was all out to hold the show. DREAMING OF JULIA was bumped between horses at the start, tucked in to save ground, was asked for run after a half, advanced reluctantly toward the inside, steadied near the seven-sixteenths pole, leveled back into stride on the second turn, worked her way to the outside with five-sixteenths to run, came six wide but was left with too much to do. MIDNIGHT LUCKY was away in good order, opened clear to dictate terms, was collared nearing the quarter pole, relinquished the lead entering the stretch, then continued to weaken in the drive. PURE FUN was jostled hard at the start, lagged well back, finished with a belated gain between horses but failed to threaten. CLOSE HATCHES was allowed to settle four wide, came five wide and made a mild improvement through the lane. ROSE TO GOLD broke inwardly and bumped DREAMING OF JULIA at the start, was straightened away and attended the pace four wide, came up empty before going six furlongs, steadied between horses as she was retreating near the three-eighths pole and showed little thereafter. SEANEEN GIRL settled off of the inside, moved up between horses on the second turn to make a mild bid but failed to sustain the drive. SILSITA was forwardly placed along the inside for six furlongs and stopped.

Owners- 6, King of Prussia Stable ; 3, Spendthrift Farm LLC ; 4, Repole Stable ; 8, Stonestreet Stables LLC ; 2, Watson, Karl, Pegram, Michael E. and Weitman, Paul ; 7, Magdalena Racing ; 11, Juddmonte Farms, Inc. ; 9, Amaya, Kathleen and Contofanti, Raffaele ; 5, Chowhan Naveed ; 1, Eclipse Thoroughbred Partners and Tanourin Stable

Trainers- 6, Pletcher Todd A.; 3, Mandella Richard E.; 4, Pletcher Todd A.; 8, Pletcher Todd A.; 2, Baffert Bob ; 7, McPeek Kenneth G.; 11, Mott William I.; 9, Santoro Sal ; 5, Flint Bernard S.; 1, Pletcher Todd A.

Breeders- 6, Ed Stanco (PA); 3, Clarkland Farm (KY); 4, Ocala Stud (FL); 8, Stonestreet Thoroughbred Holdings LLC (KY); 2, C. Kidder & J.K. & Linda Griggs (KY); 7, Royal Oak Farm, LLC (KY); 11, Millsec, LTD. (KY); 9, Joe Mulholland Sr., Joe Mulholland Jr.,John Mulholland & Karen Mulholland (KY); 5, John Trumbulovic (KY); 1, Tanourin Stable (FL)

Scratched- Flashy Gray(30Mar13 ^{7}FG^{4})

Winner - 6 - #2 FHH Contender, Best Late.

COPYRIGHT 2013 BLOODSTOCK RESEARCH INFORMATION SERVICES

IN THE LAND OF LONG SHOT HUNTERS, PATIENCE IS KING

FHH TABS 5 BAGGER IN 9TH AT ARLINGTON ON 6/2/2013!!

The race was a $7,500 starter allowance with a purse of $14,000 at 5 1/2 furlongs on the turf for fillies and mares three years old and upward which had started for a claiming price of $7,500 or less since June 2, 2011. You can see from the race conditions that there is some room for some monkey business here – even though it's legal.

Screen presented:

CONTENDER TELL POINTS

3= 11
9= 9
2= 7
4= 4
10= 4

BEST IN CATEGORY

Work= 3   4 fur :47
Start= 9   101
Mid= 9   107
Late= 1A   92

As the 9 was **double confirmed** with odds of 9/1, the system play was to bet the 9 to win and twice as much to place, then to run the

9 up and back with the screen horses in exactas, trifectas, supers, and the super high five.

Race comes 9, 4, 10, 3, 2
Winner (9) $21.60 8.60 7.00
Place (4)   6.20 4.20
Show (10)   5.20

$2 ex $123.00
$2 tri $560.00
$2 super $1,518.40

No one had the super high five so it paid an all on the bottom for $1,846.00

Using the five "tell point" numbers of the FHH program would have hit the super high five, wiping out the entire pool of $196,986.22 – a life-changing win by any measure!

I know…woulda, coulda, shoulda…and…if only.

FHH NAILS PREAKNESS: WINNER $32.50;
COLD STRAIGHT EXACTA $301.40!!

The probable winner of the 2013 Preakness was preordained by all of the usual chalk chasers. Hadn't Orb won the sloppy Derby after four straight wins? Who could possibly beat him? So the crowd bit and hammered the expert's pick down to odds on. The only problem was that his numbers didn't back up his win: his FHH late pace

IN THE LAND OF LONG SHOT HUNTERS, PATIENCE IS KING

NINTH RACE
Arlington
June 2nd, 2013

5½ FURLONGS. (1.03) (Off The Turf) STARTER ALLOWANCE. Purse $14,000 FOR FILLIES AND MARES THREE YEARS OLD AND UPWARD WHICH HAVE STARTED FOR A CLAIMING PRICE OF $7,500 OR LESS SINCE JUNE 2, 2011. Three Year Olds, 120 lbs.; Older, 124 lbs. Non-winners of a race since May 2 Allowed 2 lbs. (Races where entered for $5,000 or less not considered). Lane 5. (If the management considers it inadvisable to run this race on the Turf Course, it will be run on the main track at Five and One Half Furlongs). (Cloudy 57)

Value of Race: $15,960 ($5,684 reverts) Winner $8,400; second $3,920; third $2,240; fourth $700; fifth $420; sixth $140; seventh $140.
Mutuel Pool $107,463 Pick 3 Pool $12,891 Pick 4 Pool $23,603 Pick 5 Pool $12,195 Pick 6 Pool $8,944 Pick 9 Jackpot Pool $8,940
Daily Double Pool $12,899 Exacta Pool $86,252 Jackpot High-5 Pool $36,783 Superfecta Pool $36,893 Trifecta Pool $38,945

Last Raced	#	Horse	M/Eqt.	A/S	Wt	PP	St	¼	½	Str	Fin	Jockey	Odds $1
18May13 ⁶FP¹	9	Special Chance	L b	4F	122	6	2	1³	1²½	1³	1¹	Graham J	9.60
15May13 ²AP²	4	Fleet Encounter	L b	4F	117	3	7	6½	6²½	3ʰᵈ	2²½	Esquivel E	4.90
18May13 ⁴FP⁷	10	Cyberphobe	L b	5M	122	7	3	3¹	2¹	2²	3¹½	Castro E	6.30
02May13 ⁴CD²	3	Brezing Rain	L b	7M	122	2	5	5²	4¹	5³½	4¹½	Desormeaux K J	0.90
08May13 ²AP⁶	2	Thundering Hoofs	L b	4F	122	1	4	4²	3¹	4½	5⁴½	Thornton T	3.80
12May13 ⁵AP⁶	5	Rainy Rain	L bf	5M	122	4	1	2ʰᵈ	5½	6⁶	6¹⁹	Baird E T	20.30
12May13 ⁵AP⁵	7	Stivers Suprise	L	7M	122	5	6	7	7	7	7	Lantz J A	22.30

OFF AT 5:13 Start Good For All But FLEET ENCOUNTER. Won driving. Track Fast.
TIME :22⁰, :46¹, :58², 1:05 (:22.09, :46.26, :58.59, 1:05.08)

$2 Mutuel Prices:
9 - SPECIAL CHANCE 21.60 8.20 7.00
4 - FLEET ENCOUNTER 6.20 4.20
10 - CYBERPHOBE 5.20

$2 EXACTA 9-4 PAID $123.00 $1 JACKPOT HIGH-5 9-4-10-3-2 PAID $923.10 Carryover Pool $196,986
SUPERFECTA 9-4-10-3 PAID $75.92   TRIFECTA 9-4-10 PAID $140.00

Dark Bay or Brown Filly, (Na), by Eurosilver - Free the Magic by Cryptoclearance. Trainer Martin Dawn. Bred by Gainesway Thoroughbreds Ltd.(KY).

SPECIAL CHANCE sped clear of her rivals soon after the break, angled to the inside once establishing the advantage and held sway on a comfortable margin to late stages under firm encouragement. FLEET ENCOUNTER broke awkwardly, tracked the leaders along the inside behind the second flight, came through close turn near the inside midway through the turn, then shifted off the inside four wide racing into the gap on the winner late. CYBERPHOBE tracked the pacesetters three deep in second flight racing into the turn and continued evenly in that path into the stretch to prevail for a share. BREZING RAIN tracked off the second flight a bit off the inside early, shifted four wide racing into the stretch but offered no rally. THUNDERING HOOFS tracked the pace inside foes in the second flight to the turn but steadily faded nearing upper stretch. RAINY RAIN flashed brief pace between foes pursuing the winner but emptied out nearing upper stretch. STIVERS SUPRISE dropped out of contention early.

Owners- 9, Martin Dawn ; 4, Magana Cheryl ; 10, J B Stables, Inc. ; 3, Choctaw Racing Stable ; 2, Bahena, Fernando and Rodriguez, Jose G. ; 5, Peacock Stable ; 7, Derlacki Deborah
Trainers- 9, Martin Dawn ; 4, Brueggemann Roger A.; 10, Manley Steve ; 3, Whiting Lynn S.; 2, Lindsay Ricky ; 5, Zavash Kerry ; 7, McEwen Billy J.
Breeders- 9, Gainesway Thoroughbreds Ltd. (KY); 4, Barr Three LLC (IL); 10, J. B. Stables Inc. (IL); 3, Barbara Hunter (KY); 2, Hans Poetsch & Pat Greco (IL); 5, Sherry A. Young & Ronald D Young (KY); 7, Moises Yanez (IL)
Scratched - Lucky Gal(11May13 ¹⁰AP¹⁰), Candyonmymind(12May13 ⁵AP³), Wild Oration(12May13 ⁵AP³), Tsunami Salli(15May13 ⁵AP⁶), Cross Eyed Mary(12May13 ⁵AP⁴), Sharp Trip(17May13 ⁵AP²)

$2 Daily Double (6-9) Paid $61.00; Daily Double Pool $12,899.
$1 Pick Three (6-1/6-9) Paid $225.20; Pick Three Pool $12,891.
PICK 4 8-6-1/6-9 PAID $975.10
6-1/6-9 PAID $10,365.70 $1 Pick Six (1/2/4/6/8-3-8-6-1/6-9) 4 Correct Paid $19.20; Pick Six Pool $9,944; Carryover Po
PICK 9 JACKPOT 2-6-1-1/2/4/6/8-3-8-6-1/6-9 PAID $949.83 6 Correct Carryover Pool $35,618

FHH Screen: 3, 9, 2, 4, 10 Would have hit High Five!

COPYRIGHT 2013 BLOODSTOCK RESEARCH INFORMATION SERVICES

of 91 was slow for a graded stake. It was not so much that he put in a furious close, as it was that the field was coming back to him. The Preakness would be run on a fast track.

Screen presented:

CONTENDER TELL POINTS
6=6
9=6
1=5
2=5
8=5

BEST IN CATEGORY

Works= 1	4 fur :47
Start= 2	103
Mid= 6	130
Late= 4	107

The 130 Mid Pace number earned by Oxbow is the highest recorded since the FHH program entered the market in May of 2011. It was a monster number and was all the more remarkable because it was earned in the Derby.

The system bet was to win and twice as much to place on the 6, then to run him up and back with the screen horses in exactas, then to run the 9, Itsmyluckyday, up and back in exactas. The tri bet was to put the top two contenders, Oxbow and Itsmyluckyday, over the rest of the entire field in a 6, 9 with 6, 9 with all trifecta bet, then to do as many dime supers as affordable using 6, 9 with 6, 9 with all with all.

Race comes 6, 9, 5, 1

Winner (6)	**$32.50 12.00 6.80**
Place (9)	**7.80 5.00**
Show (5)	**5.20**

$2 ex $301.40
$2 tri $2,061.60
$2 super $3,635.60

The Late Pace number of 114 earned by Oxbow in the Preakness would carry the horse into the Belmont with the highest late pace number of the field. Amazingly, Oxbow would leave the gate in the Belmont at extremely generous odds of 10/1.

FHH NAILS BELMONT: WINNER $29.60; EXACTA $323.50!!

Most of the professional prognosticators and self-styled "experts" fell all over themselves in their praise of Orb, notwithstanding his pedestrian performance in the Preakness for which the horse had no obvious excuse. "Yes, indeed," they all agreed – the track announcer and morning line setter; Mike Battaglia; Jerry Bailey and anyone else they put a microphone in front of – Orb, of course, was the horse. Together, they led the credulous bettors down the primrose path, making the chosen one the favorite at 2/1.

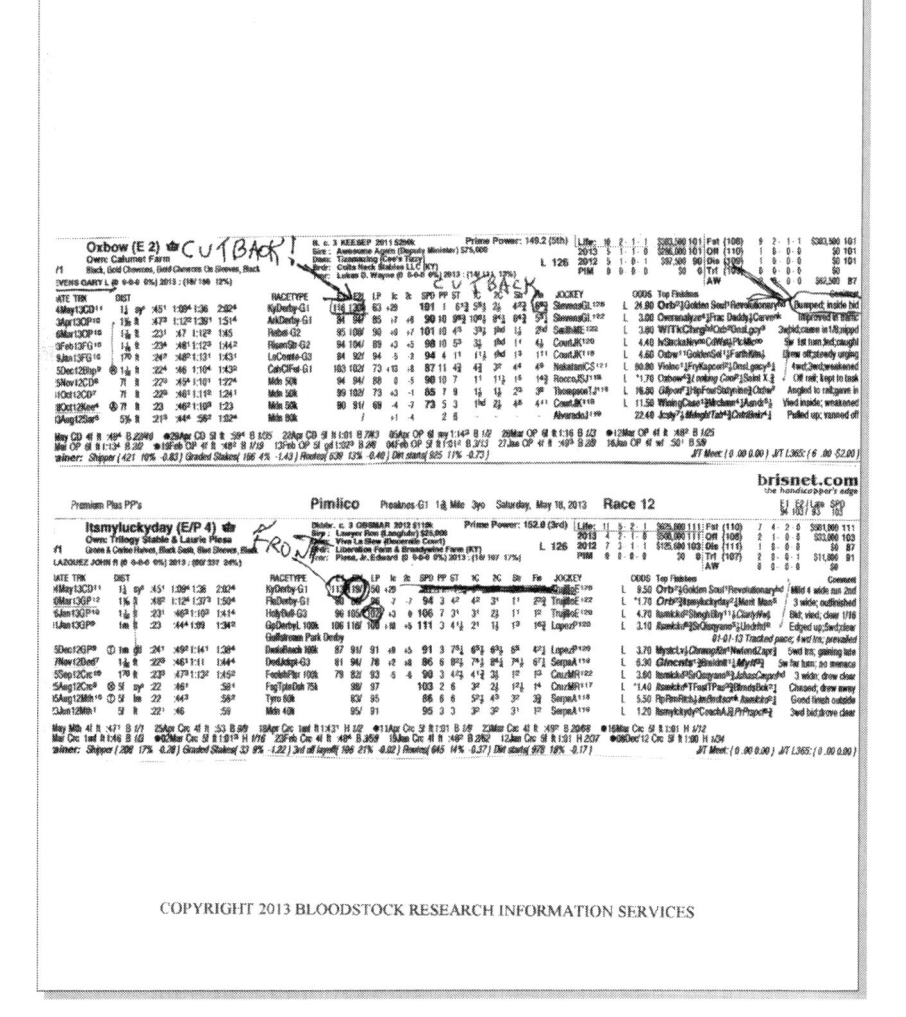

170 RUNNING A HOLE IN THE WIND: HIDDEN HORSES FOUND

TWELVETH RACE
Pimlico
May 18th, 2013

$1\frac{3}{16}$ MILES. (1.52) STAKES. Purse $1,000,000 *PREAKNESS S. (GRADE I)* FOR THREE-YEAR-OLDS, $10,000 TO PASS THE ENTRY BOX, STARTERS TO PAY $10,000 ADDITIONAL. 60% of the purse to the winner, 20% to second, 11% to third, 6% to fourth and 3% to fifth. Weight 126 pounds for Colts and Geldings. A replica of the Woodlawn Vase wil l be presented to the winning owner to remain his or her personal property. (Clear 65)

Value of Race: $1,000,000 Winner $600,000; second $200,000; third $110,000; fourth $60,000; fifth $30,000. Mutuel Pool $18,558,264 Pick 3 Pool $743,541 Pick 4 Pool $2,097,906 Pick 5 Jackpot Pool $874,838 Daily Double Pool $654,563 Daily Double Pool $695,657 Exacta Pool $11,434,368 Superfecta Pool $6,165,862 Super High Five Pool $346,821 Trifecta Pool $12,575,537

Last Raced	#	Horse	M/Eqt.	A/S	Wt	PP	St	¼	½	¾	Str	Fin	Jockey	Odds $1
04May13 $^{11}CD^{6}$	6	Oxbow	L	3C	126	6	3	$1^{1\frac{1}{2}}$	1^{2}	$1^{1\frac{1}{2}}$	1^{3}	$1^{1\frac{3}{4}}$	Stevens G L	15.40
04May13 $^{11}CD^{15}$	9	Itsmyluckyday	L	3C	126	9	5	4^{1}	4^{hd}	3^{hd}	$2^{2\frac{1}{2}}$	$2^{\frac{3}{4}}$	Velazquez J R	8.50
04May13 $^{11}CD^{5}$	5	Mylute	L	3C	126	5	9	9	9	8^{3}	3^{1}	$3^{5\frac{3}{4}}$	Napravnik R	10.90
04May13 $^{11}CD^{1}$	1	Orb	L	3C	126	1	6	$6^{1\frac{1}{2}}$	$5^{\frac{1}{2}}$	$7^{\frac{1}{2}}$	$6^{4\frac{1}{2}}$	$4^{\frac{1}{2}}$	Rosario J	0.70
04May13 $^{11}CD^{17}$	2	Goldencents	LA	3C	126	2	1	$2^{2\frac{1}{2}}$	$2^{3\frac{1}{2}}$	2^{1}	4^{hd}	$5^{\frac{1}{2}}$	Krigger K	9.50
20Apr13 $^{8}Haw^{1}$	4	Departing	L	3G	126	4	4	5^{hd}	$6^{2\frac{1}{2}}$	5^{2}	$5^{2\frac{1}{2}}$	6^{6}	Hernandez, Jr. B J	10.20
04May13 $^{11}CD^{8}$	7	Will Take Charge	L b	3C	126	7	7	$8^{2\frac{1}{2}}$	$8^{\frac{1}{2}}$	9	7^{8}	7^{16}	Smith M E	11.10
24Mar13 $^{11}Sun^{1}$	8	Govenor Charlie	L b	3C	126	8	8	7^{hd}	7^{hd}	6^{hd}	8^{2}	$8^{15\frac{1}{4}}$	Garcia M	9.40
27Apr13 $^{10}CD^{4}$	3	Titletown Five	L	3C	126	3	2	$3^{1\frac{1}{2}}$	3^{hd}	$4^{\frac{1}{2}}$	9	9	Leparoux J R	22.30

OFF AT 6:20 Start Good. Won driving. Track Fast.
TIME :23⁴, :48³, 1:13¹, 1:38, 1:57² (:23.94, :48.60, 1:13.26, 1:38.14, 1:57.54)

$2 Mutuel Prices:

6- OXBOW	32.80	12.00	6.80
9- ITSMYLUCKYDAY		7.80	5.00
5- MYLUTE			5.20

$2 EXACTA 6-9 PAID $301.40 $1 SUPERFECTA 6-9-5-1 PAID $1,817.80
$2 SUPER HIGH FIVE 6-9-5-1-2 PAID $32,187.80 $2 TRIFECTA 6-9-5 PAID $2,061.60

Bay Colt, (Mar), by Awesome Again - Tizamazing by Cee's Tizzy. Trainer Lukas Wayne D.. Bred by Colts Neck Stables LLC(KY).

OXBOW was brushed by WILL TAKE CHARGE leaving the gate, quickly recovered and cruised past GOLDENCENTS in the opening furlong, opened a daylight advantage under the wire the first time, remained off the inside while nicely rated down the backstretch, came under some hand urging leaving the five sixteenths marker, entered the lane four wide, responded when put to a strong drive leaving the three sixteenths marker and held firm to the wire. ITSMYLUCKYDAY, four wide around the first turn, edged closer within himself nearing the far turn, came six wide for the drive, made a menacing run leaving the eighth pole but flattened out a bit late while saving the place. MYLUTE was lightly steadied back at the break then was unhurried while saving ground, angled off the rail with seven furlongs remaining, picked up momentum four wide between rivals leaving the far turn, altered out seven wide straightening for the wire and steadily closed the gap. ORB bobbled inward at the break, recovered and moved up to be within range while saving ground around the first turn, eased off the inside and quickly reached a striking position between foes five furlongs out, dropped back a bit on his own entering the far turn, moved to the rail soon after, gave chase into the lane, angled out past the three sixteenths marker and finished with some interest between rivals. GOLDENCENTS, away quickest, was content to allow the winner to clear, was taken outside that one to stalk the pace, came under a ride chasing past the five sixteenths marker, continued willingly five wide to upper stretch then gave way through the final furlong. DEPARTING, three wide advancing to a stalking position past the five eighths pole, angled in and gave hard chase two wide inside rivals after seven furlongs, came three wide for the drive, failed to sustain his run and gave way through the late stages. WILL TAKE CHARGE broke inward brushing with the winner, settled off the pace, raced towards the inside past the five furlong marker but had no response. GOVENOR CHARLIE was rated back soon after the break, lost ground five wide, made a slight move near the half mile marker then had nothing from there. TITLETOWN FIVE saved ground stalking the early pace, was under strong hand urging past the five furlong pole, remained in contention to the far turn, faltered then was eased through the final three sixteenths of a mile.

Owners- 6, Calumet Farm ; 9, Trilogy Stable and Plesa, Laurie ; 5, GoldMark Farm, LLC and Whisper Hill Farm ; 1, Janney, III, Stuart S. and Phipps Stable ; 2, W. C. Racing, Kenney, Dave and RAP Racing ; 4, Claiborne Farm and Dilschneider, Adele B. ; 7, Horton Willis D ; 8, Watson, Karl, Pegram, Michael E. and Weitman, Paul ; 3, Hornung, P., Martin, E., Lukas, D., Davis, W., Miller, D. and Shade, M.

Trainers- 6, Lukas D. Wayne; 9, Plesa, Jr. Edward ; 5, Amoss Thomas M.; 1, McGaughey III Claude R.; 2, O'Neill Doug F.; 4, Stall, Jr. Albert M.; 7, Lukas D. Wayne; 8, Baffert Bob ; 3, Lukas D. Wayne

Breeders- 6, Colts Neck Stables LLC (KY); 9, Liberation Farm & Brandywine Farm (KY); 5, Mike G. Rutherford (KY); 1, Stuart S. Janney, III LLC. & PhippsStable (KY); 2, Rosecrest Farm & Karyn Pirrello (KY); 4, Claiborne Farm & Adele B. Dilschneider (KY); 7, Eaton (KY); 8, Michael E. Pegram (KY); 3, Stonestreet Thoroughbred Holdings LLC (KY)

$2 Daily Double (10-6) Paid $557.40; Daily Double Pool $654,563.
$2 Daily Double (SPECIAL/PREAKNESS 7-6) Paid $100.80; Daily Double Pool $695,657.
PICK 3 6/7/10-10-6 PAID $676.50 PICK 4 3-6/7/10-10-6 PAID $4,883.05
PICK 5 JACKPOT 1/2/6-3-6/7/10-10-6 PAID $16,686.65

Winner - 6 - FHH #1 Contender tied. Monster Mid-Pace of 130.
Place -9 - FHH #1 Contender tied.

COPYRIGHT 2013 BLOODSTOCK RESEARCH INFORMATION SERVICES

For the Belmont, the (corrected)FHH screen presented:

CONTENDER TELL POINTS

7= 7
11= 7
12= 6
8= 4
13= 4

BEST IN CATEGORY

Works= 11   5 fur :59
Start= 12   121
Mid=   7   130
Late=   7   114

The system bet was win and twice as much to place on the 7, 11, 12 (due to the odds being 10/1, 26/1, and 13/1, there would be a nice profit if just one of the three won or placed), then to box the 7, 11, 12 in exactas; then to put the 7, 11, 12 over the 7, 11, 12 over all in trifectas; finally, to do as many dime supers as affordable using the 7, 11, 12 over the 7, 11, 12 over all over all.

Race comes 12, 7, 5, 6
(The 11, Vyjack, lost all chance after being repeatedly muscled by the 10, shortly after the start.)

Winner (12) Palace Malice   **$29.60 11.20 6.70**
Place (7) Oxbow   9.90 6.10
Show (5) Orb   3.90

$2 ex $323.50
$2 tri $931.00
Dime Super $1,030.10

It was obvious which horse the insiders wanted to win when, a third of the way into the stretch, the hyperventilating announcer shouted: "And like a blue zephyr on the outside, here comes ORB!!!" It's a wonder the announcer's lungs didn't burst. Not to worry the hidden horse hunters, as Orb didn't have much left by the time he reached third.

It was puzzling that the morning line setter set Oxbow's line at 10/1 after his dazzling and easy Preakness win. Did he or she think that horse's win was a fluke, or that he couldn't get the distance? (Oxbow was sired by a Deputy Minister stallion and was out of a dam by Cee's Tizzy.) Palace Malice's lineage was equally stellar for the winner was by Curlin and out of a Royal Anthem dam; breeding suggesting the horse could run all day, not withstanding his shortening stride in the stretch in the Derby.

Who can fathom what goes on in the dusty minds of morning line setters. They are, nevertheless, the unwitting best friends of hidden horse hunters.

COPYRIGHT 2013 BLOODSTOCK RESEARCH INFORMATION SERVICES

IN THE LAND OF LONG SHOT HUNTERS, PATIENCE IS KING

ELEVENTH RACE
Belmont Park
June 8th, 2013

1½ MILES. (2.24) STAKES. Purse $1,000,000 BELMONT S. (GRADE I) FOR THREE YEAR OLDS. By subscription of $600 each, to accompany the nomination, if made on or before January 26, 2013, or $6,000, if made on or before March 23, 2013. At any time prior to the closing time of entries, horses may be nominated to The Belmont Stakes upon payment of a supplementary fee of $100,000 to the New York Racing Association, Inc. $10,000 to pass the entry box and $10,000 additional to start. All entrants will be required to pay entry and starting fees; but no fees, supplemental or otherwise shall be added to the purse. The purse to be divided 60% to the winner, 20% to second, 11% to third, 6% to fourth and 3% to fifth. Colts and Geldings, 126 lbs.; Fillies, 121 lbs. The winning owner will be presented with the August Belmont Memorial Cup to be retained for one year as well as a trophy for permanent possession and trophies to the winning trainer and jockey. (Clear 72)

Value of Race: $1,000,000 Winner $600,000; second $200,000; third $110,000; fourth $60,000; fifth $30,000. Mutuel Pool $18,123,913 Pick 3 Pool $678,185 Pick 4 Pool $2,918,807 Pick 6 Pool $1,203,178 Daily Double Pool $806,242 Daily Double Pool $755,681 Exacta Pool $10,951,504 Superfecta Pool $3,778,589 Trifecta Pool $11,410,596

[past performance chart of the Belmont Stakes with handwritten annotations "BEST START", "BEST IN L.A., BEST LATE"]

Winner: PALACE MALICE, Bay Colt, by Curlin - Palace Rumor by Royal Anthem. Trainer Pletcher A. Todd. Bred by W. S. Farish (KY).

$2 Mutuel Prices: 12 – PALACE MALICE 29.60 11.20 6.70 / 7 – OXBOW 9.90 6.10 / 5 – ORB 3.90

$2 EXACTA 12-7 PAID $323.50 $2 SUPERFECTA 12-7-5-6 PAID $20,602.00
$2 TRIFECTA 12-7-5 PAID $931.00

FHH NAILS $125.60 MOUNTAINEER WINNER; $601 EX; $7,427.60 TRI 6/11/2013!!

Go tell it on the Mountain; the track at which form seldom holds, probably because of so many lower class claiming races. Such a track is a fertile forest in which to go hunting for double digit payoffs for finding a hidden horse.

The 9th race on 6/11/2013 was a 5k claimer at 6 furlongs for three year olds which had not won a race since 6/11/2012.

Screen presented:

TELL POINT CONTENDERS
4= 6
6= 5
9= 5
10= 5

BEST IN CATEGORY

Work=0
Start= 4   98
Mid= 4   94
Late= 1   100

The key horse was the 4 as the #1 contender, double confirmed with Best Start and Best Mid Pace. The 2 long shots were the 9 and 10. The system bet was to run the 4 up and back with the screen horses in exactas and trifectas. The long shot bets were win and twice as much to place on both the 9 and 10 as the public was letting the 9 and 10 leave the gate at odds of 61/1 and 36/1, respectively.

Race comes 9, 4, 10, 3

Winner (9) Speedy Tuxedo **$125.60 42.40 26.00**
Place (4) Irish Gentleman   3.40 3.00
Show (10) B L's Land Shark   23.40

$2 exacta $601.00
$2 tri $7,427.60

Anytime you see these kinds of odds on one or more of the system's top four contenders and ties, give those horses a second look because the FHH software has identified tells that the morning line setters have overlooked or failed to consider by their usual cursory review of the past performances form.

Every so often – not nearly often enough – a race comes along in which special circumstances arise that drops into the laps of hidden horse hunters a golden opportunity for a big hit – the punter's version of a home run. Such a race was the 1st at Belmont Park on 6/15/2013; a race at 1 1/16 miles on the turf for 20k claimers three and up non-winners of two.

RUNNING A HOLE IN THE WIND: HIDDEN HORSES FOUND

NINTH RACE — Mountaineer Casino — June 11th, 2013

6 FURLONGS. (1.074) CLAIMING. Purse $8,700 FOR THREE YEAR OLDS AND UPWARD WHICH HAVE NOT WON A RACE SINCE JUNE 11, 2012. Three Year Olds, 121 lbs.; Older, 123 lbs. Claiming Price $5,000. (Clear 68)

Value of Race: $8,700 Winner $5,046; second $1,740; third $870; fourth $435; fifth $174; sixth $87; seventh $87; eighth $87; ninth $87; tenth $87. Mutuel Pool $42,316 Pick 6 Pool $2,504 Daily Double Pool $16,983 Perfecta Pool $48,480 Superfecta Pool $18,785 Trifecta Pool $39,564 Z-5 Super Hi-5 Pool $4,435

Last Raced	#	Horse	M/Eqt.	A/S	Wt	PP	St	¼	½	Str	Fin	Jockey	Cl'g Pr	Odds $1
24May13 9Mnr⁵	9	Speedy Tuxedo	L bf	7G	123	9	8	5¹	3³	2¹	1²¹	Figueroa S	5000	61.80 ← FHH #2 CONTENDER
6May13 9Mnr⁴	4	Irish Gentleman	L A f	10G	123	4	3	3²	2¹	1½	2¹¾	Bracho A	5000	1.30
24May13 9Mnr⁴	10	B L's Sand Shark	L A bf	7G	123	10	2	1¹	1½	3²	3hd	Whitacre B	5000	36.70
20May13 9Mnr⁶	3	Granite City	L A b	5H	123	3	10	8⁵	8¹⁴	5¹	4nk	Pilares C P	5000	4.70
25May13 4Mnr²	5	I'vegottabeme	L A f	9G	123	5	4	4½	6hd	4¹	5½	Ccamaque M A	5000	5.40
30Apr13 4Mnr²	7	The Big Highroller	L b	7G	123	7	5	7¹½	7½	6¹	6²¹	Oro E	5000	7.40
04May13 9Mnr⁹	2	Midnight Chase	L A b	7G	123	2	9	10	9¹²	8²	7¹	Rodriguez, Jr. L	5000	95.30
17May13 1Mnr⁴	8	A. P. Sierra	L A	5G	123	8	1	2⁰	4¹	7¹	8⁴	Hollingsworth B L	5000	33.80
24May13 9Mnr²	1	One Vote	L	7G	123	1	7	9³	10	16	9hd	Rosario, Jr. H L	5000	3.80
27Nov12 5Mnr⁵	6	Slow Nick C	L b	6G	123	6	6	6½	5¹	9³	10	Hernandez L	5000	16.70

OFF AT 10:21 Start Good. Won driving. Track Good.
TIME :22², :47, 1:00¹, 1:13⁴ (:22.49, :47.13, 1:00.30, 1:13.94)

$2 Mutuel Prices:
9 - SPEEDY TUXEDO 125.60 26.00
4 - IRISH GENTLEMAN 3.40 3.00
10 - B L'S SAND SHARK 23.40

$2 PERFECTA 9-4 PAID $601.00 $2 SUPERFECTA 9-4-10-3 PAID $56,326.20
$2 TRIFECTA 9-4-10 PAID $7,427.60 $1 Z-5 SUPER HI-5 9-4-10-ALL-ALL PAID $3,324.60

Dark Bay or Brown Gelding, (My), by Black Tie Affair (IRE) - Misty Linda by Norquester. Trainer Demczyk Virginia. Bred by Jason C Taylor (WV).

SPEEDY TUXEDO rushed up four wide on the turn, dueled abreast IRISH GENTLEMAN a sixteenth out angling in to tighten for going clear late. IRISH GENTLEMAN chased the pace wresting the lead into upper stretch, digging in from the three path dueled late steadying briefly in somewhat close quarters near the wire. B L'S SAND SHARK broke sharply setting the pace through the turn, ceded inside of rivals in upper stretch hanging on late to salvage third. GRANITE CITY away slowly saved ground to upper stretch gaining late position along the inside. I'VEGOTTABEME raced evenly in mid pack angled five wide in upper stretch lacking late surge. THE BIG HIGHROLLER a step slow early played no factor. MIDNIGHT CHASE was never involved. A. P. SIERRA chased the pace through the turn then give way in upper stretch. ONE VOTE was always outrun. SLOW NICK C raced mid pack folding to upper stretch. An objection from the rider of IRISH GENTLEMAN against the rider of SPEEDY TUXEDO for interference near the wire was disallowed by the stewards.

Owners- 9, Truman Robert W.; 4, Zook Jeff W.; 10, Four Aces Racing Stable; 3, Cline Austin; 5, Lopez Jose A; 7, Buskey, III Bob E.; 2, Silty Goose Racing Stable; 8, Just For Fun Stable, LLC and Crago, Terry; 1, Sipp Burton K.; 6, Bayley Perry H.

Trainers- 9, Demczyk Virginia; 4, Zook Donna S.; 10, Koenigsberg Mark A.; 3, Cline Berl; 5, Lopez Jose A; 7, Buskey, III Bob E.; 2, Zook Donna S.; 8, Crago Terry J.; 1, Sipp Burton K.; 6, Bayley Perry H.

Breeders- 9, Jason C Taylor (WV); 4, Catesby W. Clay (KY); 10, Four Aces Racing Stable (FL); 3, Mr. & Mrs. Michael Brickman (IL); 5, Peter Fuller (MD); 7, Lois Hawkins & Jim Hawkins (KY); 2, Ocean View Stables (NJ); 6, Just For Fun Stables (FL); 1, Palisair Place (CA); 6, William F. Outland (FL)

$2 Daily Double (9-9) Paid $156.60; Daily Double Pool $16,983.
$2 Pick Six (1-4-1-7-7/9-9) 5 Correct Paid $2,815.20; Pick Six Pool $2,504; Carryover Pool $1,368.

Winner - 9 - FHH #2 contender tied

COPYRIGHT 2013 BLOODSTOCK RESEARCH INFORMATION SERVICES

Screen presented:

TELL POINT CONTENDERS

11=6
1= 5
6= 4
2= 3
4= 3
9= 3
10=3

BEST IN CATEGORY

Work=0
Start= 4   92
Mid= 11   92
Late= 2   110

The long shots among the point contenders were the 1 at 17/1; the 6 at 27/1; the 9 at 15/1. Going inside the numbers of the FHH screen, it was plain to see that the 6 and 9 had better numbers than the 1 for the 6 had the 3rd Best Start (only two points off the Best), and the 2nd Best Mid Pace (only 1 point off the best).

When I checked the Weight Off variable, I doubted what the screen was showing on the 9 — an amazing 32 pounds lighter than the horse's last race. How could that be? Looking at the pps, I saw that the horse had been running steeplechase races, carrying no less than 154 pounds in his last four races at over 2 miles. Manacar must have thought he had little more than a feather on his back; how the crowd let him leave the gate at 14.5/1 escapes me. The 5 was a very late scratch; without which the 6 would not have drawn into the system's top contender's list.

The system play was win and twice as much to place on the 6 and 9, then to run both up and back in exactas with the screen horses, then to bet trifecta partial wheels using the 6, 9 with 6, 9 with all; then to do as many supers as affordable using the 6, 9 with 6, 9 with the screen horses 1, 2, 4, 10, 11 with all.

Race comes 6, 9, 11, 10

Winner (6) Suilleabhain **$55.50 26.20 16.40**
Place (9) Manacar   15.50 11.20
Show (11) Mr Algebra   6.30
Fourth (10) El Coriente

$2 ex $853.00
$2 tri $5,567.00
Dime Super $774.10

FHH TABS $74.60 WINNER; 406.50 EX BY BOXING
TOP 2 SYSTEM CONTENDERS

At the sprint distances, weight seldom makes a difference, but in turf route races weight frequently makes a difference; 32 pounds made a huge difference, paying a nice $15.50 to place.

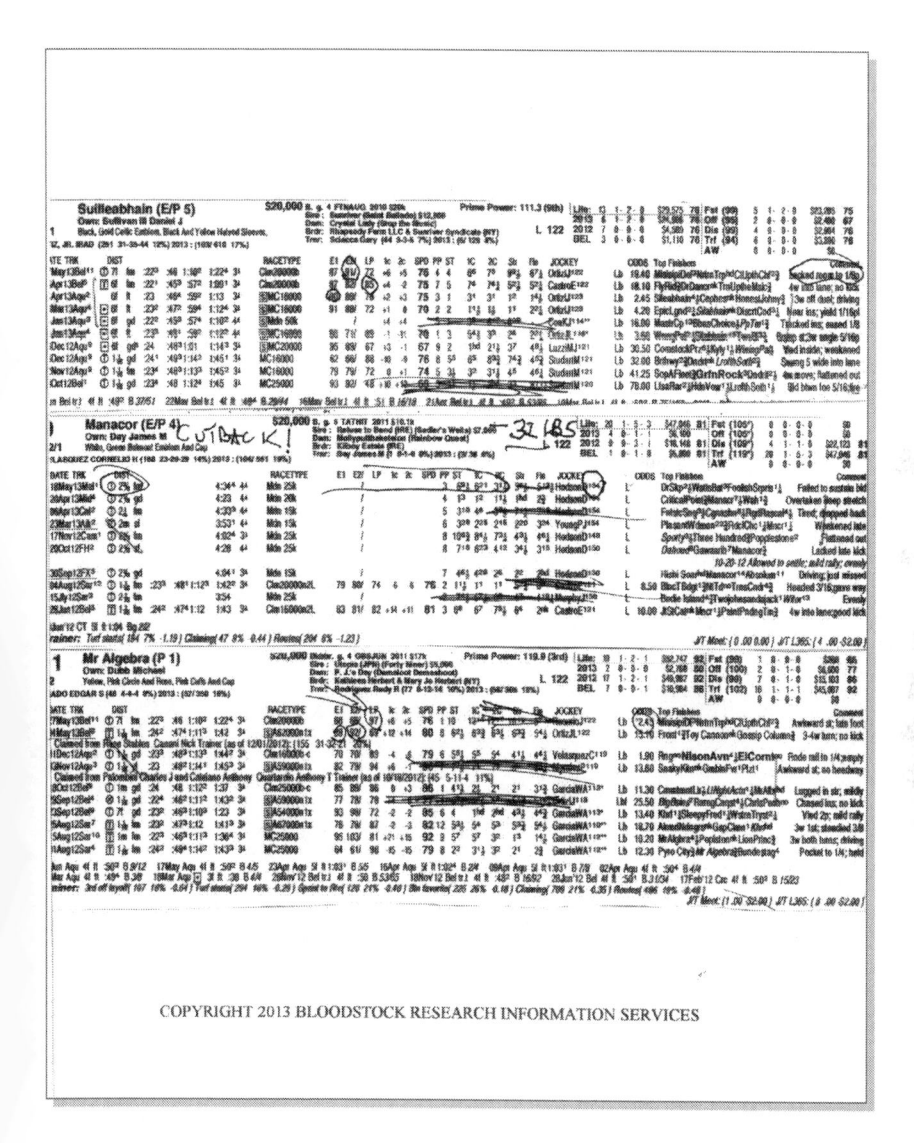

IN THE LAND OF LONG SHOT HUNTERS, PATIENCE IS KING

COPYRIGHT 2013 BLOODSTOCK RESEARCH INFORMATION SERVICES

FIRST RACE
Belmont Park
June 15th, 2013

1 1/16 MILES. (Inner Turf) (1.39^{1}) CLAIMING. Purse $31,000 INNER TURF FOR THREE YEAR OLDS AND UPWARD WHICH HAVE NEVER WON TWO RACES OR THREE YEAR OLDS. Three Year Olds, 119 lbs.; Older, 124 lbs. Non-winners Of A Race At A Mile Or Over On The Turf Since April 15 Allowed 2 lbs. Claiming Price $20,000 (Races where entered for $16,000 or less not considered) (Winners Preferred). (Clear 78)

Value of Race: $31,000 Winner $18,600; second $6,200; third $3,100; fourth $1,550; fifth $930; sixth $155; seventh $155; eighth $155; ninth $155. Mutuel Pool $278,599 Exacta Pool $279,446 Superfecta Pool $93,291 Trifecta Pool $117,363

Last Raced	#	Horse	M/Eqt.	A/S	Wt	PP	St	¼	½	¾	Str	Fin	Jockey	Cl'g Pr	Odds $1
27May13 ^{11}Bel^{6}	6	Suilleabhain	L b	4G	122	5	3	6^{2}	7^{1}	$6^{1\frac{1}{2}}$	$4^{2\frac{1}{2}}$	$1^{2\frac{1}{2}}$	Ortiz, Jr. I	20000	26.75
[illegible]May13 ^{1}Mal^{5}	9	Manacor (IRE)	L	5G	122	8	4	5^{hd}	$5^{1\frac{1}{2}}$	5^{1}	2^{hd}	2no	Velasquez C H	20000	14.50
27May13 ^{11}Bel^{5}	11	Mr Algebra	L b	4G	122	10	8	$4^{1\frac{1}{2}}$	4^{1}	$4^{\frac{1}{2}}$	$3^{\frac{1}{2}}$	3^{1}	Prado E S	20000	4.90
02Jun13 ^{5}Bel^{2}	10	El Corriente	L f	6G	122	9	5	3^{2}	3^{3}	2^{hd}	1^{hd}	$4^{3\frac{1}{4}}$	Castellano J	20000	1.40
19May13 ^{4}Bel^{4}	7	Chardsey	L bf	5G	122	6	10	8^{1}	8^{1}	$7^{\frac{1}{2}}$	6^{1}	$5^{\frac{1}{2}}$	Solis A O	20000	4.80
17May13 ^{4}Bel^{7}	3	Jackin My Style	L	4G	122	3	2	1^{1}	1^{1}	1^{1}	5^{1}	$6^{\frac{1}{2}}$	Espinoza J L	20000	52.25
02Jun13 ^{5}Bel^{5}	2	Unprecedented	L b	6G	124	2	7	7^{1}	6^{hd}	$8^{1\frac{1}{2}}$	$8^{3\frac{1}{2}}$	$7^{2\frac{1}{4}}$	Saez L	20000	5.50
02Jun13 ^{5}Bel^{8}	4	Nelson Avenue	L b	5G	122	4	6	2^{2}	2^{2}	$3^{1\frac{1}{2}}$	7^{1}	8^{10}	Lezcano A	20000	23.20
02Jun13 ^{5}Bel^{7}	1	Awesome Weekend	L b	3G	117	1	1	9	9	9	9	9	Ortiz J L	20000	17.70
05May13 ^{4}Bel^{4}	8	Impetuous Spirit (GB)	L	5G	122	7	8	10	10	10	10	10	Cohen D	20000	12.50

OFF AT 1:08 Start Good. Won driving. Track Good.
TIME :25^{1}, :50, 1:14^{3}, 1:39^{1}, 1:45^{1} (:25.36, :50.08, 1:14.62, 1:39.33, 1:45.34)

$2 Mutuel Prices:

6- SUILLEABHAIN	55.50	26.20	16.40
9- MANACOR (IRE)		15.60	11.20
11- MR ALGEBRA			6.30

$2 EXACTA 6-9 PAID $853.00 $2 SUPERFECTA 6-9-11-10 PAID $15,482.00
$2 TRIFECTA 6-9-11 PAID $5,567.00

Bay Gelding, (Feb), by Sunriver - Crystal Lady by Stop the Music. Trainer Sciacca Gary. Bred by Rhapsody Farm LLC & Sunriver Syndicate(NY).

SUILLEABHAIN settled along the inside route, contently rode it for six furlongs, got let out a notch and proceeded to angle outward, was under stronger handling spinning five wide into the stretch, got straightened away, kicked into full gear leaving the eighth pole, was the outermost of a line of four to arrive nearly at the same time at the sixteenth pole, quickly disposed of them and shook free, crossing the wire under a brisk hand ride. MANACOR (IRE) reserved from off the inside, picked up interest after being tipped into the three path midway on the far turn, entered the stretch four wide and under a drive and closed in with good energy, was briefly between rivals with a sixteenth to go, failed to keep up with the top one once that opponent went roaring by but showed good determination to garner the place. MR ALGEBRA tucked into the pocket shortly after departing the opening bend, tracked the front runners from there, was given his cue and unleashed a rail rally turning for home, missed out belatedly on place honors. EL CORRIENTE sat forwardly placed while three wide on both turns, challenged in earnest upon reaching the quarter pole, forged to a slim lead by the end of the furlong grounds, failed to shake free, yielded and weakened late. CHARDSEY swung four wide into upper stretch, lacked the needed response. JACKIN MY STYLE cut the pace from the inside, came under intensified pressure by the end of the far turn and gave way. UNPRECEDENTED placed five wide at the head of the stretch, made no impact. NELSON AVENUE prompted the leader two wide for three-quarters, folded. AWESOME WEEKEND sluggish after getting away cleanly, was never involved while undergoing a ground-saving journey. IMPETUOUS SPIRIT (GB) off slowly, was checked after becoming rank, swerved in sharply, was quickly pulled up and subsequently walked off the course.

Owners- 6, Sullivan, III Daniel J.; 9, Day James M.; 11, Dubb Michael ; 10, Corbett June ; 7, Oak Bluff Stables ; 3, Persaud, Randi and Avi's Racing Stable ; 2, Chatterpaul Naipaul ; 4, JAL Racing, Inc. and Quartarolo, Anthony T. ; 1, McConnell Racing Stable and Bilinski, Darlene ; 8, M B Racing Stables, Inc.

Trainers- 6, Sciacca Gary ; 9, Day James M.; 11, Rodriguez Rudy R.; 10, Reynolds Patrick L.; 7, Englehart Chris J.; 3, Persaud Randi ; 2, Chatterpaul Naipaul ; 4, Quartarolo Anthony T.; 1, Contessa Gary C.; 8, Kimmel John C.

Breeders- 6, Rhapsody Farm LLC & Sunriver Syndicate (NY); 9, Kilboy Estate (IRE); 11, Kathleen Herbert & Mary Jo Herbert (NY); 10, Jerry Jamgotchian LLC (KY); 7, Oak Bluff Stables, LLC (NY); 3, Flying Zee Stables (NY); 2, Betty L. Mabee & Larry Mabee (KY); 4, Stonewall Farm (NY); 1, Edition Farm (NY); 8, Darley (GB)

Scratched- Griffin Rock(07Apr13 ^{9}Aqu^{3}), Prudent Investor(08May13 ^{9}Bel^{1}), Reaganomics(19May13 ^{3}Bel^{2}), In Todd We Trust(12Jun13 ^{4}Bel^{3})

Winner - 6 - 3rd Best Start, 2nd Best Mid-Pace.
Place - 9 - Getting 32 pounds off from last race, and cutting back a full mile and 16th! Exacta $853.00

COPYRIGHT 2013 BLOODSTOCK RESEARCH INFORMATION SERVICES

IN THE LAND OF LONG SHOT HUNTERS, PATIENCE IS KING

The first race at Churchill Downs on 6/22/2013 produced a most unlikely winner if the bettor only had the pps to review. The race is a prime example of how the FHH software for handicapping thoroughbred horse races separates the wheat from the chaff. Most handicappers reviewing the first four races of the 4 horse, Contrapuntal, would not have touched the horse with a ten foot pole. But the microscopic eyes of the FHH system identified two "tells" that the morning line setter and the betting herd had completely overlooked.

In his previous race on 6/2/2013, the horse was "pulled up, vanned off" at the 2nd call. On June 18, just four days before his return to Saturday's race, he worked three furlongs in :34 3/5ths: that is "running a hole in the wind!" At least for 3/8ths of a mile. In this race he was carrying seven pounds less than in his last race. For those two variables he earned six points in the FHH system, enough to tab him as the number two contender. There should not have been any doubt that the horse was fit and ready for this race, notwithstanding his being vanned off in his previous race. Yet the crowd let him leave the gate at 36/1, an overlay from the 30/1 morning line. Understandably so, for if they just looked at the pps, few punters would have given him a second look.

The horse's trainer was new: four starts, no wins and the jockey was a bug boy with one win in sixteen starts. The horse didn't know that: the FHH numbers said he was ready to run.

Screen presented:

TELL POINT CONTENDERS

2=7
4=6
7=5
8=5

BEST IN CATEGORY

Work= 4	3 fur :34.6
Start= 3	91
Mid= 7	86
Late= 8	83

Race comes 4, 2, 8, 6

Winner (4) Contrapuntal **$74.60 26.20 16.40**
Place (2) Lucky Pursuit   4.40   3.20
Show (8)Rockfeller (BRZ)   3.40

$2 ex $406.80
$2 tri $2,412.20

The system long shot play was to bet the 4 to win and twice as much to place, then to run the 2, 4 over the 2, 3, 4, 7, 8 up and back in exactas and trifectas.

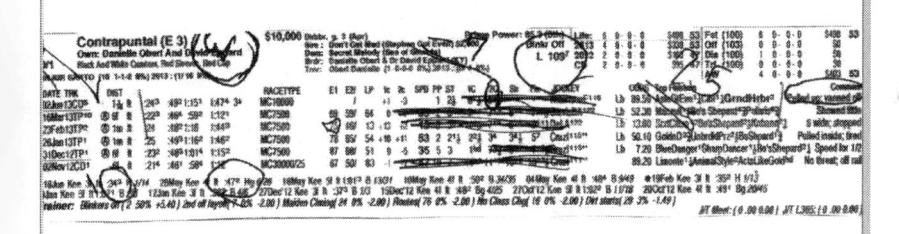

IN THE LAND OF LONG SHOT HUNTERS, PATIENCE IS KING

Example of "Pulled Up, Vanned Off" Gambit!

COPYRIGHT 2013 BLOODSTOCK RESEARCH INFORMATION SERVICES

Always give a horse that was pulled up and vanned off in its last race and is back to the track within three weeks, a long look at its workout pattern since the "pulled up" race. Contrapuntal could not have been injured in that race since he drilled a :34.6 work just 16 days later. Don't be taken in by this kind of "monkey business" trainer's too cute by half gambit.

The exceptional and unusual example of a big hitter long (in this case: long, long, long, long, long) shot horse – and unlikely horses finishing in the first four positions in a race occurred on June 16th, 2013, at Churchill Downs in (of course) the 10th and final race of the card for maiden 30k claimers three and up at a mile on the turf. A full field of 12 went to the post for the start of what was to be an exceedingly strange and absolutely amazing race. In my over forty years of punting the thoroughbreds, I have never seen a race like this one. If Robert Ripley had watched it, no doubt he would have written it up in his legendary series: Believe it or Not! Call it *the race of phantom whips.*

Screen presented:

TELL POINT CONTENDERS

11= 10
10= 6
 3= 5
 5= 4
 8= 4

BEST IN CATEGORY

Work=8, 10   4 fur :47
Start= 11   97
Mid= 11   106
Late= 3   89

Because so many long shot winners have come in the last race on the card in a maiden claiming race, I approached the FHH interface screen and the pps with a jaundiced eye, determined to pass on the favorite and to dig out the numbers for credible long shot candidates. Of the screen horses: 3, 5, 8, 10, 11 – two filled the bill; the 3, Just Tango, with a morning line of 50/1 and the 10, Cristovia, at 10/1.

In examining the Tell Point and Best in Category numbers, Just Tango was my horse. The FHH screen revealed that the horse had the best Late Pace; was tied for the 2nd best Mid Pace, and had the 3rd best Start, only 3 points off the best. About 5 minutes to post he was over 70/1 on the board. Could the morning line setter have been touting the public "off" this horse? And for what reason? (You don't get a second guess.) Granted, he was pushing class, but class in this race was not readily recognizable. (In examining the pps form, I noted that in his last race Just Tango closed some 8 lengths from the first call to the finish, and even though placing 6th, he was only 4 lengths back of the winner. That was at 6 furlongs and now he was entered at a mile. The other long shot that had decent numbers was the 10, Cristovia, being tied for the best Work with a solid :47 for 4 furlongs and tied for the 2nd best Mid Pace, yet left the gate at 28/1

The System long shot bet was on the 3 and 10 to win and twice as much to place. I was so enamored of the 3, Just Tango, that I added a stacked show bet. (Win, twice as much to place and four times as much to show as the win bet.) I reasoned that at 74/1 even the show price would be double digit. The exotic play was to run the 3 up and back with the field, minus the first and second favorites. The only way the tri was hittable was to put the 3 and 10 on the board; that is put the 3, 10 with the 3, 10 with all, then all with the 3, 10 with the 3 10 then 3, 10 with all with 3, 10: the cost of a $1 unit tri bet that way would have been just $48.

Race comes 2, 3, 10, 7

Winner (2) Courtmaster **$131.40 40.40 19.40**
Place (3) Just Tango   **59.20 23.00**
Show (10) Cristovia   **15.20**
Fourth (7) Trenton Street

$2 ex $2,085.40
$2 tri $28,824.80
Dime super $2,262.35

The respective closing odds of the top four finishers were 64.7/1, 74.2/1, 28/1, and 24.2/1. (I leave it to the reader to estimate the odds of this result occurring in an honestly run thoroughbred horse race. My guess is that the odds would be infinity to one.)

I have watched the replay a half dozen times and have concluded that this was a race of *the phantom whips* – much waving around of the sticks but not much hitting, especially in the stretch drive. For these reasons and the ridiculous odds confluence, I felt sure I had just witnessed a "boat" race, notwithstanding the fact that two of the horses that the FHH system identified as legitimate long shots finished second and third. That conclusion was reinforced when I examined the connections of the top four finishers.

The trainer for Courtmaster had a record of 17 1-1-1 6%; the jockey checked in with a record of 1-1-2 from 16 mounts. Just Tango's trainer had a record of 1 0-0-0 while his jockey posted 1-0-1 from 17 tries. Cristovia's trainer had a record of 18 1-2-6; his jockey posted 9-18-10 from 105 tries. Trenton Street's trainer had sent a horse to the post but three times, scoring 0-1-1. The jockey's record was 72 4-7-8. Of the four trainers and jockeys, the sole horse with a trainer or jockey with a winning record exceeding 6 % was the 10 who carried a jockey with a 9% record.

Let the records speak for themselves. Nevertheless the FHH system marked the top four finishers with numbers that supported the actual performances. Paraphrasing a legendary quote, mark me down as one who came to scoff and remained to.... believe in the efficacy of the Finding the Hidden Horse System for identifying long shot candidates completely overlooked by the morning line setters and the credulous betting herd that follows the touts.

RUNNING A HOLE IN THE WIND: HIDDEN HORSES FOUND

#42

TENTH RACE
Churchill
June 16th, 2013

1 MILE. (Turf) (1.33³) MAIDEN CLAIMING. Purse $29,300 FOR MAIDENS, THREE YEARS OLD AND UPWARD. Three Year Olds, 118 lbs.; Older, 125 lbs. Claiming Price $30,000, if for $25,000, allowed 2 lbs. (If deemed inadvisable by management to run this race over the turf course, it will be run on the main track at One mile.). (Rainy 77)

Value of Race: $20,608 Winner $12,180; second $4,060; third $2,030; fourth $1,015; fifth $609; sixth $102; seventh $102; eighth $102; ninth $102; tenth $102; eleventh $102; twelveth $102. Mutuel Pool $156,669 Pick 3 Pool $41,750 Pick 4 Pool $83,524 Pick 5 Pool $45,169 Pick 6 Pool $10,002 Daily Double Pool $42,178 Exacta Pool $133,789 Superfecta Pool $44,982 Super High Five Pool $5,519 Trifecta Pool $86,724

Last Raced	#	Horse	M/Eqt.	A/S Wt	PP	St	¼	½	¾	Str	Fin	Jockey	Cl'g Pr	Odds $1
02Jun13 ^{5}CD^{8}	2	Courtmaster	L	3G 118	2	6	1½	2½	4½	3½	$1^{1\frac{1}{4}}$	Rosal O	30000	64.70 2ND BEST LATE
25May13 ^{6}CD^{6}	3	Just Tango	bf	6G 123	3	4	$2^{2\frac{1}{2}}$	1½	1^{hd}	2^{1}	2¾	McMahon C	25000	74.20 BEST LATE
15Mar13 ^{2}FG^{4}	10	Cristovia	L b	5G 125	10	12	$11^{2\frac{1}{2}}$	$9^{1\frac{1}{2}}$	$10^{2\frac{1}{2}}$	6^{1}	3¾	Rocco, Jr. J	30000	28.00
31May13 ^{6}CD^{2}	7	Trenton Street	L bf	4G 125	7	5	$5^{1\frac{1}{2}}$	$4^{2\frac{1}{2}}$	2^{1}	1^{hd}	4¾	Morales R	30000	24.20
25Apr13 ^{2}Kee^{3}	8	Amazing Kitten	L b	3C 118	8	10	8^{hd}	$11^{4\frac{1}{2}}$	9½	5½	5^{1}	Bridgmohan S	30000	*1.90
18May13 ^{7}AP^{3}	12	Conserve	L bf	4C 125	12	11	9½	7½	$7^{2\frac{1}{2}}$	4½	$6^{2\frac{3}{4}}$	Albarado R	30000	9.40
27May13 ^{11}CD^{8}	4	This Ones for Tony	L b	3G 118	4	9	10½	$10^{1\frac{1}{2}}$	11^{10}	$11^{1\frac{1}{2}}$	7½	Lanerie C J	30000	7.30
24May13 ^{6}CD^{4}	5	Cat's Destiny	L	3C 118	5	2	7^{2}	8½	8^{hd}	$9^{1\frac{1}{2}}$	8^{1}	Hernandez, Jr. B J	30000	7.50
21Apr13 ^{1}Kee^{5}	11	Bill of Rights	L b	4G 125	11	8	6½	$6^{1\frac{1}{2}}$	6½	10^{1}	9^{hd}	Santana, Jr. R	30000	1.90
31May13 ^{6}CD^{3}	1	Tyler T	L b	3G 118	1	3	3^{hd}	5^{1}	5^{hd}	8^{hd}	10^{3}	Napravnik R	30000	16.50
31May13 ^{6}CD^{6}	6	Barn Stormer	L b	5G 123	6	1	4^{hd}	3½	$3^{1\frac{1}{2}}$	7½	11^{10}	Servis D A	25000	88.80
08Jun13 ^{7}Ind^{2}	9	Tuffer	L	4G 123	9	7	12	12	12	12	12	Zuniga E	25000	94.80

* Actual Betting Favorite.

OFF AT 5:26 Start Good For All But 8,12. Won driving. Track Firm.
TIME :24^{1}, :48, 1:12^{4}, 1:25^{3}, 1:38^{3} (:24.30, :48.13, 1:12.80, 1:25.67, 1:38.62)

$2 Mutuel Prices:

2- COURTMASTER	131.40	40.40	19.40
3- JUST TANGO		58.20	23.00
10- CRISTOVIA			15.20

$2 EXACTA 2-3 PAID $2,085.40 $2 SUPERFECTA 2-3-10-7 PAID $45,247.00
$1 SUPER HIGH FIVE 2-3-10-7-8 PAID $0.00 Carryover Pool $4,471 $2 TRIFECTA 2-3-10 PAID $28,824.80

Gay Gelding, (My), by Doneraile Court - Regale by Sefapiano. Trainer Bradley William. Bred by Carl Hurst, Fred Bradley &William Bradley(KY).

COURTMASTER set the early pace inside, dropped back on the second turn then came again late along the hedge to be clear. JUST TANGO closest to the pace off the inside, challenged before a half, gained a short lead soon after, stayed just off the hedge on the second turn and held on gamely to the finish. CRISTOVIA in tight at the start, was outrun for a half, advanced three wide on the second turn, angled out for the drive and closed well. TRENTON STREET within striking distance three wide, challenged from that path on the second turn, gained a short lead in midstretch but weakened late. AMAZING KITTEN bobbled at the start, was reserved along the inside, moved up on the hedge on the second turn, angled out near the sixteenth marker for a clear path, bumped CONSERVE then hung. CONSERVE outrun early three wide, made a four wide middle move, reached a forward position in midstretch, was bumped near the sixteenth marker and weakened. THIS ONES FOR TONY outrun off the inside, never threatened. CAT'S DESTINY within striking distance in the three path, lacked a rally. BILL OF RIGHTS stumbled at the start, raced within reach three wide and tired. TYLER T close up inside, moved off the rail on the second turn and tired in the drive. BARN STORMER forwardly placed early, raced in the three path on the second turn and faded. TUFFER was outrun.

Owners- 2, Bradley, Fred F. and William B. and Hurst, Carl ; 3, Caulier-Eimbcke Beatrice ; 10, Boelle Elizabeth ; 7, Boulmetis Tanya ; 8, Ramsey, Kenneth L. and Sarah K. ; 12, Mauzy, Jerry and Foley, Sharon ; 4, Considine, Dan and Snowden, Steve C. ; 5, Elm Racing LLC ; 11, Brewster Clark O.; 1, Tussey Gary K.; 6, LaFollette Autumn ; 9, Thompson Darryl

Trainers- 2, Bradley William ; 3, Caulier-Eimbcke Beatrice ; 10, Werner Ronny W.; 7, Boulmetis Tanya ; 8, Maker Michael J.; 12, Foley Vickie L.; 4, Connelly William R.; 5, McGee Paul J.; 11, Asmussen Steven M.; 1, Vance David R.; 6, Lafollette Autumn D.; 9, Burton Adam T.

Breeders- 2, Carl Hurst, Fred Bradley &William Bradley (KY); 3, Paul Robinson (KY); 10, Flying High Farm (KY); 7, Twin Creeks Farm, Tom & Nancy Clark,Taylor Made Farm Inc., et al (KY); 8, Kenneth L. Ramsey & Sarah K. Ramsey (PA); 12, Cashmark Farms, Inc. (KY); 4, Steve C. Snowden & Dan Considine (KY); 5, Hurstland Farm & James H. Greene, Jr. (KY); 11, WinStar Farm, LLC (KY); 1, Hardin Farm, LLC &The Proud Citizen Syndicate (KY); 6, Hargus Sexton, Sandra Sexton & RoseHill Farm (KY); 9, Westwind Farms (KY)

Amazing Kitten was claimed by Unlimited Equine, LLC ; trainer, McCauley Tevis Q.,
Cat's Destiny was claimed by Britton Chris ; trainer, Engler Jeff

$2 Daily Double (3-2) Paid $1,067.40; Daily Double Pool $42,178.
$2 Pick Three (1-3-2) Paid $4,979.80; Pick Three Pool $41,750.
$2 Pick Four (8-1/4-3-2) Paid $20,812.00; Pick Four Pool $83,524.
1-3-2 PAID $16,813.55 $2 Pick Six (4/10/12/13-4-8-1/4-3-2) 5 Correct Paid $679.60; Pick Six Pool $10,002; Carryover

Data provided or compiled by Equibase Company, which includes data from The Jockey Club, generally is accurate but occasionally errors and omissions occur as a result of incorrect data received by others, mistakes in processing and other causes. Equibase Company and Bloodstock Research Information Services, Inc. and Thoroughbred Sports Network disclaim responsibility for the consequences, if any, of such errors, but would appreciate being called to their attention. Copyright 2013.

Winner - 2 - 2nd Best Late
Place - 3 - Best Late
$2 exacta box on 1st and 2nd Best Late horses nails $2,085.40 payoff

COPYRIGHT 2013 BLOODSTOCK RESEARCH INFORMATION SERVICES

RUNNING A HOLE IN THE WIND: HIDDEN HORSES FOUND

Perfection is hard to come by; not only is it uncommon in men and women; it is especially uncommon in a horse race. But in the sixth race at Churchill Downs on Saturday, June 29, 2013, perfection came close, with the selections of the FHH software application for handicapping thoroughbred horse races.

The *nearly perfect race call* came in a 1 1/16 mile turf OC 62.5kn2x contest for three year olds and up which had never won two races other than maiden, claiming or starter or which had never won three races or claiming price of $62,500.

Screen presented:

TELL POINT CONTENDERS

7= 6
11=6
8= 4
10=4

BEST IN CATEGORY

Work= 11   5 fur :59.4
Start= 11   98
Mid= 8   107
Late= 1, 9   101

IN THE LAND OF LONG SHOT HUNTERS, PATIENCE IS KING

Race comes 7, 8, 11, 10

Winner (7) Seton Hall **$65.80 29.40 23.60**
Place (8) Dreaming Blue   12.20 6.40
Show (11)Cozzetti   3.60
Fourth (10) Saturday Launch (at 58/1)

$2 ex $786.60
$2 tri $3,348.00
$2 super $31,793.60

$20 to win and $40 to place on the 7, the system's #1 contender tied, returned **$1,246.00**. Putting the 7 over the other three tell point contenders in exactas at a cost of $6 returned **$786.60**. Running the 7 up and back over the other three tell point contenders in tris at a cost of $24 returned **$3,348**. Running the 7 up and back over the other three tell point contenders in supers at a cost of $24 returned **$31,793.60**; a near perfect payoff by anyone's definition. Had the 11 beaten the 8 for second, the race would have been a perfect System call.

I know, woulda…shoulda…coulda…..and if only…

RUNNING A HOLE IN THE WIND: HIDDEN HORSES FOUND

SIXTH RACE
Churchill
June 29th, 2013

$1\frac{1}{16}$ MILES. (Turf) (1.394) ALLOWANCE OPTIONAL CLAIMING. Purse $54,000 (Includes $11,400 KTDF - KY TB Devt Fund) FOR THREE YEAR OLDS AND UPWARD WHICH HAVE NEVER WON TWO RACES OTHER THAN MAIDEN, CLAIMING OR STARTER OR WHICH HAVE NEVER WON THREE RACES OR CLAIMING PRICE $62,500. Three Year Olds, 118 lbs.; Older, 125 lbs. Non-winners Of $22,200 Over A Mile On The Turf S ince April 29 Allowed 2 lbs. Claiming Price $62,500 (Races Where Entered For $50,000 Or Less Not Considered In Allowances). (If deemed inadvisable by management to run this race over the turf course, it will be run on the main track at One and One Sixteen th mile.). (Rainy 79)

Value of Race: $51,751 ($2,462 reverts) Winner $32,400; second $8,520; third $5,400; fourth $2,700; fifth $1,620; sixth $259; seventh $213; eighth $213; ninth $213; tenth $213. Mutuel Pool $245,897 Pick 3 Pool $22,263 Daily Double Pool $15,449 Exacta Pool $186,507 Superfecta Pool $87,183 Trifecta Pool $114,560

Last Raced	#	Horse	M/Eqt.	A/S	Wt	PP	St	¼	½	¾	Str	Fin	Jockey	Cl'g Pr	Odds $1
06Jun13 ^{11}CD^{4}	7	Seton Hall	L b	6G	123	5	2	3^{1}	$3^{1\frac{1}{2}}$	$2^{\frac{1}{2}}$	1^{hd}	1^{nk}	Vazquez R A		31.90
01Jun13 ^{8}CD^{3}	8	Dreaming Blue	L b	6G	123	6	7	6^{1}	$5^{\frac{1}{2}}$	5^{1}	4^{1}	2^{1}	Hernandez, Jr. B J	62500	12.30
25May13 ^{8}CD^{5}	11	Cozzetti	L b	4C	123	9	8	$2^{\frac{1}{2}}$	$1^{\frac{1}{2}}$	$1^{1\frac{1}{2}}$	$2^{1\frac{1}{2}}$	3^{1}	Bridgmohan S		2.50
25May13 ^{8}CD^{8}	10	Saturday Launch	L f	4C	123	8	3	$8^{1\frac{1}{2}}$	$8^{1\frac{1}{2}}$	3^{1}	$3^{\frac{1}{2}}$	$4^{\frac{1}{2}}$	Lebron V		58.00
08Jun13 ^{11}CD^{3}	12	Film Making	L bf	5H	125	10	9	10	10	6^{hd}	$5^{1\frac{1}{2}}$	$5^{\frac{1}{2}}$	Velazquez J R		8.20
18May13 ^{6}CD^{2}	1	Z Dager	L	4C	123	1	4	$7^{\frac{1}{2}}$	6^{hd}	7^{2}	6^{hd}	$8^{\frac{1}{2}}$	Napravnik R		2.30
08Jun13 ^{11}CD^{2}	9	Bell by the Ridge	L b	6G	123	7	6	$9^{3\frac{1}{2}}$	9^{4}	$8^{1\frac{1}{2}}$	7^{5}	$7^{15\frac{1}{4}}$	Rocco, Jr. J	62500	4.70
29May13 ^{1}Ind^{5}	2	Bronterre (GB)	L bf2	4G	123	2	10	$5^{\frac{1}{2}}$	$7^{\frac{1}{2}}$	4^{1}	8^{6}	8^{2}	Court J K		24.80
13Jun13 ^{3}CD^{2}	4	Arborville	L	4G	123	3	1	$4^{\frac{1}{2}}$	4^{hd}	10	$9^{6\frac{1}{2}}$	9^{22}	Arroyo, Jr. N	62500	12.30
06Jun13 ^{9}CD^{2}	6	Billy Two Hats	L	5G	123	4	5	$1^{\frac{1}{2}}$	$2^{1\frac{1}{2}}$	$9^{\frac{1}{2}}$	10	10	Garcia A	62500	3.60

#1 CONTENDER TIRED
BEST M-O
#1 CONTENDER TIRED
#3 CONTENDER TIRED

OFF AT 8:30 Start Good For All But SATURDAY LAUNCH. Won driving. Track Firm.
TIME :24^{2}, :48^{3}, 1:13^{1}, 1:38^{4}, 1:45^{1} (:24.58, :48.74, 1:13.38, 1:38.83, 1:45.36)

$2 Mutuel Prices:

7- SETON HALL	65.80	29.40	12.60
8- DREAMING BLUE		12.20	6.40
11- COZZETTI			3.60

$2 EXACTA 7-8 PAID $786.60 $2 SUPERFECTA 7-8-11-10 PAID $31,793.60
$2 TRIFECTA 7-8-11 PAID $3,438.00

Chestnut Gelding, (Feb), by Lion Heart - New Jersey by Kingmambo. Trainer Wilkes R. Ian. Bred by Aleyrion Bloodstock Ltd.(KY).

SETON HALL close up while off the inside, moved out a path on the second turn, challenged with a furlong to go and proved best under pressure. DREAMING BLUE within striking distance three wide, moved in to be in the two path on the second turn, angled in with less then a furlong to go for a clear path then closed well but missed. COZZETTI vied for the lead off the inside, drew clear on the second turn, responded willingly when challenged in midstretch and held on gamely. SATURDAY LAUNCH stumbled at the start, was outrun four wide, made a good four wide middle move but went evenly in the final quarter. FILM MAKING angled to the inside when outrun early, made a five wide run on the second turn but lodged only a mild late bid. Z DAGER reserved inside, moved off the rail on the second turn and lacked the needed closing bid. BELL BY THE RIDGE outrun for a half along the inside, moved out a path with three furlongs to go and had little left late. BRONTERRE (GB) within striking distance off the inside, tired. ARBORVILLE forwardly placed along the inside, faded. BILLY TWO HATS vied for the lead along the inside and stopped.

Owners- 7, Windridge Farms Inc and Donahoe, Donald ; 8, Hamilton Terry ; 11, Albaugh Family Stable ; 10, Oak Haven Farm ; 12, Courtlandt Farms ; 1, Zayat Stables, LLC ; 9, Scarlet Stable ; 2, Riverside Bloodstock, LLC, Beaty, D., O'Callaghan, K., Ryan, D. et al. ; 4, Cella Charles J.; 6, Thunderhead Farms

Trainers- 7, Wilkes Ian R.; 8, Stidham Michael ; 11, Romans Dale L.; 10, Frederick Edward Harrison; 12, Baker James E.; 1, Asmussen Steven M.; 9, Maker Michael J.; 2, Murphy Conor ; 4, Whiting Lynn S.; 6, Thomas Gary A.

Breeders- 7, Aleyrion Bloodstock Ltd. (KY); 8, Mr. Dale Caraway (KY); 11, Soc. Agr. Santa ElenaDe Chimbarongo Ltd. (KY); 10, Bloodstock Holdings LLC (KY); 12, Courtlandt Farm (KY); 1, Glencrest Farm LLC (KY); 9, Joseph J. Sullivan (FL); 2, Swettenham Stud & Lofts Hall Stud (GB); 4, Nelson Bunker Hunt (KY); 6, W. S. Farish (KY)

Dreaming Blue was claimed by Grum Mary ; trainer, Borel Cecil P.

Scratched- Workin for Hops(08Jun13 ^{4}AP^{3}), Sound Effect(15Jun13 ^{3}AP^{2}), Southern Parkway(05Jun13 ^{8}AP^{3}), River Boss(09Jun13 ^{8}CD^{1})

$2 Daily Double (6-7) Paid $291.00; Daily Double Pool $15,449.
$2 Pick Three (1-6-7) Paid $3,788.60; Pick Three Pool $22,263.

[illegible]

NEARLY PERFECT FHH SYSTEM PICK FOR BOXCAR PAYOFFS!

COPYRIGHT 2013 BLOODSTOCK RESEARCH INFORMATION SERVICES

One of the few criticisms my father made of me as an adult was the often voiced admonition: "Brother, you have got to learn patience, good things usually take time." After all these years of chasing the big hit, calm and calculating patience has brought me and mine more than I had any right to hope for. So many punters are committed to grinding the wins out, hoping to make a marginal profit from apparent form. My experience at this frustrating yet majestic game has taught me that in the long run, swinging for the fences is the punter's best bet to win over time and their only chance of hitting a life-changing score. Of course, you can't go for the big hit until you get on track money. And getting on track money is what these long shot plays are all about, for - in the land of long shot hunters - patience is king.

Chapter 12

WHERE WOULD WE BE WITHOUT NUMBERS?

*Handicapping thoroughbred horse
races is a mathematical problem...*
CONRAD CREASE

The saddest words of gambling mice and betting men comes after the race has run, for then: Oh! What *might* have been! Algorithms are fine in determining long shot candidate winners, but the timely *execution* of your wagers is half the battle in the punter wars. The previous chapters have examined the mechanics of the FHH software application for handicapping thoroughbred horse races and the technical aspects of how the formula consistently produces so many double digit winners; but solid selections, backed up by solid numbers, are worthless without well judged execution in getting your bets down before the bell rings.

The years have taught me that ten minutes before post is too long and one minute to the bell is too late to get your bets confirmed. One of the real downers for the experienced punter is to watch the horse that he or she attempted to make a solid bet on (too late) win the race. It's remarkable to see how much the odds-board can change in five minutes, especially at the second tier tracks. The larger the handle, the less the volatility; another good reason for confining your handicapping to the big league tracks. Practice making five minutes to post your drop dead deadline for placing your bets. If you haven't landed on a horse or horses with confidence by then, you're probably wrong anyway. Last minute bets are usually not well thought out propositions, but the compulsive-obsessive punters seem to prefer that method.

Most of the online sites, such as Twinspires or ExpressBet, will let you cancel a bet prior to post. This can be a double edged sword. Just as there is nothing worse than a punter being shut out with winning bets that were intended, only to watch those bets come in; it's worse yet if the bet that was cancelled turns out to be a winner. Take it from me, that more than messes with your mind. When that happens, the punter may as well call it a day. When you lose your equanimity at the track, the loss of your bankroll usually follows sooner rather than later.

Advance betting has its advantages, but that is tempered by its considerable disadvantages. I hit my $15,000 super with a bet made some six hours before the race. While I would like to take credit for the win, the truth is that it was an impulse bet — a hunch upon which Lady Luck smiled. Little handicapping (in the usual sense of the word) was involved. I have no idea what triggered me to bet the runners with the four highest odds in the race. It came to me from nowhere, but I executed on the idea as I was up over $500 for the day when I made the bet and would go home a winner, no matter if the swing-for-the-fences gamble missed. When you are handed a gift from the *goddess of chance*, accept it without question as eventually the *king of misses* will see that you get nothing for something when you least expect it. Remember the gift of which you got something for little of nothing. My forty years in the punter's wilderness has taught me that, generally, advance betting is a losing proposition.

Several FHH software users have asked about my personal betting strategy, using the system as my handicapping methodology to which I apply my gambling theory developed over forty years of trial and error. At this point it should be clear to the readers and users of the FHH software that I'm basically a long shot player. My ten years as a thoroughbred owner, breeder, and managing partner of the Prairie Pride Farms Racing Stable has given me an insider's view to which the average punter has not been privy. I have always been a numbers man; analytical to a fault in my four children's view — a mixed-blessing trait to which I readily confess.

Saturday is my favorite day to play for that's when the largest crowds show up and the day on which most substantial stakes races are run. Normally, I limit my play to no more than three days a week and usually just two. I've found that I can't adequately cover more than two tracks simultaneously, or my synapses cry *no mas!* I prefer the big league tracks as their handles are substantial as well as their purses. The odds are not as volatile as at the second tier tracks where often a two hundred dollar win bet will change the odds by two or three points.

As a hidden horse hunter, I don't usually pay much attention to the records of the top trainers and jocks; long shots are not usually trained or ridden by the cream of the crop. I realize this is counter-intuitive, but that's how you have to play the game if you are shooting for the bomber horses. Let the form players and the chalk chasers risk their money on favorites that will over time lose two out of three races. The theorem of *regression to the mean* and the *law of probabilities* will discriminate against the form players. The hidden horse hunters will be more discriminating in their wagering decisions and will worship at the feet of Patience for without mastering that invaluable character trait, their punting efforts are fated to fail.

Let's talk about winning!

When I go to the track, I travel by internet to Twinspires and the backup of ExpressBet. In addition to the frustration of being shut out because the bettor cut too thin the timing of getting the bet down, it's doubly galling to get the message "Twinspires (or ExpressBet) is not responding" as you attempt to get your hopeful money down. Unless the bettor has waited until the last minute, there is usually time to pull up the backup betting site.

The first steps in preparation for the day's punting are to download the comma delimited single data files from the site and then to download the Brisnet PPs for the tracks you want to play. The next step is to note the scratches for each race and apply them. The formula that the FHH application uses to determine the top four contenders and ties and the Best in Category column is dependent on getting the scratches correct.

The next step is to analyze the interface screen. At the top of each specific variable column is a white box: clicking that box will arrange in descending order the best numbers to the worst for that variable; Work, Trouble, Cutback, Start, Mid, Late, and Weight. Those are the seven variables used in the construction of the mathematical formula applied to each horse to produce the contenders displayed, and their "tell" point totals.

I'm basically a long shot player; many of the FHH program users are not. Not to worry, for the system will tell the user whether or not it has found any long shots. If not, then the user can assume that the system is telling you that the race is probably a current form contest, and that – with its microscopic eyes – it has not been able to find a long shot contender or Best in Category horse with long shot morning line odds.

Over many years I have found that it is extremely difficult to beat this challenging game by playing the obvious. Historically, favorites win one of three races: in order to just break even you have to get a minimum of 2/1 odds on the winning favorite. That is not to say that on occasion favorites win two, three, four or more races in a row: but, over time, favorites are discriminated against by the theorem of *regression to the mean*. Long shots are not so tightly bound by that theory, because of the prices they pay. You may also have times when a long shot wins two, three, or even four races in a row (which the records show is much more unlikely than a winning streak of chalk horses). Long shot winners are equally ruled by the theory; the difference is that their winning prices make *all the difference*.

Of course, a long shot winner is just that – a winner at long odds (arbitrarily setting the definition at odds of 10/1 or more).

Others might set the definition at eight or nine to one and others might set the criteria at twelve to fifteen to one or more. Over many years of study, including three years of algorithmic research, the records show that the average frequency of long shot winners is about one in ten races, or one long shot per race card; thus, the requirement that long shot hunters possess a high degree of patience .

The next step in analyzing the interface screen is to examine the morning line on each of the system's top four contenders and ties; using paper and pencil I circle any of the system contenders having odds of 10/1 or more. I then examine the printed out Brisnet pps of each of the system's long shot contenders.

The next step is to examine the horses in the Best in Category column. Are there one or more of any long shots from the top Tell Point Contenders that also have a Best in Category? Double confirmed horses (that is, a horse appearing in the top four and ties in the top contender's column and also has two Best in Category designations; for instance, Best Start and Best Late) have a good win rate. And *triple* confirmed horses are golden.

If there are no horses with a morning line of at least 10/1 in the Top Contenders, I have to make the decision as to whether or not to go for the middle odds horses (7/2 to 9/1). I only use the first or second favorite in exotic bets. The next question is: Do I play or pass the race? I pass a lot of races; those with six or fewer runners, or a two year old race with four or more first time starters. As a general rule, I only play about half of the races I examine. My favorite kind of race is a turf route maiden claimer, especially if it is the last race on the card.

Once I make the decision to pass or play, and have landed on my pick or picks, I usually bet $20 to win and $40 to place. Rarely do I make a show bet. In the exotic betting I usually run my pick or picks up and back with the screen horses (ie: the remaining Contender column horses and the Best in Category horses) in exactas. If I feel strongly enough about my key horse or horses, I will run it up and back in trifectas. For example: suppose my horse is the 3 and there are 5 other screen horses (after allowing for duplicates) such as 1, 2, 4, 5, 6. The bet would be 3 with 1, 2, 4, 5, 6 with 1, 2, 4, 5, 6 then putting the 3 in second in another trifecta. For a one dollar unit bet this would cost $40. Frequently there may only be 5 screen horses, reducing the cost of that bet to $24. Superfecta bets are similarly constructed. Ideally, the top contenders consist of just four horses. If there are no additional horses other than the top contenders in the Best in Category column, those bets would cost just $12 each for an exacta, trifecta, or superfecta using a $2 betting unit.

Once I'm up for the day, I gradually increase the size of my bets. On a really good day – when I get up by five or six hundred – and I find a horse that the system numbers support and that I really like, I will bet up to half my winnings; for instance, in this case $300 in a $100 win $200 place bet. I limit my losses to $100 a day; if I lose two days in a row, I back off – like a horse being turned out for a freshening – I take a breather and the time to analyze my mistakes before returning to the punter wars.

I favor playing only at the big league tracks: Arlington, Aqueduct, Belmont, Churchill Downs, Del Mar, Gulfstream, Hawthorne, Keeneland, Oaklawn, Santa Anita, Saratoga, TampaBay and Woodbine. Your best insurance against a monkey business race is to go where the "elephants" play for the big money and the jockeys ride for substantial pay.

My favorite races are on the turf, especially routes. I don't much care for dirt sprints of six furlongs or less. My favorite type of long shot race is the last one on the card, especially if it's a distance maiden claimer for any age.

Basically, that's my strategy. I'm looking for the big hit, fully realizing that it doesn't come along very often. I realize that it's an unorthodox method, but it has made me good money since the formula for the software was completed in May of 2011. The FHH System has proved invaluable in pinpointing long shot candidates that the betting public and the generally wrong morning line setters have overlooked. Without this software, I wouldn't have touched many of the system's double – and frequently triple – digit winners with a ten foot pole.

Most professional handicappers are quick to caution the public bettor that there are so many variables involved in handicapping a thoroughbred horse race that it is nearly impossible to reduce them to just a few; they further tell us that the problems are far too complicated for the average credulous punter to comprehend. The FHH software program isn't complicated. Following Einstein's scientific admonition: "*Everything should be as simple as possible, but not simpler,*" the program was scientifically researched and the final formula scientifically designed; its efficacy proven in its performance over the past two years in producing an abundance of long shot winners from the system's *horn of cornucopia*.

The program accomplishes in a millisecond what the player would have to spend at least half an hour on per race, using just their brain and pencil and paper. Brains are subject to fatigue, followed by mistaken calculations; computers never get tired. The system crunches the numbers to produce the horses that appear on the interface screen in the tell point contenders and best in category columns. It is up to the punters' common sense and experience to make their selections from the numbers put before them. The many illustrations set out in this work should prove to any reasonable bettor the consistent efficacy of the program.

Let's thank the gambling gods for numbers, because without them all would be little more than an educated guess: there would be no theorem of *regression to the mean* or *law of probabilities,* without which chaos would reign. Let me leave you with some food for thought by Peter L. Bernstein, author of the best-selling *Against the Gods: The Remarkable Story of Risk.* (John Wiley & Sons, Inc. New York, New York 1996.)

"Likeness to truth is not the same as truth. Without any theoretical structure to explain why patterns seem to repeat themselves across time or across systems, these innovations provide little assurance that today's signals will trigger tomorrow's events. We are left with only the *subtle sequences of data that the enormous power of the computer can reveal.* Thus, forecasting tools based on nonlinear models or on computer gymnastics are subject to many of the same hurdles that stand in the way of conventional probability theory: *the raw material of the model is the data of the past.*"(Emphasis added.)

Good luck in finding the hidden horse that can run a hole in the wind!

Addendum

Many users have asked for the data to date on the relative importance of each of the variables used in the formula constructed on which the FHH application is based. Over two years of back data support the following list:

1. Works – At any distance, on any surface.
2. Late Pace – At any distance, but most important in routes, and on the turf.
3. Mid-Pace – Primarily in sprints, Flat Mile in routes.
4. Start – At any distance.
5. Trainer Change – (Substitution for Trouble) Whether by claim or owner's decision.
6. Cutback – Primarily when cutting back from a route to a sprint.
7. Weight Off – Routes only.

As the reader no doubt has recognized from the 41 examples illustrated in this work, over time the two most important variables appearing in a thoroughbred winner's performance are – far and away – the winning twin variables of Works and Late Pace.

The Finding the Hidden Horse Software available:
vkress15@hotmail.com
www.RPMhandicappinggiant.com

Bibliography

RUNNING A HOLE IN THE WIND: HIDDEN HORSES FOUND

Bernstein, Peter L.: *Against the Gods: The Remarkable Story of Risk*. New York: John Wiley and Sons, Inc., 1998.

Beyer, Andrew: *The Winning Horseplayer*. Boston-New York: Houghton Mifflin Company, 1994.

_____*Beyer on Speed*. Boston-New York: Houghton Mifflin Company, 1994.

Crease, Conrad: *Finding The Hidden Horse: Profiles of Long Shots*. Myrtle Beach: Blue Max Press, LLC, 2010.

Davidowitz, David and Beyer, Andrew: *Betting Thoroughbreds: a Professional's Guide for the Horseplayer*. New York: Penguin Books, 1995.

Dostoyevsky, Fyodor: *Notes From Underground*. London: Penguin Books, 1972.

_____*The Gambler*. London. Penguin Books, 1972

Le Bon, Gustave: *The Crowd: A Study of the Popular Mind.* (1895) London: Dover Publications, 2008.

Mackay, Charles: *Extraordinary Popular Delusions and the Madness of Crowds.* Radford, VA: Wilder Publications, 2008.

Malmuth, Mason and Sklansky, David: *Gambling for a Living.* Las Vegas: Crest Printing Co., 1998.

Mamis, Justin: *The Nature of Risk.* New York: Addison-Wesley Publishing Company, 1991.

Meadows, Barry: *Money Secrets at the Racetrack.* Anaheim, CA: TR Publsihing, 1990.

Pizzola, Michael: *Handicapping Magic.* Las Vegas: I.T.S. Press, 2000.

Wong, Stanford and Spector, Susan: *Gambling Like a Pro.* Indianapolis: Alpha Books, 2003.

Made in the USA
Lexington, KY
27 May 2014